THE WAY
of
CHINESE CHARACTERS

漢字之道

THE ORIGINS
OF 450 ESSENTIAL WORDS

Expanded Edition

JIANHSIN WU
ILLUSTRATED BY CHEN ZHENG AND CHEN TIAN

CHENG & TSUI COMPANY
Boston

18 17 16 15 14 13   3 4 5 6 7 8 9 10

Published by
Cheng & Tsui Company, Inc.
25 West Street
Boston, MA 02111-1213 USA
Fax (617) 426-3669
www.cheng-tsui.com
"Bringing Asia to the World"™

ISBN 978-0-88727-760-3

Illustrated by Chen Zheng and Chen Tian

The Library of Congress has cataloged the first edition as follows:

Wu, Jian-hsin.
  The Way of Chinese characters : the origins of 400 essential words = [Han zi zhi dao] / by Jianhsin Wu ; illustrations by Chen Zheng and Chen Tian.
      p. cm.
  Parallel title in Chinese characters.
  ISBN 978-0-88727-527-2
  1. Chinese characters. 2. Chinese language--Writing. I. Title. II. Title: Han zi zhi dao.

PL1171.W74 2007
808'.04951--dc22

                                                                    2007062006

Printed in the United States of America.

CONTENTS

ABOUT THE AUTHOR

Jianhsin Wu received her Ph.D. from the Department of East Asian Languages and Literatures at University of Wisconsin, Madison. A professor of Chinese at Pomona College since 1990, she concentrates her research on etymology, the pedagogy of teaching Chinese to heritage students, classical Chinese novels, and modern Chinese poetry.

PREFACE

Mastering characters is often the most challenging task for learners of Chinese. Unlike an alphabetical language with a writing system composed of a limited number of letters, the Chinese writing system is built upon about 200 radicals, which are the most basic components of Chinese characters. (Radicals, along with stroke counts, also provide the organizing principle for Chinese dictionaries.) Although there are over 50,000 Chinese characters, 2,500 characters are required for basic literacy. Furthermore, the pronunciation of a particular character does not necessarily relate to its meaning. The sheer number of Chinese characters, in addition to the frequent lack of visual pronunciation guides, makes character memorization a significant challenge for many.

Paradoxically, this complexity is precisely what draws many people to learn Chinese. The presence of pictographic elements in Chinese characters is one of the unique and fascinating aspects of the language. Most radicals, for example, are pictographs, or visual representations of objects or concepts. Given a pictograph, learners can turn the character into a vivid picture, or associate the character with a shape, color, sound, smell, feeling, emotion, movement, or action. When using this method of employing pictographs as memory aids, students will find that learning Chinese characters can be enjoyable, and can provide valuable insight into Chinese culture.

We believe that each and every Chinese character is a crystallization of the wisdom and creativity of our ancient Chinese ancestors. When given the logical and historical origins of each character, as described in this book, learners can also remember characters in an efficient and intelligent manner, rather than mechanically reproducing strokes that may seem meaningless to them. Students can also acquire knowledge of Chinese history and culture while learning the origins and evolution of characters, as their pictographic features often reflect vivid aspects of ancient life, such as agricultural and domestic life, war, trade materials, crafts, rituals, etc.

After studying *The Way of Chinese Characters*, learners will understand pictographic forms, interpret the logic behind the meanings of characters, and know something about the ancient forms of the most commonly occurring characters.

Selection and Presentation of Characters

The characters included in this book are frequently used in modern Chinese, and correspond with the glossary of the Second and Third Editions of *Integrated Chinese, Level 1, Part 1 Textbook* (by Tao-chung Yao, Yuehua Liu, et. al.), a Chinese textbook used at colleges and high schools across the United States.

Explanations are given in both English and Chinese. The English entries are meant for students, while the Chinese entries may serve as references for teachers and advanced learners.

For each entry, we display the character in its various ancient scripts (see **Types of Script** below), and we include each character's classification, which indicates how the character was constructed (see **Types of Characters** below). Illustrations help readers instantly connect the characters' pictographic elements to their meanings, both ancient and modern.

Also included are four indices, organized by chapter, *pinyin*, and stroke count (of both traditional and simplified characters), respectively. We hope all readers will find these indices convenient and practical.

Types of Script

The characters in *The Way of Chinese Characters* are written in "Regular Script" (or traditional characters) and simplified characters. Regular Script can be traced to the late Han Dynasty (207 B.C.–220 A.D.) and is still used in Taiwan, Hong Kong, and many overseas Chinese communities. Simplified characters were introduced and promoted by the government of the People's Republic of China in the 1950s, and have since remained the standard in mainland China.

In this book we focus on Regular Script, or traditional form, because we have found that it is often difficult for beginning learners to appreciate the visual flavor of simplified Chinese characters. We present the ancient forms of the characters and provide illustrations, so that students can identify characters' original pictographic traits. We hope

Preface

that with such imagery in mind, students will have a much easier time remembering Chinese characters.

This book also introduces other forms of Chinese script including "Oracle-Bone Inscriptions 甲骨文," "Bronze Inscriptions 金文," "Seal Script 篆文," and "Cursive Script 草書." "Oracle-Bone Inscriptions" come from carvings on ox bones or tortoise shells, which were used during the Shang Dynasty (ca.1600–ca.1100 B.C.) to record events and devise predictions. "Bronze Inscriptions" are found on bronze vessels of the Shang and Zhou Dynasties (Zhou Dynasty: ca.1100–ca. 221 B.C.). "Seal Script" includes both "Big Seal Script" and "Small Seal Script." The former was used in the Qin State during the Eastern Zhou Dynasty (ca.770–ca.221 B.C.) and the latter became official in the Qin Dynasty (221–207 B.C.). As an abbreviated form of traditional Chinese characters, "Cursive Script" originates from the Han Dynasty (207 B.C.–220 A.D.). These characters are written swiftly such that the strokes flow together, and were thus considered an artistic form of Chinese calligraphy. Many of the simplified characters used in mainland China today were born out of this cursive style.

In the book, we display each character in its various forms: Oracle-Bone Inscriptions, Bronze Inscriptions, and Seal Script, alongside Regular Script and simplified forms. You will notice that some characters are without ancient forms, however, such as 她 (tā, she), 您 (nín, polite form of the pronoun you), and 啤(pí, beer), as these were created in later periods. Cursive Script is also shown for those simplified characters which were derived from the cursive style.

Types of Characters

Chinese characters are constructed differently from alphabetic languages. According to the Han dynasty scholar Xu Shen, in his *Analysis and Explanation of Characters*, they can be divided into six basic categories: pictographs (象形), explicit characters (指事), associative compounds (會意), picto-phonetic characters (形聲), mutually explanatory characters (轉注), and phonetic loan characters (假借).

Pictographs delineate the shape of certain objects or their parts. Examples include:

木 (mù, wood; tree), 刀 (dāo, knife), 女 (nǚ, woman), and 馬 (mǎ, horse). Although such characters are relatively easy to identify, the limitation of this particular category is that pictographs cannot convey more abstract meanings.

Explicit characters are simple diagrammatic indications of abstract ideas, such as 上 (shàng, above), or 下 (xià, below). Others are formed with the addition of a symbol to an existing pictograph, such as 本 (běn, root; basic), or 刃 (rèn, edge). Explicit characters constructed via this method comprise only a small proportion.

The meanings of associative characters are derived from their components, which may combine two or more ideographs. Examples include 明 (míng, bright, the combination of 日 rì, sun and 月 yuè, moon), and 森 (sēn, forest, the combination of three trees 木 mù).

The majority of Chinese characters are picto-phonetic, which combine semantic and phonetic components. For instance, the character 媽 (mā, mother) consists of 女 (nǚ, female) and 馬 (mǎ, horse). 女 suggests the general meaning of the character while 馬 signals its pronunciation.

According to Xu Shen, mutually explanatory (or synonymous) characters refer to those that are of the same or similar meanings, and thus can be used to define one another, e.g., 老 (lǎo, old; aged) and 考 (kǎo, aged; long life; test). However, the exact meaning of this category is ambiguous. Some contemporary scholars consider that the characters in this category actually refer to those later invented characters for recovering their original meanings. A common way to make this type of characters is to add radicals or other components to the original characters. The character 蛇 (shé, snake) is an example from this category. The character 它 (tā) was a pictograph of a cobra-like snake and originally meant "snake". Later 它 was borrowed to mean "other," "it," etc., and these meanings overwhelmed its original meaning. Therefore, a worm radical 虫 was added to the left of 它 to make a new character 蛇. Other examples are 灸/久 (L. 4), 燃/然 (L. 9), and 鼻/自 (L.11).

Phonetic loan characters refer to those that originally had no written form, and so borrowed existing characters of the same or similar pronunciation. For example, the character 我 resembles a weapon with a saw-toothed blade and long shaft, and originally referred to a kind of ancient weapon. Because the pronunciation of this character is similar to that of the pronoun "I," 我 was borrowed to mean "I," or "me."

Using This Book as a Teaching Tool

This book is the result of a serious, meticulous, and extensive study of the origins of Chinese characters. Many of the books currently on the market on this topic offer learners imaginative, yet inaccurate pictorial representations of characters. While imagination can help learners remember Chinese characters, such historically groundless explanations may misinform them. This book's academic, accurate, and straightforward explanations allow learners to study Chinese characters thoughtfully, but without the risk of becoming overwhelmed by overly detailed information on origin and evolution.

It is our belief that this book will provide teachers with a new, efficient, interesting, and scholarly way to teach Chinese characters to learners of Chinese, as well as learners of Japanese and Korean, whose writing systems employ Chinese characters. At Pomona College, where this book is required reading material for our beginners' classes, the explanation of certain characters, such as 沒 (méi, have not, **Lesson 2**), 家 (jiā, family; home, **Lesson 2**), 教 (jiāo, teach, **Lesson 7**), 黑 (hēi, black, **Lesson 9**), often induce laughter and excitement. We give tests weekly, asking students to briefly explain how some characters came into being, in addition to identifying the characters' *pinyin* spellings and English definitions. We have noticed that our students not only memorize Chinese characters more quickly and logically, but also retain far more knowledge about the Chinese language in general.

It is our expectation that this book will benefit all learners of Chinese characters, especially those who have difficulty memorizing numerous characters. In short, we hope that reading *The Way of Chinese Characters* helps learners overcome the obstacles to memorizing Chinese characters in an academically sound and creatively engaging way.

Jianhsin Wu
August 2009

BIBLIOGRAPHY

Gu, Yankui 谷衍奎, ed. *Hanzi yuanliu zidian*,《漢字源流字典》. Beijing: Huaxia chubanshe, 2003.

Hanyu dazidian bianji weiyuanhui 漢語大字典編輯委員會, ed. *Hanyu dacidian* 《漢語大字典》. Chengdu: Sichuan cishu chubanshe & Hubei cishu chubanshe, 1993.

Jiang, Lansheng 江藍生 and Zunwu Lu 陸尊梧, eds. *Jianhuazi fantizi duizhao zidian*《簡化字繁體字對照字典》. Shanghai: Hanyu dacidian chubanshe, 2004.

Jiang, Shanguo 蔣善國. *Hanzixue*《漢字學》. Shanghai: Shanghai jiaoyu chubanshe, 1987.

Liu, Yuehua 劉月華 and Tao-chung Yao 姚道中, et. al. *Integrated Chinese* 《中文聽説讀寫》, *Level 1, Part 1 Textbook*. 3rd ed. Boston: Cheng & Tsui Company, 2009.

Rong, Geng 容庚, ed. *Jinwen bian*《金文編》. Beijing: Zhonghua shuju, 1985.

Shi, Dingguo 史定國, et al., eds. *Jianhuazi yanjiu* 《簡化字研究》. Beijing: Shangwu yinshuguan, 2004.

Wan, Zhiwen 宛志文, et al., eds. *Gujin hanyu changyong zidian*《古今漢語常用字典》. Wuhan: Hubei renmin chubanshe, 2002.

Weng, Zhifei 翁志飛, et al., eds. *Xinbian caoshu zidian* 《新編草書字典》. Hangzhou: Zhejiang guji chubanshe, 2005.

Xie, Guanghui 謝光輝, et al., eds. *Hanyu ziyuan zidian* 《漢語字源字典》. Beijing: Beijing daxue chubanshe, 2002.

Xu, Shen [漢] 許慎. *Shuowen jiezi* 《說文解字》. Beijing: Zhonghua shuju, 1978.

Xu, Shen. Preface to *Analysis and Explanation of Characters* in Zang, Kehe 臧克和 and Ping Wang 王平, ed. *Shuowen jiezi xinding* 《說文解字新訂》. Beijing: Zhonghua shuju, 2002.

Xu, Zhongshu 徐中舒, et al., eds. *Hanyu guwenzi zixingbiao* 《漢語古文字字形表》. Chengdu: Sichuan renmin chubanshe, 1981.

Xu, Zhongshu 徐中舒, et al., eds. *Jiaguwen zidian* 《甲骨文字典》. Chengdu: Sichuan cishu chubanshe, 1998.

Yao, Tao-chung 姚道中 and Yuehua Liu 劉月華, et. al. *Integrated Chinese* 《中文聽説讀寫》, *Level 1, Part 1 Textbook*. 2nd ed. Boston: Cheng & Tsui Company, 2005.

Zhang, Shuyan 張書岩, et al., eds. *Jianhuazi suyuan* 《簡化字溯源》. Beijing: Yuwen chubanshe, 2005.

RADICALS

Key: 甲 refers to the Oracle-Bone Inscriptions, 金 the Bronze Inscriptions, 篆 the Seal Script, and 草 the Cursive Script. See the Preface for more information.

甲 金 篆

人 rén (man; person; humankind)

Pictograph. In the Oracle-Bone and Bronze Inscriptions, the character 人 presents the profile of a figure with a head, arched back, arms, and legs, which could indicate the early stage of humankind as evolved from primates. Later, the character came to resemble a person with two long legs. The person radical 亻 is often used in characters related to human beings and their activities, such as 你 (nǐ, you), 他 (tā, he; him), 住 (zhù, to live), and 休 (xiū, to rest).

人 象形。甲骨文、金文像有頭、背、臂、腿的側面人形。

甲 篆

刀 dāo (knife)

Pictograph. In ancient writing systems, the character 刀 resembles a knife, with the upper part as the handle and the lower part as the edge. In Regular Script, the handle is shortened so that it becomes almost unnoticeable. Characters with the knife radical 刂 usually have something to do with knives, or cutting, such as 別 (bié, to separate), 刺 (cì, to stab), and 利 (lì, sharp).

刀 象形。像刀形。上像刀柄，下像刀刃及刀背。

 甲 金 篆

力 lì (physical strength; power)

Pictograph. In both the Oracle-Bone and Bronze Inscriptions, the character 力 resembles an ancient plow, with the upper part as the handle and the lower part as the plowshare. Since plowing requires great physical strength, 力 means "strength." In Regular Script, 力 is similar in form to 刀 (dāo, knife) except that its top sticks out.

力 象形。甲骨文、金文均像耕田用具。因耕田要有力，引申為力氣。

 甲 金 篆

又 yòu (right hand; again)

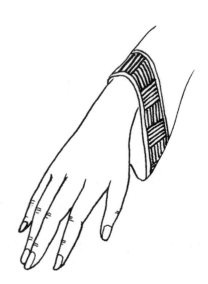

Pictograph. In the ancient writing systems, the character 又 represents a right hand. Later 又 came to mean "again," possibly because most people are right-handed and therefore use their right hands again and again in daily life.

又 象形。像右手形。

甲 ﹀ 金 ﹀ 篆 ﹀

口 kǒu (mouth; entrance)

Pictograph. The character 口 looks like an open mouth. Characters with the mouth radical are often associated with the movement of the mouth, e.g. 吃 (chī, to eat), 喝 (hē, to drink), 唱 (chàng, to sing), and 叫 (jiào, to shout).

口 象形。像人口形狀。

篆 ▢

囗 wéi (enclose)

Pictograph. 囗 represents the periphery or border of an area. Characters relating to boundaries often include the radical 囗, such as 國/国（gúo, country; state）, 園 /园 (yuán, garden; park), 圖/图 (tú, map). Note that 囗 is larger than the radical 口 (kǒu, mouth), indicating a large area that can contain many objects.

囗 象形。像環围形。從囗的字多有外圍或邊界。

甲 △ 金 ⼟ 篆 ⼟

⼟ tǔ (earth; soil)

Pictograph. In the Oracle-Bone Inscriptions, the upper part of ⼟ represents a small hill or mound of soil, while the bottom line stands for the ground. In Regular Script, a cross replaces the mound.

⼟ 象形。像一⼟塊狀，下方 "一" 字意指⼤地。

甲 ⟁ 金 ⅅ 篆 ?

夕 xī (sunset; evening)

Pictograph. In its ancient forms, the character 夕 resembles a half moon, meaning "sunset," "dusk," "evening," or "night." Sometimes the moon can be seen rising from the east at dusk.

夕 象形。像半個⽉亮，傍晚或夜晚之意。

 甲 金 篆

大 dà (big; great)

Pictograph. In its ancient forms, the character 大 portrays a figure standing with arms outstretched and legs apart. The ancient Chinese believed that human beings were the greatest creatures on earth.

大 象形。像伸展雙臂的正面人形。天地萬物中以人為大為貴，故用人形表示"大"意。

 甲 金 篆

女 nǚ (female; woman)

Pictograph. In the Oracle-Bone Inscriptions, the character 女 depicts a woman kneeling with her arms lowered and hands clasped on her lap, reflecting the lower social status of women in ancient times. In later forms, the kneeling component is transformed as women are recognized as having a status more equal to men. The Regular Script forms of 女 and 大 are similar, but 女 emphasizes the female bosom.

女 象形。甲骨文像女子俯首，雙臂交叉下跪形。

甲 金 篆

子 zǐ (baby; child)

Pictograph. In its ancient forms, the character 子
resembles a baby swaddled in cloth, with a large
head sticking out and outstretched arms. In
Regular Script, a horizontal hook replaces the
round baby's head.

子 象形。像繈褓之中的嬰兒。

篆 ヨ

寸 cùn (inch)

Explicit character. In Seal Script, 寸
combines 又 with 一. 又 means "right
hand" while 一 indicates the section of the
forearm one inch from the wrist, where a
traditional Chinese doctor would feel a
patient's pulse and diagnose ailments.

寸 指事。從又，從一。"又"為右手，
"一"指手后一寸之处。中醫所言寸口。

甲 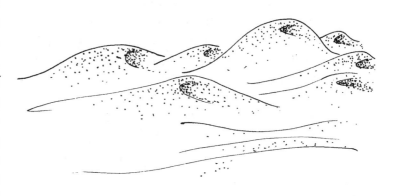 金 篆

小 xiǎo (small)

Associative compound. In the Oracle-Bone and Bronze Inscriptions, the character 小 consists of three dots, representing three grains of sand, therefore meaning "small." In its later forms, 小 indicates the action of cutting something into smaller pieces with a knife, which is represented by the vertical hook in the middle.

小 會意。甲骨文、金文作三點，表示沙粒微小的意思。

甲 金 篆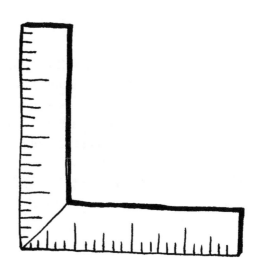

工 gōng (tool; to work; labor)

Pictograph. In its ancient forms, the character 工 looks like a carpenter's square or ruler. Its original meaning is "tool," from which derived the meanings: "work" and "labor"

工 象形。像工匠用的曲尺。

幺 yāo (tiny; the youngest)

Pictograph. In the Oracle-Bone Inscriptions and Bronze Inscriptions, the character 幺 represents a wisp of silk. Since a wisp is a small quantity, 幺 extends to mean "small," "tiny," or "youngest."

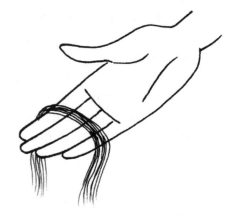

幺 象形。像一小把細丝。甲骨文幺、糸（mì）、丝为同源字。糸、丝都像丝束形，不同的是糸为一束絲， 絲為兩束絲。系(xì) 字在甲骨文中為一隻手握兩束絲。

弓 gōng (bow)

Pictograph. In the Oracle-Bone Inscriptions, the character 弓 resembles an entire bow. In the Bronze Inscription form, 弓 depicts a bow without its string, which is how a bow should be stored. Just like human beings, bows need time for relaxation!

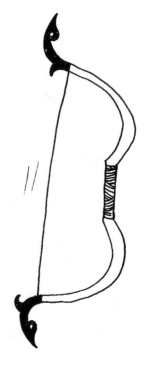

弓 象形。甲骨文像有弓弦弓背的完整弓形。金文简化。

心 xīn (heart)

Pictograph. In its ancient forms, the character 心 represents a heart. There are two forms of the heart radical, 心 and 忄. 心 is usually positioned at the bottom of a character while 忄 is on the left, as in 想 (xiǎng, to think), 愁 (chóu, to worry), 忙 (máng, busy), and 怕 (pà, fear). Characters with heart radicals are often associated with feelings or other mental activities.

心 象形。像人的心臟。

戈 gē (dagger-ax)

Pictograph. The dagger-ax 戈 is a weapon from the Shang (ca.1600–C.1100 B.C.) and Zhou Dynasties (ca.1100–221 B.C.). In the Oracle-Bone and Bronze Inscriptions, the character 戈 delineates such a weapon with a long shaft and a blade at the end. 戈 is used as a component of many characters, such as 我 (wǒ, I), 國/国 (guó, nation), and 錢/钱 (qián, money).

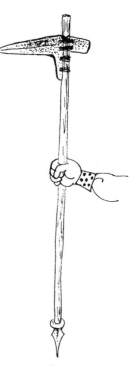

戈 象形。戈是古代常用的一種長柄橫刃的兵器。

金 ⼿　篆 ⼿

⼿ shǒu (hand)

Pictograph. The ancient form of the character ⼿ looks like an outspread hand, with five fingers comprising the upper part, and the forearm below. Characters with the hand radical 扌 are often related to acts performed with the hands, e.g., 打 (dǎ, to beat), 推 (tuī, to push), and 擦 (chā, to wipe).

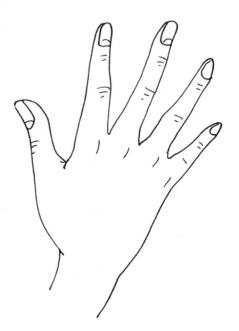

⼿ 象形。像五指伸開的⼿掌。

甲 ⽇　⾦ ⽇　篆 ⽇

⽇ rì (sun; day)

Pictograph. In the Oracle-Bone and Bronze Inscriptions, ⽇ represents the sun. Since the sun rises daily, ⽇ extends to mean "day." Regular Script is also called "Square Script" and usually there are no round components, so the character ⽇ in Regular Script is drawn as a rectangle with a horizontal line through its middle, which indicates that the sun is not just a circle but a solid thing, and distinguishes ⽇ from the character ⼝.

⽇ 象形。甲骨⽂、⾦⽂像太陽的輪廓。⽇字寫成⽅形則出於楷书書寫的習慣。

 甲 金 篆

月 yuè (moon; month)

Pictograph. In the Oracle-Bone and Bronze Inscriptions, the character 月 depicts a crescent moon, which may be compared to a large eye, following and watching people quietly at night. The dot or lines in the character 月 represent the darker areas of the moon's surface. Given that the moon's orbit takes approximately thirty days, the extended meaning of 月 is "month."

月 象形。像彎月形。

 甲 金 篆

木 mù (tree; wood)

Pictograph. In its ancient forms, the character 木 depicts a tree with branches on top and roots at the bottom. "Tree" is the original meaning of 木, while extended meanings today are "wood" or "lumber."

木 象形。像一棵樹。上像樹枝，中像樹幹，下像樹根。

甲 水 金 水 篆 水

水 shuǐ (water)

Pictograph. In its ancient form, the character 水 represents flowing water, with the middle line as the main stream and the dots on the two sides as the water's spray. In Regular Script, the dots extend into lines, resembling the tributaries of a river. The original meaning of 水 was "river," but later came to mean "water." Since life is closely associated with water, there are over five hundred characters with the water radical 氵, such as 河 (hé, river), 海 (hǎi, sea), and 酒 (jiǔ, wine).

水 象形。甲骨文字形中間像流水，旁似浪花或水的支流。

甲 火 篆 火

火 huǒ (fire)

Pictograph. In the Oracle-Bone Inscriptions, the character 火 represents flames. In Regular Script, 火 resembles flames on firewood. There are two forms of the fire radical: 火 and 灬, as in 燙/烫 (tàng, scalding), 燒/烧 (shāo, burn), and 熱/热 (rè, hot).

火 象形。像火焰形。

甲 囲 金 田 篆 田

田 tián (a surname; farmland; field)

Pictograph. The character 田 depicts plots of land, divided by vertical and horizontal lines, as if seen from above.

田 象形。像阡陌縱橫的田地。

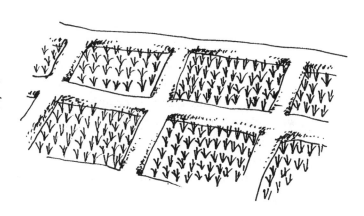

甲 👁 金 👁 篆 目

目 mù (eye)

Pictograph. In the Oracle-Bone and Bronze Inscriptions, the character 目 represents an eye. In Seal Script, this eye becomes vertical and the curves in the character are straightened. 目 is often used as a radical in characters related to eyes, e.g., 看 (kàn, see), 瞎 (xiā, blind), and 睡 (shuì, sleep).

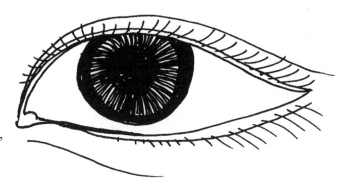

目 象形。甲骨文、金文像人眼形。為書寫方便，小篆將橫目改為豎目。

甲  篆

示 shì (to show)

Pictograph. In the Oracle-Bone Inscriptions, the character 示 looks like a T-shaped stone table upon which sacrificial offerings to gods or ancestors were placed. In Seal Script, more lines are added beneath, as if to make the altar more stable. This show radical 礻 often appears in characters related to religious ritual, such as 禮/礼 (lǐ, rite), and 祝 (zhù, pray).

示 象形。甲骨文中像用石塊搭起的簡單祭臺。

甲 金 篆

糸 mì (silk)

Pictograph. In the Oracle-Bone and Bronze Inscriptions, 糸 depicts a silk string. Characters with the silk radical 糸/纟 often relate to the process of making cloth, including dyeing, such as 織/织 (zhī, weave), 線/线 (xiàn, thread), 紅/红 (hóng, red), and 綠/绿 (lǜ, green). The character 糸 combines 幺 (yāo, tiny) and 小 (xiǎo, small).

糸 象形。像丝束形。

耳 ěr (ear)

Pictograph. In the Oracle-Bone and Bronze Inscriptions, the character 耳 delineates the contour of an ear. In Regular Script, 耳 still somewhat resembles the shape of an ear, with the two lines in the middle representing the helix, earlobe, and internal structure.

耳 象形。像耳朵的形狀。

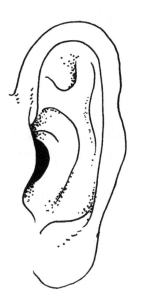

衣 yī (clothing)

Pictograph. In its ancient form, the character 衣 outlines a garment, with its collar and sleeves in the upper part, and hemline in the lower part. In Regular Script, 衣 looks like a garment on a clothes hanger. Characters with the clothing radical 衤 usually relate to clothing or cloth, e.g. 襯衫/衬衫 (chènshān, shirt), 袖 (xiù, sleeve), and 被 (bèi, quilt).

衣 象形。像有領、袖、長襟的衣服。

甲 金 篆

言 yán (to speak; speech)

Associative compound. In the Oracle-Bone and Bronze Inscriptions, the character 言 looks like a tongue (the upper part) sticking out from a mouth (the bottom part), referring to the act of speaking with excitement and energy. In Regular Script, the mouth 口 comprises the lower part of 言, but the upper part resembles a sound wave more than a tongue.

言 會意。甲骨文字形下像嘴，上像伸出的舌頭。意指言乃是從舌上發出的聲音。

甲 金 篆 草

貝/贝 bèi (cowry shell)

Pictograph. In the Oracle-Bone and Bronze Inscriptions, the character 貝 resembles a cowry shell. Since cowry shells were used as currency in ancient times, characters with 貝 as a component often relate to money, trade, or wealth, e.g., 買/买 (mǎi, buy), 賣/卖 (mài, sell), 貴/贵 (guì, expensive), and 財 (cái, fortune). The simplified character 贝 derives from the cursive style of the traditional character 貝.

貝 象形。像貝殼形。簡體字贝是由繁體字貝的草書楷化而來。

金  篆

走 zǒu (to walk)

Associative compound. In the Bronze Inscriptions, the upper part of 走 looks like a person walking rapidly, with swinging arms, while the lower part represents a human foot. In Regular Script, the lower part looks like a person striding forward with one arm swung high, and the upper part becomes 土 (tǔ, earth), being ground upon which to walk.

走 會意。金文上像人擺動雙臂，下從止（腳），表示人用腳快步前行。

甲  金 篆

足 zú (foot)

Pictograph. In the Oracle-Bone Inscriptions, the upper part of 足 represents the calf of a leg, while the lower part presents an image of a foot, which is the same as the lower part of 走. In Regular Script, the calf part is replaced by 口. Characters with the foot radical 𧾷 are often associated with acts that involve using one's feet, such as 跟 (gēn, follow), 踢 (tī, kick), and 跳 (tiào, jump).

足 象形。從口、從止。口像小腿；止是腳。合起來表示人足。

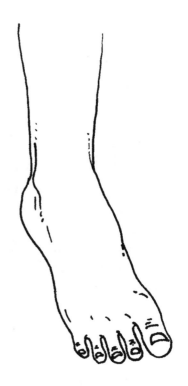

金 二主 篆 金

金 jīn (gold; metal)

Pictograph and associative compound. In the Bronze Inscriptions, the character 金 consists of three parts: 人 (arrowhead), 王 (axe) and two dots (representing bronze ingots), suggesting that both arrowheads and axes are made of bronze. The primary meaning of 金 is "metal," with the extended meaning "gold."

金 象形兼會意。金文左邊像兩塊青銅塊，右邊上是箭頭下是斧，指可用來製作箭、斧等器具的金屬。本义为金属，引申為黃金。

甲 𦥑 金 𦥑 篆 門 草 〜

門/门 mén (door; gate)

Pictograph. The character 門 depicts a door with two panels. Characters with the 門 radical include: 開／开 (kāi, open), 關／关 (guān, close), 問／问 (wèn, ask), etc. The simplified character 门 derives from the cursive style of 門.

門 象形。像兩扇門之形。门是門字的草書楷化字。

 甲 金 篆

隹 zhuī (short-tailed bird)

Pictograph. In the Oracle-Bone and Bronze Inscriptions, the character 隹 depicts a short-tailed bird. In Regular Script, the bird's head shrinks and the claws disappear, but its body and feathers are still apparent. 隹 is often used in characters pertaining to birds, or as a phonetic symbol, e. g. 雞/鸡 (jī, chicken), 雁 (yàn, wild goose), and 錐/锥 (zhuī, awl)

隹 象形。意指短尾巴鳥。

甲 金 篆

雨 yǔ (rain)

Pictograph. The character 雨 could indicate heavy rain, as one can see four large rain drops. Characters with the rain radical often relate to natural phenomena, e.g. 雪 (xuě, snow), 雷 (léi, thunder), 霧/雾 (wù, fog), and 雲/云 (yún, cloud).

雨 象形。像水滴從天上落下形。

甲 金 篆

食 shí (to eat)

Associative compound. In the Oracle-Bone Inscriptions, the lower part of 食 resembles a high-legged container full of food, while the upper part represents an open mouth, referring to the act of eating. In Regular Script, the lower part of 食 looks like legs in movement, which could suggest that one derives energy from eating. The food radical 食／饣 always appears on the left side of a character, e.g., 飯／饭 (fàn, food; cooked rice), 餓／饿 (è, hungry), and 餅／饼 (bǐng, pancake).

食 會意。甲骨文中"食"字上邊像是向下張開的嘴，下邊像是盛滿了食物的容器，表示張口向下吃容器中的食物。一説下像裝滿食物的容器，上則為蓋子。

甲 金 篆 草

馬／马 mǎ (horse)

Pictograph. In the Oracle-Bone Inscriptions, the character 馬 delineates a horse. In its later forms, the character becomes more simple and abstract. Yet the shape of a horse, complete with body, mane, and legs, can still be seen in the Regular Script form. The simplified character 马 derives from the cursive style of the traditional character 馬.

馬 象形。上像馬頭與鬃毛，下像身、腿、尾。簡體的马字保留了繁體馬字的大體輪廓，十分接近馬字的草書。

NUMERALS

甲 一　金 一　篆 一

甲 二　金 二　篆 二

甲 三　金 三　篆 三

一 yī (one); 二 èr (two); 三 sān (three)

Explicit character. In Chinese writing systems, one horizontal stroke represents the number one; two horizontal strokes stand for the number two, and three for the number three. 一, 二, 三 are probably the easiest Chinese characters for one to remember. From ancient times until now, these three characters have not changed much.

There is a Chinese joke about a silly boy who began to learn numerals. After the boy learned 一, 二, 三 from his teacher, he told his father he was able to write any number. His father was very proud of him. One day he asked his son to write the number "ten thousand" to show his guests. The boy remained in the study for half a day and used up many pieces of paper, but was still unable to finish the task. When the guests saw what he wrote, they all laughed. On the paper there were thousands of horizontal strokes! In fact, numbers larger than three are expressed in different patterns.

一 二 三 指事。以一至三画表示数字一到三，是原始的记数符号。

甲 三　金 四　篆 四

四　sì (four)

Phonetic loan character. In the Bronze Inscriptions, the character 四 resembles a big nose, or nostrils on a face. Therefore it originally meant "gasp" or "pant." Later 四 came to mean the numeral "four."

四 在甲骨文中是四橫。金文"四"像臉部的口鼻。本義為喘息，是呬的本字，因讀音相近而借用為四字。

甲 Ⅹ　金 Ⅹ　篆 Ⅹ

五　wǔ (five)

In the Neolithic signs around 4,000 B.C., the symbol "X" was used to indicate "five." In the Oracle-Bone and Bronze Inscriptions, a line was added above and below the X. In Regular Script, the middle part of 五 resembles a cross that corners at its right end.

五 在西安半坡仰韶文化遺址出土的陶器上，Ⅹ 即五。 甲骨文、金文在 Ⅹ 上下各加一橫。

甲 金 篆

六 liù (six)

Phonetic loan character. In the Oracle-Bone and Bronze Inscriptions, the character 六 outlines a hut or shed, possibly some sort of prehistoric dwelling. Later, 六 came to indicate the number six. In Regular Script, 六 still resembles a simple house, with the roof on top and two pillars beneath.

六 在甲骨文、金文中為茅棚狀，本義為廬。由於讀音相近的關係，借用為六字。

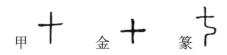

甲 金 篆

七 qī (seven)

In the Neolithic signs, Oracle-Bone, and Bronze Inscriptions, 十 represented the number seven. However, in Seal Script, 十 was used to mean "ten" and the vertical line of 十 was bent to mean "seven." In Regular Script, you may still see similarities between 十 (shí, ten) and 七 (qī, seven), as 七 looks like 十 with a tail.

七 在半坡陶器上以及甲骨文、金文中，十的意思皆是七。小篆將十的意思改為十，而將十的一豎彎曲，另造七字，以區別于十。

甲 乂　金 八　篆 八

八 **bā (eight)**

Phonetic loan character. The character 八 suggests is the act of dividing something into parts. Originally the character did mean "to divide" or "to separate." Later 八 came to mean the numeral eight.

八　甲骨文中用兩劃來表示將一物分開，是分字的初文，後借用位數字。

甲 乙　金 乙　篆 九

九 **jiǔ (nine)**

Phonetic loan character. In the Oracle-Bone and Bronze Inscriptions, the character 九 looks like the posterior of an animal with a long tail, possibly a monkey. Hence, the original meaning of 九 is "behind" or "buttocks." Later 九 came to mean the number nine.

九　甲骨文像是獸類臀部上長出的尾巴，是尻（kāo 屁股）的初文。後借為數目字。

十 shí (ten)

In the Neolithic signs, as well as in the Oracle-Bone Inscriptions, one vertical line stood for ten, two lines for twenty and three for thirty. In the Bronze Inscriptions, a circular dot was added in the middle of the vertical line. Later, in Seal Script, this dot became a horizontal line, making the character for "ten" look like a cross.

十 指事。在半坡陶器上，十字為一竪畫，甲骨文同。金文中間加一點，篆文又由一點延長為一橫。一説在一根繩上打一個結表示一个十。

LESSON 1

先 xiān (first; before; earlier)

Associative compound. In the ancient form, the upper part of 先 is a foot and the lower part is a person, indicating one person walking ahead of another. In Regular Script, the upper part is 土 (tǔ, soil; earth), with a stroke on the left, and the lower part still resembles a person.

先 會意。甲骨文從之（足）在 儿（人）前，本義為走在他人前面。

生 shēng (to be born; to grow)

Associative compound. In the Oracle-Bone inscriptions the character 生 looks like a seedling growing out of the ground. Hence the original meaning of 生 is "the growth of plants." It can also mean "grow," "life," "give birth to," "unripe," "student," etc. In Regular Script the bottom part of 生 is 土 (tǔ, soil; earth), and the upper part resembles grass or plants growing above.

生 會意。像地面上剛長出的一株幼苗，本義指草木生長。

甲  金 篆

你 nǐ (you)

Phonetic loan character. The character 你 is derived from 爾 (ěr). In the ancient form, 爾 looks like silkworms spinning silk to make cocoons. Later this character was borrowed to represent the pronoun "you." since the pronunciation of "you" is similar to that of 爾. In Regular Script 爾 is simplified to 尔 with the person radical 亻 added on the left.

你 古時寫作爾，像蠶吐絲結繭。一說像花枝垂下之形。假借為第二人稱的代詞。楷書加人字旁。

甲  金 篆

好 hǎo (good; fine; O.K.)

Associative compound. In the Oracle-Bone Inscriptions and Bronze Inscriptions, the character 好 shows a woman holding a child. In traditional Chinese society, giving birth to children, especially sons, was a married woman's main responsibility. The inability to bear children was considered a legitimate reason for a husband to divorce his wife. Mencius said: "There are three major sins against filial piety, and the worst is to have no heir." It follows that women who had sons were considered good. You have already learned both 女 (nǚ, female) and 子 (zǐ, child) in the Radicals Section.

好 會意。從女、從子，以能生兒育女使家族興旺的婦女為好。

甲  金 篆

小 xiǎo (small)

Associative compound. In the Oracle-Bone Inscriptions and Bronze Inscriptions, the character 小 consists of three dots, like three tiny grains of sand. In its later forms, 小 resembles a knife (represented by the vertical hook in the middle) cutting something into two smaller pieces.

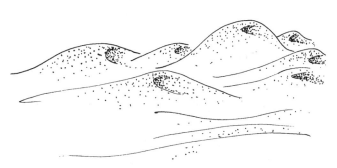

小 會意。甲骨問及金文作三點，像細小的沙粒形，表示微小的意思。

篆

姐 jiě (elder sister)

Pictophonetic character. The character 姐 contains 女 (nǚ, female) as the radical and 且 (qiě) as the phonetic element. This combination shows that the character relates to something female and is pronounced as, or similar to, the sound of 且 (qiě)[*]. In the Oracle-Bone and Bronze Inscriptions, the character 且 looks like a memorial tablet used in ancestral worship. The original meaning of 且 is "ancestor."

姐 形聲。從女，且聲。且在甲骨文金文中像代表祖先之靈的牌位，供祭祀時用。

---

[*]Please note that this book uses Mandarin pinyin to show pronunciation, which may not reflect ancient pronunciation. Some characters contain phonetic elements that seem unrelated to pronunciation; this may be because the remaining phonetic element within the character refers to the ancient pronunciation. It is difficult to trace the history of such pronunciation changes due to changes in the pronunciations of phonetic elements themselves.

王 wáng (king; a surname)

Pictograph. In the Oracle-Bone and Bronze Inscriptions, the character 王 looks like an ax-type tool, with the handle on the top and the blade at the bottom. This 王 symbol of an ax suggests power and authority, therefore meaning "king." In Regular Script, one can hardly find the ax in the character 王, as it evolved into a simple 三 with a vertical stroke running down the middle.

王 象形。甲金文中像斧形，上像其柄，下像其圓弧形的鋒刃。王是一種斧狀的的兵器，後來成為執法的刑具，是權威的象徵。引申意指以武力征服天下者為王。

篆

李 lǐ (plum; a surname)

Associative and pictophonetic compound. The character 李 has 木 (mù, tree; wood) on the top and 子 (zǐ, child) underneath, meaning "plum." The character 李 resembles a child under a plum tree, trying to reach the fruit. Both 木 and 子 help to reveal the meaning of the character 李. 子 also functions as a phonetic symbol.

李 會意兼形聲。從木，子聲。本義為果木。孩子站在樹下看樹上的李子，考慮如何摘下。

金 請 篆 請 草 请　青 金 青 篆 青 草

請/请 qǐng (please; to invite)

Pictophonetic character. In the character 請, 言 (yán, word) is the radical and 青 (qīng, green) is the phonetic element, meaning "ask," "please," "invite." In the Bronze Inscriptions, the upper part of 青 is 生 (shēng, grow) and the lower part 丹 (dān, color), indicating that the color of a growing plant is green. In Regular Script, the upper part of 青 is 生 without the downward left stroke, and the lower part changes from 丹 to 月 (yuè, moon; month). In the simplified character 请, the radical 讠 is derived from the cursive of the radical 言. As a radical, 言 is always written as 讠 in simplified characters.

請 形聲。從言，青聲。青，會意兼形聲。金文從生，從丹，丹為顏色。用植物生長的顏色來表示綠色之意。後楷書寫作青。丹，象形。四周像丹砂井，中間一點像丹砂形。簡體字请的部首讠 是由繁体部首言 的草书楷化而來。

甲 問 金 問 篆 問

問/问 wèn (to ask)

Associative and pictophonetic compound. In the character 問, 口 (kǒu, mouth) suggests the meaning and 門 (mén, door) the pronunciation. (See 門 and 口 in **Radicals**). 門 also helps to reveal the meaning, as it indicates someone at the door, opening her/his mouth to ask a question. In the simplified character 问, the radical 门 derives from the cursive style of the character 門. As a radical or character, 門 is always written as 门 in simplified characters.

問 形聲。從口，門聲。像人到門下張口問事。簡體字问的部首门是繁體字門的草书楷化字。

您 nín (polite form of "you")

The character 您 was first seen in writing from the Jin and Yuan Dynasties (1115–1368). 您 consists of 你 (nǐ, you) on the top and 心 (xīn, heart) at the bottom, signifying a heartfelt respect towards "you." (See 心 in **Radicals** and 你 in this lesson.)

您 會意。你的敬稱。

篆

貴/贵 guì (honorable; expensive)

Associative compound. In the Seal Script, the top part of 貴 delineates two hands holding something and lower part is a cowry. Since cowries were used as money in ancient times, the basic meanings of 貴 are "valuable," "expensive," and "costly." Extended meanings include "noble," "honorable," etc. In the simplified version of the character 贵, the radical 贝 (bèi, cowry shell) is developed from the cursive style of the character 貝. As either radical or character, 貝 is written as 贝 in simplified characters.

貴 會意。篆文上像雙手捧物，下從貝。貝代表錢，凸顯出手捧之物十分貴重。簡體字贵下部的贝是繁體貝的草書楷化字。

甲 𡘹 篆 姓

姓 xìng (surname)

Associative and pictophonetic compound. The character 姓 consists of 女 (nǚ, female) and 生 (shēng, give birth), meaning "surname." In the matrilineal society of ancient times, children adopted their mothers' surnames since women were considered superior to men. In the character 姓, 生 also functions as the phonetic element.

姓 會意兼形聲。從女，從生；生亦聲。姓是母系社會的反應。上古姓是族號，隨母系。

甲 𢦔 金 𢦔 篆 𢦔

我 wǒ (I; me)

Phonetic loan character. In the Oracle-Bone Inscriptions, the character 我 is the sketch of a weapon with a saw-toothed blade and a long shaft and originally referred to a kind of ancient weapon. Later 我 was borrowed to represent the personal pronoun "I" since the pronunciation of "I" was similar to that of 我. Consequently the character 我 no longer carried its original meaning, In Regular Script, the left part of 我 is 手 (shǒu, hand) and the right part 戈 (gē, dagger-ax), representing a hand holding a dagger to protect oneself.

我 甲骨文像兵器之形。後借為第一人稱，遂失本義。從手，像手執戈以自衛。

尼 篆

呢 ne (question particle)

Pictophonetic character. 呢 is made up of the mouth radical 口 (kǒu, mouth) and the phonetic element 尼 (ní). In ancient form, 尼 looks like two people close to each other, therefore meaning "close" or "intimate." In Chinese, question markers sometimes contain the radical 口, since one needs to open one's mouth to ask a question. 嗎 (ma), also introduced in this lesson, is another example of a question marker.

呢　語氣詞。會意兼形聲。從口，尼聲。尼，像二人從后相近之形，意為二人親昵，後作"昵"。

니 甲　金　篆

叫 jiào (to call; to shout)

Pictophonetic character. The character 叫 consists of the mouth radical 口 and the phonetic element 니 (jiū), meaning "call" or "shout." 니 (jiū) is the phonetic symbol of the character 叫 (jiào) because the pronunciations of jiū and jiào are similar. In ancient form, 니 looks like tangled vines or silk, and it means "entangle."

叫　形聲。從口，니聲。니意為糾纏，像籚蔓糾結狀。一說像絲綫纏繞。

什 shén (what)

Phonetic loan character. The character 什 is the combination of the person radical 亻 and 十 (shí, ten). In ancient times, a group of ten soldiers or ten households was named 什. Later 什 came to represent an interrogative without any change in form.

什 會意。從人，從十。古代戶籍十家為什，兵制十人為什。"什"後借用為疑問代詞。

篆

麼/么 me (interrogative auxiliary)

The character 麼 consists of the phonetic indicator 麻 (má, hemp) and the component 幺 (yāo, tiny), functioning as an interrogative auxiliary. In the Oracle-Bone and Bronze Inscriptions, 幺 and 么 (me) are used interchangeably to mean a "wisp of silk." The character 麻 combines 广 (guǎng, shed; roof; shelter) and 枼 (pài, to peel hemp), suggesting people processing hemp in a workshop. 麻 originally meant "hemp" or "flax." Since the surfaces of hemp and flax are not smooth, 麻 extends to mean "rough," "coarse," "numb," etc. The simplified character 么 is derived from the bottom part of the traditional 麼.

麼 助詞，語氣詞。從么，麻聲。么同幺，像一把細絲。麻，像在敞屋下（或屋簷下）劈麻晾麻。簡體字么取繁體字麼的下半部。

名 míng (name)

Associative compound. The character 名 has 夕 (xī, sunset; evening) on the top and 口 (kǒu, mouth) at the bottom, suggesting a person calling someone's name in the dark. Hence, 名 means "name," and also extends to mean "given name," "excuse," "reputation," "famous," etc. (See both 夕 and 口 in **Radicals.**)

名 會意。從口，從夕。夕，夜裏。夜裏色昏暗，相互看不見，只好叫名字。

字 zì (character)

Associative and pictophonetic compound. The character 字 has the roof radical 宀 on the top and 子 (zǐ, child) underneath, indicating a child in a house. The original meaning of 字 was to "give birth to" or "bring up," but later evolved to mean "characters." Children were supposed to remain at home, practicing their characters every day. You could probably memorize all the characters you have learned if you did the same!

字 會意兼形聲。從寶蓋頭，從子；子亦聲。用房屋中有子意指生養孩子。現可想象為孩子在屋中寫字。

甲 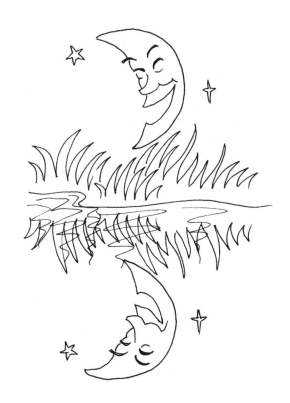 金

朋 péng (friend)

Pictograph. In the Oracle-Bone and Bronze Inscriptions, the character 朋 represents two strings of cowry shells, suggesting a monetary unit. Later 朋 extended to mean "friend" because the strings of shells are together. In Regular Script, the two strings of shells are replaced by two moons 月.

朋 象形。甲骨文、金文像兩串貝殼形，本義為古代貨幣單位，後引申為朋友。楷書寫作朋。

甲 𣎴 金 𢏚 篆 𦦙

友 yǒu (friend)

Associative compound. In its ancient form, the character 友 delineates two right hands together, to represent two people shaking hands, as friends would. You have learned in the Radicals Section that 又 (yòu) means "right hand." In Regular Script, the right hand in the upper part of 友 looks slightly different, but the one underneath remains the

same as the radical. In ancient times, people used 朋 (péng, friend) and 友 separately. Although they both mean "friend," 友 refers to a closer friend than 朋.

友 會意。甲骨文以兩人右手握在一起來指志同道合的朋友。

是 shì (to be)

Associative compound. In its ancient form, the character 是 is a combination of 日 (rì, sun) and 正 (zhèng, straight), indicating high noon. 是 originally meant "straight," and has evolved to mean "correct," "yes," "to be," etc. In Regular Script, the lower part of 是 is no longer 正, but instead like the lower part of 足 (zú, foot) and 走 (zǒu, to walk).（See 足 and 走 in **Radicals.**）

是 會意。金文從日，從正，表示日正當午。本義為正、直，引申意有正確、是非、肯定等。

老 lǎo (old)

Pictograph. In the Oracle-Bone and Bronze Inscriptions, the character 老 sketches an old man with long hair and a bent back, leaning on a walking stick. Although the character looks significantly different in its regular script form, one can still see evidence of the older forms.

老 象形。像長髮長鬚老人弓腰扶拐杖之形。

金 跃 篆 師 草 师

師/师 shī (teacher)

Associative compound. The character 師 consists of 自 (duī, hill) on the left and 帀 (zā, circle; surround) on the right, suggesting numerous people gathered on a hill. The original meaning of 師 is "mass," "army," and later came to mean "study," "teacher," etc. The simplified character 师 derives from the cursive style of the traditional character 師, and 自 is replaced by two vertical strokes.

師 會意。師字左邊 自 (duī)意為小土山，右部帀（zā）是環繞的意思，意指眾人環繞在土山旁。本義指眾人，軍隊、都邑，引申為學習、老師等。师是師字的草書楷化字。

嗎/吗 ma (question particle)

Pictophonetic character. The character 嗎 combines the mouth radical 口 with a phonetic 馬 (mǎ, horse). 馬 is a pictograph of a horse. The mouth radical 口 is often used as a component of interrogatives and onomatopoeic words. In the simplified form of the character (吗), the 马 part derives from the cursive form of 馬. (See 馬/马 in **Radicals**.)

嗎 形聲。部首"口"用於疑問詞或象聲詞。馬，象形字。簡體字右邊用了簡化的马字。

不 bù (not; no)

Phonetic loan character. In the Oracle-Bone Inscriptions, the horizontal stroke of the character 不 represents the ground, and the three strokes underneath signify a germinating seed. The original meaning of 不 was "seed of a plant," but later was borrowed to mean "no" or "not."

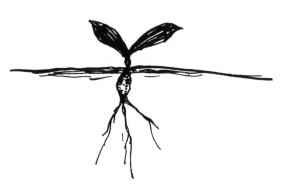

不 像種子萌芽即將破土而出時的形狀，是胚的本字。後多借為否定詞，本意遂不用。

學/学 xué (to study)

Associative compound. In the Bronze Inscriptions, the upper part of 學 represents two hands playing with four sticks, and the lower part shows a child under a roof, thereby representing a child learning math at home. You will find only the tops are different if you compare the character 學 with 字 (zì, character, see **Lesson 1**). The simplified character 学 derives from the cursive of the traditional form 學.

學 會義。金文像屋裏一個孩子雙手擺佈小木棍，學習計算。簡體学字是繁體學字的草書楷化字。

 金 篆

也 yě (also; too)

Phonetic loan character. In the Bronze Inscriptions and the Seal Script, 也 looks like a snake with a large head, and its original meaning was "snake." Later 也 was borrowed to mean "also" or "too," but the character still looks like a snake with a big head, a cobra perhaps.

也 在金文中 "也" 是一條拖著尾巴、頭部突出的蛇形。本義為蛇，后被借為語氣詞、助詞與副詞。

甲 金 篆 中

中 zhōng (center; middle)

Associative compound. In the Oracle-Bone Inscriptions, the character 中 represents streamers fluttering in the wind, perhaps at the center of a square. The original meaning of 中 is "flag" and it now means "center" or "middle."

中 會意。甲骨文、金文像樹立在場地中央迎風飛舞的旗幟。本義為旗幟，引申為中央。

甲 金 篆

國/国 guó (country; nation)

Associative compound. The character 國 represents its meaning in a concise and vivid way. Within the character 國, 囗 (wéi, enclose) stands for the boundary or moat surrounding a city, 一 represents the land, 口 (kǒu, mouth) the population, and 戈 (gē, dagger, ax) the weapon protecting the country. In the simplified character 国, the inside of the enclosure is replaced by the character 玉 (yù, jade), as an emperor's jade seal represents the highest authority of a country.

國 會意。囗像城池，一為土地，
口指人口，戈用以守衛。簡體字將中間部分改為玉字。國有玉璽，是會意字。

甲 金 篆

人 rén (man; person; humankind)

Pictograph. In the Oracle-Bone and Bronze Inscriptions, the character 人 presents the profile of a person with a head, an arched back, arms and legs, possibly indicating a figure from an early stage of human evolution. In Regular Script, 人 looks like someone with two rather long legs.

人 象形。甲骨文、金文像人側立之形。

甲 金 篆

美 měi (beautiful)

Associative compound. In the Oracle-Bone Inscriptions, the top part of 美 shows the front view of a goat's head with horns (羊), and the bottom part the front view of a person (大). In ancient times, men often wore horns or feathers on their heads as part of decorative costumes in celebrations or dances, which were considered beautiful. Hence, the meaning of 美 is "beautiful." In Regular Script, the character 美 is still a combination of 羊 (yáng, goat; sheep) and 大 (dà, big).

美 會意。從羊，從大。男子頭戴羊角作裝飾，是男性健美的表現。一說是羊肥大則肉味鮮美。

甲 金 篆

京 jīng (capital)

Pictograph. In the Oracle-Bone and Bronze Inscriptions, 京 (jīng, capital) resembles a large grand building at the top of a hill or mountain. "Capital" is the extended meaning of 京. You may compare 京 with 高 (see gāo, tall, in **Lesson 2**) and 亮 (see liàng, bright, in **Lesson 5**).

京 象形。像建于高丘之上的華屋大廈，引申為京城，首都。

紐/纽 niǔ (knob; button)

Associative and pictophonetic compound. The character 紐 consists of the silk radical 糸 and 丑 (chǒu) as both the phonetic and signifying component. Its original meaning was "to tie a knot." In its ancient form, 丑 looks like a hand twisting an object and its original meaning was "twist" or "wrench," but later was borrowed to mean "the second of the twelve Earthly Branches."

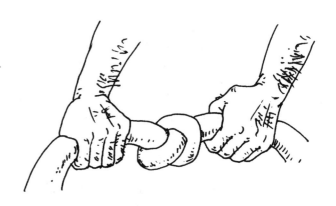

紐 會意兼形聲。從糸，丑聲。本義為打結，鈕扣為其引申義。丑，古字像以手用力扭曲一物，本義為擰扭，后借用表示地支的第二位而另造"扭"字表示擰扭之意。丑現也是繁體字醜的簡化字。

LESSON 2

篆

那 nà/nèi (that)

Associative compound. In the Seal Script, 那 is the combination of 冄 (rǎn, whiskers) and 邑 (yì, town; city), referring to foreigners with long beards and hair who lived west of ancient China. Later 冄邑 came to mean "that," and was simplified to 那. 阝 is a commonly used radical. When 阝 appears in the right part of a character, it means "town" or "city," which was derived from the character 邑. When 阝 is on the left side of a character, it signifies "mound" or "plenty," which was derived from the character 阜 (fù, mound; plenty), such as 郊 (jiāo, suburbs), or 陡 (dǒu, steep).

那 會意兼形聲。篆文從邑（城邑），冄 rǎn 聲，本義指留有長髮長鬚的西夷國人。楷書寫作那。

篆 張 長甲 金 篆 草 长

張 / 张 zhāng (open; MW; a surname)

Pictophonetic character. The character 張 consists of the bow radical 弓 (See 弓 in **Radicals**) and the phonetic element 長 (cháng; long). Its original meaning was "to draw a bow," and extended meanings include "open" and "display." 張 is also used as a measure word for things with flat surfaces. In the ancient writing systems, the character 長 looks similar to 老, as it also resembles an old figure with long hair and a walking stick. In the simplified character 张, the right part 长 derives from the cursive version of the character 長.

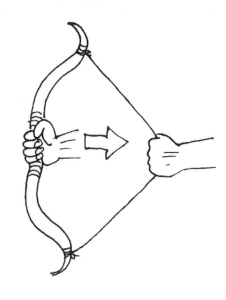

張 形聲。從弓，長聲。本義指把弦綳在弓上，引申為拉開弓。引申義有張開、擴張等。長，象形。甲骨文中像一長髮長鬚的老人弓腰拄拐形。簡體字张的右部长是由繁體字長的草書楷化而來。

金 𤎩 篆 照

照 zhào (to shine)

Associative and pictophonetic compound. The character 照 consists of the signifying parts 日 (rì, sun) and 灬 (fire radical), and the phonetic element 召 (zhāo, call), meaning "shine," "illuminate," "reflect," etc. The character 召 is the phonetic element that combines 刀 (dāo, knife) and 口 (kǒu, mouth).

照 會意兼形聲。金文左邊像手持火把狀，右邊召是聲旁。篆文改為火字旁，昭聲，昭也有日光明亮之意。

甲 片 篆 片

片 piàn (slice; piece; film)

Explicit character. You have learned the radical 木 (mù, wood). In Seal Script, 片 stands for the right part of 木, meaning to split wood into pieces. In Regular Script, 片 still resembles a piece of the character 木.

片 指事。從半木，是樹木劈開后右邊的一半。

篆 明　勺 金 ⼮ 篆 勺

的 de (noun modifier)

Associative compound. The character 的 consists of 白 (bái; white) and 勺 (sháo, ladle; spoon). Its original meaning was "bright-colored" or "distinctive." Now 的 is used to connect an attributive to a noun. Both 白 and 勺 are pictographs. In its ancient form, 白 may resemble the bright rays spreading from the sun or a grain of white rice—scholars differ on the explanation. 勺 is the outline of a ladle containing something.

的 形聲。篆文從日，勺聲，楷書寫作"的"。白 象形。像日出光芒射出狀。一說像白米粒。勺 象形。像用勺舀物。

篆 遣

這/这 zhè/zhèi (this)

The character 這 is a combination of 辶 (walk radical) and 言 (yán, word; to speak), indicating the action of walking somewhere to speak. 這 originally meant to "go to a certain place," and came to mean "meet," "welcome," "here," and "this." The walk radical 辶 is often used in characters pertaining to movement with the feet, e.g., 進/进 (jìn, enter), 過/过 (guò, pass), and 逛 (guàng, stroll). In the simplified character 这, 文 replaces 言.

這 本義為迎接。從辶，表示前去；從言，表示以言語相迎。簡體字这以文取代言，屬符號替代字。清代已見此字。

父 甲 ㄅ 金 ㄈ 篆 ㄓ 巴 篆 ㄅ

爸 bà (dad)

Pictophonetic character. The character 爸 is made up of the radical 父 (fù, father) and the phonetic 巴 (bā, cling to). In its ancient form, 父 delineates a hand holding a stone ax—an important tool and weapon in primitive society. In Seal Script 巴 looks like a snake with a mouth supposedly large enough to swallow an elephant. The original meaning of 巴 was "snake." Later it came to mean "cling to" or "stick to" because when a snake moves, its body always clings to something.

爸　從父、巴聲。父　象形。甲骨文、金文字形像手持石斧工作狀。巴，象形。篆文中像一條張著大嘴的蛇。

媽/妈 mā (mom)

Pictophonetic character. The character 媽 is composed of 女 (nǔ, female) and 馬 (mǎ, horse). 女 shows the character's meaning relates to someone female and 馬 indicates the pronunciation. 媽 does not mean female horse, though! In the simplified character 妈，马 derives from the cursive form of 馬. (See 馬/马 in **Radicals** and 嗎/吗 in **Lesson 1**.)

媽　形聲。從女，馬聲。簡體字妈右邊的馬簡化為马。

篆

個/个 gè (MW)

Associative compound. The character 個 consists of the person radical 亻 and the phonetic element 固 (gù, solid; consolidate). 個 is a commonly used measure word for people and other nouns. 固 has 囗 (wéi, enclose) outside and 古 (gǔ, ancient) inside, indicating an invincible city. 古 is the combination of 十 (shí, ten) and 口 (kǒu, mouth), suggesting the way in which ancient stories are passed down orally generation to generation. Thus, the meaning of 古 is "ancient." Many complex Chinese characters are the combinations of a few simple characters. If you have learned the character 個, you have also learned 固 and 古. The character 個 was originally written as 个, and the simplified character 个 restores this original form.

個/个 象形。竹像兩根並生的竹子，个為一根竹子，本用以指竹子的數量，擴大範圍以後用作量詞。後另造"個"字。個，從人，固聲，簡化後仍為"个"。固，從口，從古，指城四周有墻保護，便可永固不破，引申為堅硬，牢固等。古，從十從口，十代表衆多，意指在有文字記載以前，衆口相傳遠古之事。

甲  金 篆 男

男 nán (male)

Associative compound. The character 男 consists of 田 (tián, field) and 力 (lì, plow, also meaning physical strength or power). (See 田 and 力 in **Radicals**.) In ancient agricultural societies, men provided most of the manpower in the fields, and it was the men's duty to plow the fields.

男 會意。從田，從力(甲骨文像犁形)，借用犁耕田來代表男子。"男耕女織"在田裏耕種主要是男人的事。

篆 **𩠹** 亥甲 **𠄏** 金 **𠂈**

孩 hái (child)

Pictophonetic character. 孩 consists of the radical 子 (zǐ, child; son) and the phonetic symbol 亥 (hài; cut). Its original meaning was children's laughter. Later it came to simply mean "child." In the Oracle-Bone and Bronze Inscriptions, 亥 is a pictograph of a pig without a head and feet, meaning "to cut." In Regular Script, the character 亥 still resembles a pig, but one with its head on the top and two legs and a tail as the lower part.

孩 形聲。從子，亥聲。本義為小兒笑聲，引申為兒童，孩子。亥，象形。甲骨文像切掉頭、蹄的豬，是"刻"的本字，本義為切割。

甲 **𝍦** 金 **𝍦** 篆 **𝍦**

子 zǐ (baby; child)

Pictograph. In its ancient form, the character 子 shows a baby swaddled in cloth, with its head sticking up and arms stretching out. In Regular Script, the head of the baby is represented by a horizontal hook instead of a round shape.

子 象形。像頭部突出、手臂在外、裹在襁褓中的嬰兒。

Lesson 2

金  篆 誰

誰/谁 shéi (who)

Pictophonetic character. The character 誰
is the combination of the word radical 言
and the phonetic element 隹 (zhuī;
short-tailed bird). (See both 言 and 隹
in **Radicals**). 誰 does not mean the
speech of a bird, but the personal
interrogative pronoun "who." In the
simplified character 谁, the speech radical
is simplified. (See 請/请 in **Lesson 1**.)

誰 形聲。從言，隹聲。簡體字偏旁簡化。

他 tā (he)

他 is built with the person radical 亻 and the
character 也 (yě, also). It originally meant
"other" and is used today as the third person
pronoun for males. You learned 也 in **Lesson 1**.

他 第三人稱代詞。人字旁加也。也，見第一
課的解釋。

弟 dì (younger brother)

Associative compound. In its ancient form, the character 弟 looks like a man with a bow on his shoulder. Some scholars believe the character 弟 refers to a cord wound around something. The original meaning of 弟 was "order" and came to mean "younger brother." In Regular Script, we can still see the bow (see 弓 in **Radicals** and the character 張 in this lesson) in the character 弟. Other than the bow, the top part of 弟 looks like a child's hair twisted in two knots and the lower part the two legs.

弟 象形。像人身上背弓箭形，古時年輕人挂弓箭祭奠死去的長者。一説上像總角，下像腿形。另一説弟本意指以繩捆物的次第。

女 nǚ (female; woman)

Pictograph. In the Oracle-Bone Inscriptions, the character 女 shows a woman kneeling down with her arms lowered and hands clasped in front, signifying the lower social status of women in ancient times. In the later forms, the kneeling part is removed and women are shown standing up, like men.

女 象形。甲骨文像女子双臂交叉，跪坐在地形。

甲  金 篆

妹 mèi (younger sister)

Pictophonetic character. The character 妹 is made up of the female radical 女 and the phonetic 未 (wèi, future). In its ancient form, 未 is a pictograph of a tree with many leaves. (Compare 未 with 木.) 未 originally meant "luxuriant," and later came to mean "future." "Younger sister," therefore, is a young girl with bounteous future.

妹 形聲。從女，未聲。未，甲骨文像樹木生長旺盛，枝葉繁茂狀。本義為繁茂，引申義為將來。

她 tā (she)

她 consists of the female radical 女 and the character 也 (yě, also). It is used as the third person pronoun for females. Both 他 (tā, he) and 她 (tā, she) have the component 也 in the right part, but the character 他 has the person radical 亻 while 她 has the female radical 女.

她 從女，從也。女性第三人稱代詞。

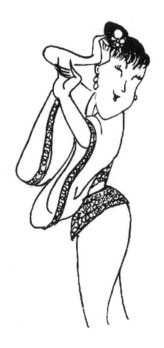

兒/儿 ér (son; child)

Pictograph. In its ancient form, 兒 looks like a baby whose fontanel has not finished forming. 兒 means "small child" and "son." In Regular Script, 兒 resembles a baby with a big head and two thin legs. The simplified form of the character (儿) uses only the bottom part of the traditional form (兒).

兒 象形。像頭囟未合的嬰兒。簡體字儿僅保存兒字的下半部。

有 yǒu (to have; there are)

Associative and pictophonetic compound. In the Bronze Inscriptions and Seal Script, the character 有 delineates a right hand (yòu, 又) holding a piece of meat (yuè, 月), meaning "to possess" or "to have." 又 also serves as the phonetic component of the character. The character 月 means moon, but when used as a radical, usually means "flesh." For example, the characters 腿 (tuǐ, leg), 臉/脸 (liǎn, face), 腦/脑 (nǎo, brain), and 腳/脚 (jiǎo, foot) all have the flesh radical 月. Be careful not to confuse 有 (yǒu, to have) and 友 (yǒu, friend).

有 會意兼形聲。金文、篆文從又（右手）持肉（肉月旁），意為持有。

篆

沒/没 méi (to not have)

Associative compound. In Seal Script, 沒 consists of a circle or whirlpool 回 on top, and a right hand 又 at the bottom, indicating a person sinking in a whirlpool with one hand sticking out. It makes sense that the original meaning of 沒 was "to sink" or "disappear." Current meanings include "disappear," "end," and "to not have." In Regular Script, a water radical 氵 is added on the left of the character and the component 回 on the top has been simplified to 几 or 勹.

沒 會意。從水。篆文像人淹沒在漩渦中，水面上只能看見一只手狀。本義為淹沒，引申為沒有。

 甲 金 篆

高 gāo (tall; high)

Pictograph. In the Oracle-Bone and Bronze Inscriptions, the character 高 looks like a tall building with a tower above and wall with a gate underneath, conveying the meanings "tall" or "high." When you memorize the character, try to imagine a two-story building with a gate on each level. Don't forget the tower on the top!

高 象形。像高聳的樓臺。

 甲

家 jiā (family; home)

Associative compound. In the Oracle-Bone and Bronze Inscriptions, the character 家 consists of the roof radical 宀 on top and a pig 豕 underneath. In an agricultural society, a household without pigs or other livestock would be considered poor. In its ancient forms, 豕 is the pictograph of a pig with a head, rounded body, legs, and a short tail. Distinguish between 豕 and 亥, the pig without head and feet. (See 亥 in the character 孩 in this lesson.)

家 會意。從寶蓋頭，從豕，表示在家中養豬。農業社會中不養牲畜不像一個家。

 金 篆

幾/几 jǐ (how many; a few)

Associative compound. The character 幾 consists of two wisps of silk 幺幺 (yāo, tiny; small) on top, and a person with a dagger-axe 戍 (shù, guard; defend) at the bottom. Originally 幾 meant signs of danger to guard against. Later it came to mean "few" or "how many." Whether used in a statement or a question, 幾 refers only to a small number (between one and nine). Originally the character 几 (jī) meant a small table. In simplified characters, 几 is used to replace 幾 and means "how many" or "a few" because the pronunciations of the two characters are very similar.

幾 會意。上部"幺幺"表示微小，下部"戍"意為防備。表示在發現細微跡象時就要警惕，加以防備。本義為細微跡象、先兆，後作為數詞、疑問詞。戍，會意。甲骨文、金文像人持戈。几字早已存在，如茶几。簡體字用几代替幾，屬同音替代字。

篆 哥

哥 gē (elder brother)

Associative compound. In the Oracle-Bone Inscriptions, 可 (kě) resembles a mouth exhaling, and meant "approve" or "okay." The character 哥 consists of two 可 characters, one on the top of the other, showing someone opening his or her mouth to sing. Therefore, the original meaning of 哥 was "to sing," but later came to mean "elder brother." For the word "sing," 欠 (qiàn, yawn; breathe) is added to the right part of 哥 (歌 gē, sing). Does anyone have a big brother who always opens his big mouth to sing?

哥 會意。從二可。可有歡樂的意思，表示聲聲相連歌不斷，樂在其中，是歌的本字。后稱兄為哥，遂加欠作歌。

金 帀 篆 兩

兩/两 liǎng (two; a couple)

Associative compound. In the Bronze Inscriptions, the character 兩 resembles a chariot with two yokes, meaning "a couple" or "two." In Regular Script, 兩 retains the same basic structure as that of the Bronze Inscription form. In the simplified character 两, the inside is composed of two 人, differing slightly from the traditional character 兩.

兩 會意兼形聲。金文像車衡上有兩個軛的戰車，引申為並列成雙之物。簡體字两去掉兩字中間一豎，並把中間的兩個入字改為兩個人字。這種寫法元代已見。

甲  金 篆

和 hé (and; harmonious)

Pictophonetic character. 和 is a simplification of the character 龢. In its ancient form, 龢 has 龠 (yuè, the pictograph for a flute-like instrument) as the signifying component and 禾 (hé, a pictograph for a ripe rice plant) as the phonetic symbol, meaning "harmonious." Today it also means "echo," "and," "peace," "mild," etc. In Regular Script, 龠 is replaced by 口 (kǒu, mouth) since one uses one's mouth to play wind instruments (like flutes). 禾 remains part of the character today, but is found on the left side instead of the right.

和 形聲。甲骨文從龠，禾聲，意指樂聲和諧。引申為和諧、協調、和睦、和好等意，也可用作連詞。古文簡化，改龠為口。龠，像一由多條竹管做成的笙簫。禾，像一株禾形。上像禾穗，下像根部。

甲 篆 金

做/作 zuò (to do)

Associative compound. In the Oracle-Bone and Bronze Inscriptions, the character 作 is written as 乍 (zhà). 乍 looks like the stitching of a collar, and its original meaning was therefore "to do" or "to make." In Seal Script, the person radical 亻 is added to 乍 to form 作. 做 developed later than 作, and is the combination of 亻 and 故 (gù, former). When 作 is used as a verb, it is often interchangeable with 做.

做/作 會意。從人，從乍。甲骨文、金文寫為"乍"，意指縫製衣領。後加人字旁為"作"。"做"是後起字，在一些意思上二字相通。

篆

英 yīng (flower; hero)

Pictophonetic character. The character 英 is the combination of the grass radical 卄 and the phonetic 央 (yāng, center). Its original meaning was "flower" and extended meanings include "hero," and "outstanding." In Chinese, "England" is translated as 英國/国 (yīngguó) and "English" as 英文 (yīngwén), based on the English pronunciation of these words. The grass radical 卄 derives from the character 艸 (cǎo, grass), which looks like two blades of grass. In the Oracle-Bone Inscriptions, the character 央 looks like a figure carrying something on a shoulder pole. Since the figure stands in the middle, 央 means "middle" or "center." In Regular Script, 央 resembles a figure from the front (dà, 大) with something on his or her shoulders.

英 形聲。從卄，央聲。本義指花，引申為美好、傑出、才能出眾。央，古文像一人挑擔，意為正中、中心。

甲　　金　　篆

文 wén (script; language)

Pictograph. In the Oracle-Bone and Bronze Inscriptions, the character 文 shows a man with a tattoo on his chest. The original meaning of 文 was "tattoo" or "pattern." Later it came to mean "script," "language," "writing," etc. In Regular Script, the character 文 still looks like a man with a broad chest, but without the tattoo.

文 象形。甲骨文像一正面站立、胸有刺青的人形。

篆 律 書 甲 ※ 金 ※ 篆 肃

律 lǜ (law; rule)

Pictophonetic character. The character 律 combines the radical 彳 (left step; walk slowly) with 聿 (yù, pen; then) as the phonetic symbol, meaning "rule" or "law." In the Oracle-Bone and Bronze Inscriptions, 聿 shows a hand holding a brush. 聿 is often used in characters pertaining to brushwork, such as 書 (shū, book), 筆 (bǐ, pen), and 畫 (huà, painting).

律 從彳（左腳走半步為彳，一説彳為小步走走停停的樣子，一説指半條街），聿聲。意為法律、規則。聿，象形。甲骨文像以手持筆狀，本義為筆。

金 都 篆 都

都 dōu (all; both)

Pictophonetic character. When the radical 阝 appears on the right side of a character, it means "town" or "city" as 阝 is derived from 邑 (yì, town; city; county). (See 阝 in the character 那 in this lesson.) In the Bronze Inscriptions and Seal Script, 都 consists of the phonetic symbol 者 (zhě) and 邑 as the signifying component，meaning "big city" or "capital" (pronounced as dū). 都 is also used as an adverb, meaning "all" (pronounced dōu). In Regular Script, the upper part of 者 is the same as that of 老, but the bottom part is 曰.

都 形聲。金文從邑，者聲。本義為都市，引申義為全部（副詞）。者，會意。甲骨文、金文中像將食物投到鍋中煮。者是煮的本字。

篆

醫/医 yī (doctor; cure; medicine)

Associative compound. The character 醫 combines 医 (yī, an arrow 矢 in a quiver 匚), with 殳 (shū, an ancient weapon), and 酉 (yǒu, a wine jar), indicating the use of alcohol to heal a wound. Both 矢 and 酉 are pictographs in the Oracle-Bone and Bronze Inscriptions. 殳 looks like a hand holding a weapon. The simplified character 医 retains only the left top of the traditional character 醫.

醫 會意。医，古時盛箭的器具。殳 shū，會意。甲骨文像一只手拿一件圓頭兵器，意指一種古代兵器。酉，象形。像一個尖底的酒壇子。酒可以用以治病。醫指受到箭傷或兵器的傷害，可以用酒來消毒治病。簡體字医僅保留醫字左上方的部分。

篆  草

愛/爱 ài (love; be fond of)

Associative and pictophonetic compound. In the Seal Script, the top part of 愛 is both the phonetic and signifying component (pronounced ài, meaning "love") and the bottom part is the signifying element (夊 suī, walk back and forth; hover). It seems a man is deeply falling in love with a woman, hovering around her house and being reluctant to leave. The simplified character 爱 derives from the cursive style of the traditional form 愛.

愛 會意兼形聲。篆文上部標聲兼表意(ài, love)，下部從夊(suī 腳)，表示心有所愛而腳下徘徊不忍離去，有慈愛、情愛、喜愛等意。爱是愛字的草書楷化字，去掉愛字中間的心字而將夊字改為友。

LESSON 3

甲) 金 D 篆 ⟨moon glyph⟩

月 yuè (moon; month)

Pictograph. In the Oracle-Bone and Bronze Inscriptions, the character 月 shows a crescent moon. In Chinese legend, the dark part is believed to be the reflection of the beautiful Chang'E and her jade rabbit. The Chinese are very fond of the moon, and descriptions of it can be found in hundreds of poems. During the Moon Festival holiday on August fifteenth of the lunar calendar, family members get together to watch the full moon while eating moon cakes. Since the change from new moon to full moon to new moon again takes about thirty days, 月 is also used to mean "month."

月 象形。像彎月形。

篆 ⟨glyph⟩ 虎 甲 ⟨glyph⟩ 金 ⟨glyph⟩ 篆 ⟨glyph⟩

號/号 hào (number)

Associative compound. The character 號 is the combination of 号 (hào, cry) and 虎 (hǔ; tiger), indicating the roar of a tiger. The original meaning of 號 was "shout," and extended meanings include "command," "order," "mark," "number," and "date." The character 号 consists of 口 (kǒu, mouth) and 丂 (kǎo, breathe), meaning "to cry." In the Oracle-Bone Inscriptions the character 虎 vividly depicts a tiger. In Regular Script, 虎 is made up of 虍 (hū, tiger radical) and 几 (jī, small table).

號 會意兼形聲。從号，從虎；号亦聲。本義為虎叫，引申為呼叫、日期等。号像口中出氣，意指呼喊。虎，象形。像老虎之形。簡體字号僅保留繁體的左邊一半。

星 xīng (star)

Pictophonetic character. In the Bronze Inscriptions, the character 星 consists of three 日 shaped stars in the upper part and the phonetic indicator 生 (shēng, born, **Lesson 1**) on the lower part. In Regular Script, 星 has only one star on top of 生.

星 形聲。從日，生聲。甲骨文像光芒閃耀的群星，金文改成三顆星，下加聲旁，楷書減為一顆星。

期 qī (period of time)

Pictophonetic character. The character 期 is composed of the moon radical 月 and the phonetic element 其 (qí), meaning "period of time," "expectation" or "appointment." Since people observe the cycles of the sun or the moon to tell time, in Chinese 日 (rì, sun; day) and 月 (yuè, moon; month) are sometimes used as radicals in characters pertaining to time, such as 朝 (zhāo, early morning), 晚 (wǎn; evening; late) and 昨 (zuó, yesterday; past). In the Oracle-Bone Inscriptions, the

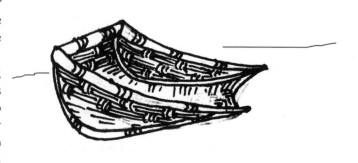

character 其 is a pictograph of a dustpan or winnowing pan (used to sift grain), meaning "dustpan." Later 其 was primarily used as a third person pronoun.

期 形聲。從月，其聲。其，象形。甲骨文像簸箕形，本義為簸箕。後因用為語氣詞，遂另造箕字。

甲 金 篆

天 tiān (sky; heaven; day)

Explicit character. As explained in the Radicals Section, the character 大 (dà, big) represents the front view of a figure. In the character 天, the horizontal stroke above 大 symbolizes "sky" or "heaven." 天 is also used to mean "God," "weather" or "day."

天 指事。從一、大。"大"為正面人形，"一"指頭上有天。

甲 金 篆

日 rì (sun; day)

Pictograph. In the Oracle-Bone and Bronze Inscriptions, 日 represents the sun. Since the sun rises daily, 日 extends to mean "day." Regular Script is also called Square Script and there are usually no round components, so the character 日 in Regular Script is drawn as a rectangle with a horizontal line through its middle, which indicates that the sun is not just a circle, but a solid thing.

日 象形。像太陽的輪廓。

今 jīn (today; now)

Pictograph. In the Oracle-Bone and Bronze Inscriptions, 今 looks like a figure with an open mouth, sticking out his or her tongue in preparation to drink. 今, therefore means "now" and "the present."

今 象形。像一人正張口喝下面罐子裏的酒，表示此時、現在的意思。

年 nián (year)

Associative compound. In the Oracle-Bone and Bronze Inscriptions, the character 年 depicts a figure carrying crops on his or her back. The original meaning of 年 was "harvest." Since a harvest is the result of a year's hard work, 年 extends to mean "year."

年 形聲兼會意。從禾，從人。甲骨文像人背禾形，表示五穀成熟是一年勞作的成果，引申為一年。

66

甲  金 篆

多 duō (many)

Associative compound. In its ancient form, the character 多 looks like two pieces of meat, meaning "extra," "large amount," or "many." In Regular Script, 多 became one 夕 (xī, sunset, evening) on the top of another 夕. (See 夕 in **Radicals.**)

多 會意。多字像兩塊肉形。古時祭祀用肉，用兩塊以表示多。

甲 金 篆

大 dà (big; great)

Pictograph. In the ancient writing systems, the character 大 portrays a figure standing with arms stretching out and legs spread apart. This posture seems to suggest that humans are the greatest creatures on earth. The primary meanings of 大 are "big," "large," and "great."

大 象形。像正面人形。天地萬物中以人為大為貴，故用人形來表示大。

甲  金 篆

歲/岁 suì (age; year)

Associative compound. In the Oracle-Bone and Bronze Inscriptions, the character 歲 contains a tool with a long shaft and two footprints next to the tool, meaning "step forward to harvest." Since crops are harvested once a year, 歲 extends to mean "year" and "age." In Regular Script, 歲 consists of an ax-type tool 戌 (xū), with a footprint 止 (zhǐ) on the top and another footprint under 戌. The two footprints together become the character 步 (bù, footstep; pace). When you memorize the character 歲, you will have learned three additional characters: 止, 步, and 戌. A variant form of 歲 is 崴. The simplified character 岁 replaces the bottom part of 崴 with 夕.

歲 會意。甲骨文、金文從戉 （yuè 斧形，此處象徵收割用具），從步，指在田裏邁步向前用鐮刀之類農具收割莊稼。戉也兼表聲。歲本義為收割，引申為一年的收成、年齡等。篆文改戉為戌（xū 斧形兵器）。歲有異體字崴，簡體岁字保留了繁體崴字上部的山，而下部改為夕字。

篆

吃 chī (to eat)

Pictophonetic character. The character 吃 combines the mouth radical 口 and the phonetic 乞 (qǐ), meaning "to eat." The character 乞 is derived from the character 气 (qì, air) meaning "to supplicate" or "beg for alms," etc. In the Oracle-Bone and Bronze Inscriptions, 气 looks like three thin clouds in the sky, meaning "air" or "breath." Be sure to note the difference between 气 and 乞.

吃 形聲。從口，乞聲，意為進食。乞，本為气，像天上的雲氣浮動狀。后省去一筆為乞。乞由气字分化而來，意為請求、乞討。

免 金 宁

晚 wǎn (evening; late)

Pictophonetic character. The character 晚 combines the sun radical 日 with the phonetic 免 (miǎn), meaning "evening" or "late." In its ancient form, 免 looks like a person with a big hat, meaning "take off," "remove," or "exempt" (even though the hat is still on the person's head).

晚 形聲。從日，免聲。免，會意。
像人帶著冠冕形，意為脫去，赦
免等。

篆 飯 草 饭

飯/饭 fàn (meal; food)

Pictophonetic character. The character 飯 consists of the food radical 飠 and the phonetic element 反 (fǎn), meaning "cooked rice," "meal," or "food." In its ancient form, 反 depicts a hand next to a cliff, suggesting a person climbing. Its original meaning was "to climb," and extended meanings included "against," "opposite" and "turn over." Note the difference between the food radical 飠 and the character for food 食 (see 食 in **Radicals**). The food radical 饣 developed from the cursive of 飠 and is always written as 饣 in simplified characters.

飯 形聲。從食，反聲。反, 會意。從厂 (hǎn
山崖)，從又（右手），表示以手攀崖。簡
體字中，作為部首的食 一律簡化為饣。饣
由食 的草書楷化而來。

怎 zěn (how)

Pictophonetic character. The character 怎 consists of the heart radical 心 and the phonetic symbol 乍 (zhà/zuò), meaning "why," or "how." In the Oracle-Bone and Bronze Inscriptions, 乍 looks like the stitching of a collar. The original meaning of 乍 was "to make" or "to do," (see 做/作 zuò, in **Lesson 2**) and later extended to mean "for the first time," "spread," or "abruptly."

怎 代詞，表示疑問。從心，乍聲。乍，像用針縫製衣領。

篆

樣/样 yàng (shape; kind)

Pictophonetic character. The character 樣 combines the wood radical 木 and the phonetic element 羕 (yàng). Its original meaning was "acorn." Later it came to mean "shape," "kind," or "type." The character 羕 is made up of the phonetic 羊 (yáng, goat) and the signifying part 永 (yǒng, swim), meaning "undulate." (See 羊 in the character 美 měi, beautiful, in **Lesson 1**.) The ancient form of 羊 depicts a goat head and the character 永 to show a figure swimming. In the simplified character 样, 羊 replaces 羕 since their pronunciations are similar.

樣 形聲。從木，羕聲。羕，形聲。從永，羊聲，形容水長。永，會意。甲骨文從人，像人在水流中游泳狀。本義指游泳，是泳的本字。後加水旁作泳，而以永為永久意。羊，象形。像羊頭之形。簡體字样把繁體右部的聲旁羕改為羊。

甲  金 篆

太 tài (too; extremely)

Explicit character. The character 大 means
"big." A dot is added under 大 to emphasize
the large size or scale. Consequently, 太
means "too," "excessively," or "extremely."

太 指事。為強調事物過大，在大字下再加
一點。

篆

了 le (particle for the completion of an action)

Pictograph. In Seal Script, 了 looks like a baby
who is wrapped in swaddling clothes. The original
meaning of 了 was to finish wrapping a baby in a
blank or swaddling clothes. Now 了 is used to
mean the end or completion of an event or action.
Compare 了 with 子 (see zǐ, son, in **Lesson 2**).

了 象形。從子，但無臂，像嬰兒在縕褓中束其
兩臂。本義為收束，引申為完畢，了解，結束等。

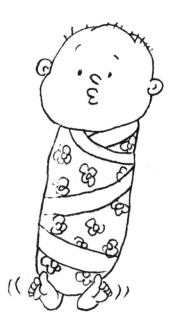

射 甲  金 篆

謝/谢 xiè (thank)

Pictophonetic character. The character
謝 consists of the radical 言 and the
phonetic symbol 射 (shè). The
original meaning of 謝 was "resign."
Its extended meanings are "decline,"
"apologize," and "thank." In the
Bronze Inscriptions, the character 射
depicts a hand drawing a bow,
meaning "to shoot." In Seal Script, the
bow is replaced by a human body 身 (shēn). In its ancient form 身 is a pictograph of
a pregnant woman. In Regular Script, 謝 is the combination of three characters: 言
(yán, word), 身 (shēn, body), and 寸 (cùn, inch). (See 寸 in **Radicals**.) As a
radical, 言 is always written as 讠 in simplified characters.

謝 形聲。從言，射聲。射，會義。甲骨文像張弓射箭形。金文加手。篆文將弓
改為身，從寸。寸有手義。意指用手張弓射箭始于身而及于遠。身，像人腹有身
孕形。簡體字中，作為字左邊部首的言 一律簡化為讠 。

甲  金 篆

喜 xǐ (to like; happy)

Associative compound. The character 喜 is the
combination of 壴 (zhù; drum) and 口 (kǒu, mouth),
indicating laughing while beating a drum. In its ancient
form, 壴 looks like a drum with decoration on top and
a stand underneath. 喜 means "happy," "happy event,"
"to be fond of," or "to like."

喜 會意。從壴（zhù 鼓），從口，意指張口笑着，歡
樂击鼓。

篆

歡/欢 huān (joyful)

Pictophonetic character. The character 歡 consists of 欠 (qiàn, breathe; yawn) as the radical and the phonetic element 雚 (guàn), meaning "joyous," or "vigorously." The ancient form of 雚 looks like an owl with a large head and eyes, and also means "owl." In Regular Script, 雚 is the combination of 艹 (grass radical), two 口 (kǒu, mouth), and 隹 (zhuī, short-tailed bird). (See 隹 in **Radicals.**) In the Oracle-Bone Inscriptions, 欠 looks like a person with a mouth open wide to breathe or yawn. In the simplified character 欢, 又 replaces 雚.

歡 形聲。從欠，雚 guàn 聲。雚，小雀或貓頭鷹。欠，象形。甲骨文中像人張口出气狀。人像鳥一般張口嘰嘰喳喳般説話，意為歡喜快樂。簡體欢字左邊以又取代雚。明清已有欢字。

金  篆

還/还 hái/huán (still; yet)

Pictophonetic character. The character 還 consists of the walk radical 辶 and the phonetic component 睘 (qióng/huán, look around with fear; lonely). The original meaning of 還 was "go back" or "return" (pronounced huán). Today it is also used as the adverb "still" (pronounced hái). In Seal Script, 睘 is the combination of an eye 目 on the top and the phonetic symbol 袁 (yuán) underneath. 袁 looks like a garment with a jade ring in the middle, meaning "long garment." Compare the lower part of 睘 with the character 衣 (yī, clothes) in the **Radicals** section. In the simplified character 还, 不 replaces 睘.

還 形聲。從辶，睘(qióng/huán)聲，返回、交還之意。亦用作副詞，表示持續。睘，回首驚視之意。簡體字还用不取代睘。元代已有此字。

甲 可 金 可 篆 可

可 kě (but; may; to permit)

Associative compound. In the Oracle-Bone Inscriptions, 可 resembles a mouth exhaling, and means "approve." The extended meanings of 可 include "fit," "okay," "may," "can," and "but." You have learned the character 哥 (see gē, elder brother, in **Lesson 2**), which contains two 可 characters, one on top of the other.

可 會意兼形聲。從口，從丂(kǎo)；丂亦聲。丂，气欲舒出狀。本義為口中舒气以示認可，引申為許可、同意等。

們/们 mén (plural suffix)

Pictophonetic compound. 們 is the plural marker for people. It consists of the person radical 亻 and the phonetic component 門 (mén; door, see 門 in **Radicals**). 門 is always written as 门 in simplified form.

們 形聲。從人，門聲。簡體字中，門皆簡化為门。

篆 黑占 占 甲 占 篆 占

點/点 diǎn (dot; o'clock)

Pictophonetic character. The character 點 combines the radical 黑 (hēi, black) and the phonetic symbol 占 (zhàn, divination), meaning "speck" or "spot." Extended meanings include "drop," "point," "a little," "o'clock," etc. In the Bronze Inscriptions, the character 黑 looks like a sweaty person whose face is blackened from the smoke of fire. (See **Radicals** to find the character 火 (huǒ, fire) and the fire radical 灬.) The character 占 consists of 卜 (bǔ, a crack on an oracle-bone) and 口 (kǒu, mouth), suggesting the interpretation of cracks on oracle bones. The simplified character 点 retains the fire radical 灬 under 占.

點 形聲。從黑，占聲。黑 會意。甲骨文、金文中像一個被煙熏火烤、大汗淋漓、滿面污垢的人。占 會意。從卜（龜殼燒裂後出現的兆紋），從口，意指觀察兆紋解釋凶吉。簡體字点去掉黑字的上半部，把灬移到占字下。明清已有此字。

篆 鐘 草 鍾 童 金 童 篆 童

鐘/钟 zhōng (clock)

Pictophonetic character. The character 鐘 consists of the radical 金 (jīn, metal; gold, see 金 in **Radicals**) and the phonetic component 童 (tóng), meaning "bronze bell" or "clock." In Regular Script, 童 is made up of 立 (lì, stand), 田 (tián, field), and 土 (tǔ, earth; soil, see 田 and 土 in **Radicals**), meaning "male slave" or "child." You may imagine male slaves turning over the soil with plows in the fields or children playing with earth in the fields. In the simplified character 钟, the gold/metal radical 金 is simplified into 钅, and the right part 童 is replaced by 中 (the pronunciation of 中 is the same as 鐘).

鐘 形聲。從金，童聲，意指古代鐘樂。童，會意兼形聲。金文從辛（刑刀），從人，從東（東西），指人頭上有刀，身負重物。本義為男奴隸，引申為兒童。金作為部首時，在簡體字中簡化為钅，是由草書楷化而來。钟字右邊以中替代童，屬近音替代。

金 辛 篆 半

半 bàn (half)

Associative compound. In its ancient form, the character 半 consists of 八 (bā, divide; eight) and 牛 (niú, ox), indicating cutting an ox in half. In the Oracle-Bone Inscriptions, the character 牛 depicts the front view of an ox's head. In the character 半 in Regular Script, 八 is upside down and 牛 loses one stroke on the left.

半 會意。上從八（分開），下從牛。表示將牛從中切為兩半，意為事物的二分之一。

甲 ⌣ 金 二 篆 上

上 shàng (above; top)

Explicit character. In the Oracle-Bone and Bronze Inscriptions, 上 consists of two horizontal lines. The longer line on the bottom represents the horizon; the short line on top represents something above the horizon. In Regular Script, a vertical line is added on top of the longer horizontal line. The primary meaning of 上 is "above," "upper" or "top." Extended meanings of 上 include: "up," "on," "go to," and "last."

上 指事。表示在一物在另一物之上。

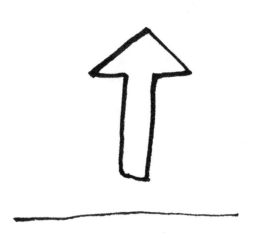

甲 金 篆 草

見/见 jiàn (to see)

Associative compound. In the Oracle-Bone and Bronze Inscriptions, the character 見 looks like a person with one large eye in place of a head, meaning "to see" or "meet." In Regular Script, 見 looks like a cartoon rendition of a figure with a big eye above two thin legs. The simplified character 见 derives from the cursive style of the traditional form 見.

見 會意。從目從儿。儿指人，表示人看東西時要睜大眼睛。簡體字见是繁體字見的草書楷化字。

甲 金 篆

再 zài (again)

Associative compound. In its ancient form, the character 再 looks like two fish in a basket, meaning "twice" or "once again." In Regular Script, the upper part of 再 resembles the handle of the basket, the middle part resembles the bodies of two fish and the lower part resembles the fish tails.

再 會意。甲骨文中其上下橫為二，當中像篆中的魚形，意指提兩條魚。本義為第二次，兩次。一說像兩魚相遇狀。

甲  金 篆

白 bái (white)

Pictograph. In its ancient form, 白 resembles a grain of rice or bright rays spreading from the sun. The original meaning of 白 is "white." Extended meanings include "pure," "clear," and "in vain." 白 is also in the character 的 (de, see **Lesson 2**).

白 象形。像太陽初升、光芒四射狀。一説像一粒白米。

玉 甲

現/现 xiàn (now; present)

Pictophonetic character. The character 現 combines the character 王 (wáng, king; a surname) as the radical with the phonetic element 見 (jiàn, to see). You have learned both 王 (**Lesson 1**) and 見 (**Lesson 3**). As a radical, the meaning of 王 is "jade," rather than "king." In Chinese there is also an independent character for "jade": 玉. In the Oracle–Bone Inscriptions, 玉 looks like a cluster of jade pieces. Since 現 consists of "jade" and "see," it originally meant "the revealing of jade by its light." Extended meanings include "appear," "existing," "present," and "now." In the simplified character 现, 见 derives from the cursive form of 見.

現 從玉, 見聲, 本意指玉光外射, 引申為顯露、出現、此刻之意。玉, 象形。甲骨文像一串玉。金文和篆文改為三片玉。玉作為偏旁寫作王。簡體字现的右部簡化。

 甲 中 金 杜 篆 杜

在 zài (at; in; on)

Associative and pictophonetic compound. The character 在 consists of 土 (tǔ, earth; soil) as the radical and 才 (cái, just) as both the phonetic and signifying element. In its ancient form, 才 is the pictograph of a seed just sprouting from the ground,  therefore meaning "just," "ability," etc. The character 在 uses the sprout breaking through the soil to indicate the existence of something. Therefore, 在 means "existence," "present" or may be used to mean "at," "in," or "on."

在 形聲兼會意。從土，從才；才亦聲。像草木從土中長出，以此表示存在。才，象形。像小苗破土而出，本義指才長出的草木。

 篆

刻 kè (quarter hour; carve)

Associative and pictophonetic compound. The character 刻 is composed of the knife radical 刂 and the phonetic and signifying component 亥 (hài), meaning "cut" or "carve." 刻 extends to mean "quarter" (of an hour). In its ancient form, 亥 looks like a pig without a head or feet. Its original meaning was "cut," but later was borrowed to mean "the last of the twelve Earthly Branches." The 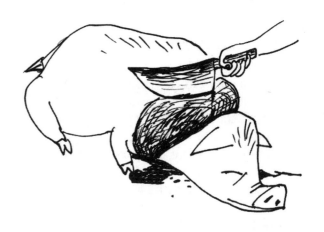 character 刻 is a later invented character for covering the original meaning of 亥. 亥 is also in the character 孩 (see hái, child, in **Lesson 3**).

刻 形聲兼會意。從刂，亥聲，本義為切割，後用於計時單位。亥，甲骨文中像割了頭蹄的豬形，是"刻"的本字。

甲  金 篆

明 míng (bright)

Associative compound. The character 明 is a combination of the sun 日 (rì, sun) and the moon 月 (yuè, moon). Since both the sun and moon are luminous, the original meaning of 明 is "bright." Extended meanings of 明 include "daybreak," "clear," "wise," and "next."

明 會意。從日，從月。日月皆明亮之物，所以用來表示明亮。

亡 甲 金 篆

忙 máng (busy)

Pictophonetic character. The character 忙 has the vertical heart radical 忄 and the phonetic component 亡 (wáng, to flee), meaning "busy" or "hurry," states which can affect one's heart. In its ancient form, the character 亡 looks like a person (the upper part) hiding in a corner (the lower part). Its original meaning is "run away," from which derived the meanings "lose," "perish," and "decease."

忙 形聲。從忄，亡聲。《說文》認為亡字從人，從乚。乚為隱蔽，意指人逃亡時躲在於隱蔽之処。

很 hěn (very)

Associative and pictophonetic compound. In the Oracle-Bone and Bronze Inscriptions, the upper part of 艮 is one large eye and the lower part a person, indicating someone turning back to stare at something. The meanings of 艮 include "disobey," "tough," "blunt" and "straightforward." The character 很 has the radical 彳 (left step; walk slowly) and the character 艮 (gěn) as both the phonetic and signifying component. 很 originally meant "defy," "violate," or "fierce," but today is used as the adverb "very" or "quite."

很　會意兼形聲。從彳（走路，道路），艮(gěn)聲，指人在走路時回頭瞪眼怒視。本義指不順從、凶狠，引申義為程度高。艮，會意。甲骨文從人，像人回首瞪視狀。

事 shì (affair; matter)

Associative compound. In the Oracle-Bone Inscriptions, the character 事 looks like a hand holding a hunting fork to catch a wild animal. Hunting was an essential part of primitive society, so the character 事 became used to mean "matter," "affair," or "event." In Regular Script, the animal is simplified to a horizontal stroke on top; the square in the middle and the vertical hook stand for the fork, while the component in the lower part refers to a hand. This is similar to the character 又, which originally meant right hand. (See 又 in **Radicals**.)

事　會意。在甲骨文中像一手持獵叉狀。因古代狩獵是經常發生的事，故以此來泛指做事。

甲 金 篆 草

為/为 wèi/wéi (for)

Associative compound. In the Oracle-Bone Inscriptions, the character 為 delineates a hand (the upper part) leading an elephant (the lower part), suggesting a man using an elephant to help with his work.

Therefore, 為 means "to do," "to do something for someone," or "for the sake of." In Regular Script, 為 becomes more simplified and abstract, but one can still see traces of the elephant's trunk and body (with its four legs underneath). The simplified character 为 derives from the cursive style of the traditional form 為.

為 會意。甲古文中像一只手牽象鼻形。因古代用大象為人做事，故本義為做。簡體字为是繁體字為的草書楷化字。

甲 金 篆

因 yīn (because)

Associative compound. The character 因 looks like a figure (大) laying on a mat (囗), meaning "rely on," "on the basis of," or "in accordance with." It also extends to mean "cause," "reason," or "because."

因 會意。從囗，從大。像人仰臥于席上。意為憑藉、依靠等。

甲 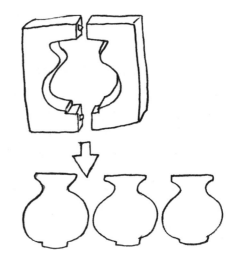 金 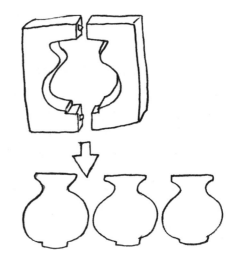 篆 同

同 tóng (same)

Associative compound. In its ancient form, the upper part of 同 depicts a mold and the lower part 口 resembles a casting from the mold. Castings made from a mold are the same, so 同 therefore means "same" or "alike."

同 象形。上像模子，下像模子製出的產品。指用同一個模子製造相同的東西。

忍 金  篆

認/认 rèn (to recognize)

Pictophonetic character. The character 認 consists of the word radical 言 and the phonetic component 忍 (rěn; tolerate), meaning "recognize," "know," or "identify." The character 忍 is the combination of 心 (xīn, heart) and 刃 (rèn, the edge of a knife; blade), suggesting that tolerating or enduring something or someone you do not like can be compared to bearing the thrust of a knife into one's heart. You have learned the character 刀 (dāo, knife) in **Radicals**. In the word 刃, the dot on the left side points to the cutting edge of a knife. In the simplified character 认, the speech radical is simplified into 讠 and 人 replaces the right part 忍, since the pronunciation of 忍 (rěn) and 人 (rén) are similar.

認 形聲。從言，忍聲。忍，會意兼形聲，從心，刃聲。忍的滋味就像一把刀插在心上。刃 指事。從刀，一點指向刀刃処。簡體认字部首由言 簡化為讠，聲旁由人替代忍。

戠 甲  金 篆

識/识 shí (to recognize)

Pictophonetic character. 識 is made up of the word radical 言 and the phonetic symbol 戠 (zhī, sign; mark), meaning "to recognize," "know," or "knowledge." 戠 is the combination of 音 (yīn, sound) and 戈 (gē, dagger-ax), suggesting the sound of a small bell or ring attached to a weapon, from which the meanings "sign" or "mark" are derived. 音 and 言 are cognate characters. In their ancient forms, both look like a tongue sticking out from a mouth, indicating sounds made by the mouth. Later the two characters differ in their usage. 言 now refers to "word," "speech," or "speak," while 音 means "sound" or "musical sound." In the simplified character 识, the speech radical on the left side is simplified and 只 (zhǐ) replaces the right side 戠 (zhī), as the two are similarly pronounced.

識 形聲。從言，從戠(zhī)；戠也兼表聲。戠，甲骨文像戈上挂有鈴、環之類的飾物，本義為標誌、記住。音，會義。表示口舌發出的聲音。戈，象形。是一種長柄橫刃的兵器。簡體字识左邊部首簡化，右邊聲旁用只替代戠，屬于近音替代。

采 甲  金 篆

菜 篆

菜 cài (vegetable; dish; food)

Associative and pictophonetic compound. The character 菜 is composed of the grass/plant radical 艹 and phonetic and signifying component 采 (cǎi), meaning "vegetable." In the Oracle-Bone Inscriptions, the character 采 looks like a hand picking fruits from a tree, and means "pick," "pluck," or "gather." When vegetables are ripe, people will gather them.

菜 會意兼形聲。本義為蔬菜。從艸，采聲。采亦有採摘之意。采，會意。像以手採樹上果實。

LESSON 4

甲 申 金 𝌀 篆 周

週/周 zhōu (week)

Associative compound. In the Oracle-Bone Inscriptions, the character 周 consists of 田 (tián, field) and four dots, suggesting crops planted in an orderly fashion in a field. The primary meanings of 周 are: "circumference," "surround," and "all around." Extended meanings include: "period," "cycle," and "week." The walk radical 辶 was eventually added to 周 to specifically mean "week." In Regular Script, 土 and 口 are found inside 冂. The simplified character 周 is without the walk radical 辶.

週 周 會意。甲骨文像田地形，中間四點代表田裏種的莊稼。本義為農田，引申為周圍、環繞、一定循環的時段等。簡體周字去掉辶。

金 木 篆 末

末 mò (end)

Explicit character. The character 末 consists of the radical 木 (mù, wood, tree), with a horizontal stroke on the top, indicating the tip of a tree. The extended meanings of 末 include "top," "end," "last stage," etc. You have learned 未 (wèi, future) in the character 妹 (see mèi, younger sister, in **Lesson 2**). In the character 末 (mò, end), the top line is longer than the lower line, suggesting that there is no space for development; whereas in the character 未 (wèi, future), the top line is shorter, indicating that there is room for growth.

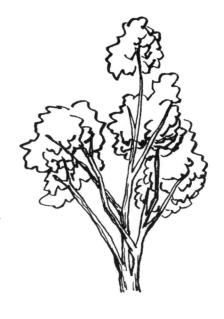

末 指事。從木，木上一橫表示樹梢所在的位置。

篆

打 dǎ (to hit; to strike)

Associative compound. The character 丁 (dīng) depicts a nail, and originally meant "nail." Later, the radical 金 (metal) was added to the left of 丁 (釘). The character 打 combines the hand radical 扌 with the nail 丁, conveying the act of striking a nail with a hammer. Hence 打 means "to strike," "hit," or "beat."

打 會意。從手，從丁。丁本義為釘，用手釘釘子來表示敲打。

篆 球 求 甲

球 qiú (ball)

Pictophonetic character. The character 球 consists of the jade radical 王 and the phonetic 求 (qiú, request). Its original meaning was "beautiful jade." Later it came to mean "ball." In the Oracle-Bone Inscriptions, 求 is a pictograph of a fur coat. Since a fur coat represents warmth, shelter, and material comfort as things that people seek, later 求 came to mean "seek," "request," "beg," etc.

球 形聲。從玉，求聲，意為美玉或球形的物體。求，象形。像毛翻在外的皮裘。 後求加衣字為裘。"求"引申為尋求、乞求等。

篆 看

看 kàn (to see; to look)

Associative compound. The character 看 is the combination of 手 (shǒu, hand) and 目 (mù, eye), indicating the act of looking into the distance with a hand over one's eyes. Its original meaning was "look into the distance," and extended meanings include "to see," "look at," "read," "visit," etc.

看 會意。從手，從目。表示以手掌置於目上遮光遠望。

金 電　篆 電

電/电 diàn (electricity)

Associative compound. In the Oracle–Bone Inscriptions, the character 電 has 雨 (yǔ, rain) in the upper part and 申 (shēn, lightning) in the lower part, symbolizing lightning in a rainstorm. The extended meanings of 電 are "swift," "electricity," and "electric shock." The character 申 resembles lightning streaking across a field, with extended meanings such as: "stretch," "express," and "state." The simplified character 电 is without the rain radical 雨.

電 會意。金文從雨，從申，像雷雨時閃電划過長空狀。簡體字去掉上部的雨字。

甲  篆

視/视 shì (to view)

Associative compound. The character 視 consists of the radical 礻 (reveal; show) and 見 (jiàn, see), suggesting acts of predicting future events according to astronomical phenomena. Therefore it means "to view," "look at," "regard," "treat," etc. 礻 derived from the character 示. In the Oracle-Bone Inscriptions, 示 resembles a stone altar upon which sacrifices are offered to gods or ancestors. Hence, characters with the  礻 radical are often associated with religious ceremonies or divination activities, e.g., 禮/礼 (lǐ, ceremony; rite), 祝 (zhù, wish; bless), and 神 (shén, god; deity). (See 示/礻 in **Radicals**.) In the simplified version (视), the 见 part is in its simplified form.

視 會意兼形聲字。甲骨文從示，從目，指用眼觀看天象。示也兼表聲。示 象形。甲骨文字形像用石塊搭起來的祭臺。視字右邊簡化。

篆 唱 昌 篆 昌

唱 chàng (to sing)

Pictophonetic character. The character 唱 contains the mouth radical 口 and the phonetic component 昌 (chāng, flourishing), meaning "to sing." 昌 consists of 日 (rì, sun) on top and 曰 (yuē, speak; say) at the bottom. Its original meaning was "to speak openly" or literally "speak under the sun" and symbolizes being truthful and frank. 昌 can also mean: "prosperous" or "flourishing."

唱 形聲。從口，昌聲。昌，會意。從日，從曰（説話）。本義指光明磊落的言詞，引申為美好、昌盛等。

金 𪔛 篆 歌

歌 gē (song)

Pictophonetic character. The character 歌 is composed of the radical 欠 (qiàn, to yawn; breathe) and the phonetic component 哥 (gē, elder brother), meaning "song" or "sing." In the Oracle-Bone Inscriptions, 欠 looks like a kneeling person yawning or breathing with an open mouth. Characters containing 欠 often have something to do with the mouth, for instance, 吹 (chuī, blow), 歎/叹 (tàn, sigh). 欠 also appears in the character 歡/欢 (see huān, joyful, in **Lesson 3**).

歌 形聲。從欠（人張口出氣），哥聲。本義為高聲吟誦。

篆 𨂿

跳 tiào (to jump)

Pictophonetic character. The character 跳 consists of the foot radical 足 and the phonetic component 兆 (zhào, omen; foretell). (See 足 in **Radicals**.) In its ancient form, 兆 resembles the cracks on an ox bone or tortoise shell after baking. Since a diviner would tell fortunes by reading crack marks on such shells, 兆 means "portend" or "omen."

跳 從足，兆聲。兆，象形。古文像龜甲燒裂後出現的紋路，意為徵兆。

甲  金 篆

舞 wǔ (to dance; wave)

Pictograph. In the Oracle-Bone Inscriptions, the character 舞 looks like a person dancing with ox tails or ribbons in both hands. In Seal Script, 舛 (chuǎn, two feet) was added to the bottom of the character, indicating dancing with both hands and feet. In the Bronze Inscriptions and Seal Script, 舛 is a pictograph of a pair of feet, meaning "opposite" or "run counter to."

舞 象形。甲骨文中像一人雙手持物起舞。

甲 金 篆

聽/听 tīng (to listen)

Associative compound. In the Oracle-Bone Inscriptions, the character 聽 consists of only an ear and a mouth. Later the character becomes more complex. In Regular Script, one can see the radicals 耳 (ěr, ear), 王 (wáng, king), 十 (shí, ten), 目 (mù eye), 一 (yī, one), and 心 (xīn, heart) within the character 聽. Perhaps you should listen to every Chinese word whole-heartedly eleven times in order to become a master at understanding Chinese! In the simplified character 听, the mouth radical 口 suggests the meaning, while the character 斤 (jīn) indicates the pronunciation.

聽 會意兼形聲。甲骨文中從耳、從口，表示用耳聽別人説話。後加悳 dé。悳，真誠。直，會意。甲骨文字形像用眼睛正對標杆以測量物體是否直正。聽字強調要認真用心領悟所聞之事。簡體听字左邊口字表意，右邊斤字表聲。

Lesson 4

甲  金 篆

音 yīn (sound; music)

Associative compound. 音 and 言 (yán) are cognate characters. In their ancient forms, both resemble a tongue sticking out from a mouth, representing a sound made by the mouth. Later the two characters differ in usage. 言 refers to words or speech, while 音 means (musical) sound. In Regular Script, 音 is the combination of 立 (lì, stand) and 曰 (yuē, speak; say). In the Oracle-Bone and Bronze Inscriptions, the character 立 depicts a person standing on the ground, and 曰 signifies the sound coming out of his or her mouth. 音 also appears in 識/识 (see shí, to recognize, in **Lesson 3**).

音 會意。音與言同源，是由同一個甲骨文字演變來的。金文在口中加一橫，表示發音時舌頭的位置。

甲 金 篆 草 乐

樂 / 乐 yuè; lè (music; happy)

Pictograph. In the Oracle-Bone Inscriptions, the character 樂 consists of 幺幺 (two strings) as the upper part and 木 (mù, wood) in the lower half, indicating a stringed musical instrument. In the Bronze Inscriptions, the

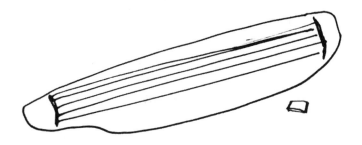

representation of a "pluck" (白) is added between the strings. The original meaning of 樂 is musical instrument. Extended meanings are "music," (yuè) and "happy" (lè). The simplified character 乐 derives from the cursive form of 樂.

樂 象形。甲骨文從絲，從木。表示將絲弦繃于木上，意指琴瑟之類的樂器。簡體字乐字是繁體字樂的草書楷化字。

甲  金 篆

對/对 duì (correct; toward)

Associative compound. In the ancient form, the character 對 delineates a hand (寸) holding a tablet, meaning "to answer" or "respond," because in the past, an official often referred to his notes on a small narrow tablet made of jade, ivory, or bamboo, which he held in his hands when discussing state affairs with his sovereign or answering questions. The extended meaning of 對 is "right" or "correct." In the simplified character 对, 又 replaces the left part of the traditional character 對.

對 會意。篆文左邊一半是板子，右邊從寸（手），本義為手持笏板回答，引申為對答，正確，面對等。簡體对字左邊以又替代。明代已有此字。

甲 金 篆 草 时

時/时 shí (time)

Pictophonetic character. The character 時 combines the radical 日 (rì, sun) and the phonetic element 寺 (sì, temple), meaning "season," "time," or "often." In the Bronze Inscriptions, 寺 consists of 止 (zhǐ, stop) and 又 (yòu, hand), meaning "hold," "handle," or "manage." Later 寺 came to mean "temple" or "monastery." The simplified character 时 is developed from the cursive style of the traditional character 時, with 寸 replacing 寺 on the left.

時 形聲。從日，寺聲。寺，形聲。金文從又（手），從止。手之所止為持，本以為持有。簡體字时是繁體字時的草書楷化字，右邊以寸代替寺。

篆

候 hòu (to wait; time)

Pictophonetic character. In Seal Script, 候 consists of the person radical 亻 and the phonetic component 矦 (hóu, marquis), meaning "await" or "wait for," also extending to mean "time." In the Bronze Inscriptions, 矦 is comprised of 厂 (hǎn, target for archery) and 矢 (shǐ, arrow). The original meaning of 矦 was "target." Later it came to mean "marquis," "duke," or "prince under an emperor." In its ancient form, 矢 is represented by the drawing of an arrow. 矢 also appears in the character 醫/医 (see yī, medicine; doctor, in **Lesson 2**). Notice how 候 has changed in its Regular Script form.

候 形聲，篆文從人，矦聲，本義是等候。矦，會意。從厂從矢（箭），厂像靶子，矢在靶上，本義為箭靶。

甲  金 篆 草

書/书 shū (book; to write)

Associative compound. In the Oracle-Bone Inscriptions, the upper part of 書 shows a hand holding a brush (聿 yù, see 律, in **Lesson 2**) and the lower part resembles a box (口), indicating the act of writing on something. Besides "write," 書 also means "script," "book," or "letter." The simplified character 书 derives from the cursive style of the traditional character 書.

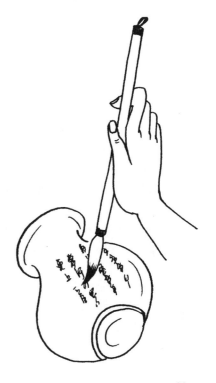

書 會意。甲骨文上是手持筆形，下為一器物，指手持筆在器物上書寫。书是書字的草書楷化字。

京 甲  金 篆 京

影 yǐng (shadow)

Associative and pictophonetic compound. The character 影 consists of the radical 彡 (彡 can indicate decorative patterns; hair; beards; carvings; or shadows) and 景 (jǐng, sunlight; view) as both the phonetic and signifying element, meaning "shadow," "reflection," and "film." 景 consists of 日 (rì, sun) and 京 (see jīng, capital, in **Lesson 1**). In the Oracle-Bone Inscriptions, 京 looks like a palatial structure built on a terrace. 京 originally meant "man-made highland." Later it came to mean "national capital."

影 形聲兼會意。三撇意為飾紋、光影等。景（日光），有影子就有光，景还兼表聲。景，形聲。從日，從京（高）。表示太陽高照。京 指事。甲骨文、金文中像在高丘上建宮觀之形，有高大、國都之意。

篆

常 cháng (often)

Pictophonetic character. In Seal Script, 常 consists of the radical 巾 (jīn, scarf) and the phonetic indicator 尚 (shàng, uphold; esteem). The original meaning of 常 was "skirt" or "clothes," but later came to mean "often," "constant," and "ordinary." In its ancient form, 巾 is a pictograph of a scarf, whereas 尚 resembles smoke drifting from a window.

常 形聲。篆文從巾，尚聲。本義指裙子，与裳本為一字，后分開，常意為經常，常規，日常等。

甲 　金 　篆

去 qù (to leave; to go)

Associative compound. In the Oracle-Bone and Bronze Inscriptions, the character 去 consists of 大 on top and 口 at the bottom, indicating a person (大) leaving her or his cave (口). In Regular Script, the upper part is 土 (tǔ, earth, soil) and the lower part 厶 (sī, private).

去 會意。甲骨文從大（人），從口（洞穴出口），表示人離開洞穴。

金 　篆

外 wài (outside)

Associative compound. The character 外 is made up of 夕 (xī, sunset; evening) and 卜 (bǔ, fortune telling). The original meaning of 外 is "outside," but can also mean "other" or "foreign." In the Oracle-Bone Inscriptions, 卜 resembles a crack on an oracle bone. You have learned a few characters pertaining to divination. For example, 占 (zhàn, divine) is the combination of 卜 and 口 (see 點 in **Lesson 3**). 兆 (zhào, omen) represents more cracks on an oracle bone or shell. (See 跳 in **Lesson 4**.)

外 會意。從夕，從卜。古人在早上占卜。晚上占卜，則不在常規之內了。

金  篆

客 kè (guest)

Associative compound. The character 客 consists of the roof radical 宀 and the character 各 (gè, arrive; each), suggesting someone arriving at a house. It follows that the meaning of 客 is "visitor," "guest," or "traveler." In the Oracle-Bone and Bronze Inscriptions, 各 is a combination of 夊 (zhǐ, a moving foot) and 口 (kǒu, the entrance of a dwelling). The original meaning of 各 was "arrive." Later it came to mean "each" or "every." Be careful not to confuse 各 and 名 (míng, name, in **Lesson 1**).

客 會意兼形聲。從宀，從各；各亦聲。指人自外面進屋之意。各，會意。甲骨文、金文中從止（腳趾），從口（古人穴居洞口），本意指來到，引申為每個。

篆

昨 zuó (yesterday)

Pictophonetic character. The character 昨 consists of the sun radical 日 and the phonetic component 乍 (zhà/zuò). In the Oracle-Bone and Bronze Inscriptions, 乍 indicates the stitching of a collar. The original meaning of 乍 was "to make" or "to do." Later the character came to mean "for the first time," "spread," or "abruptly." Please compare 昨 with 怎 (zěn, how) in **Lesson 3**.

昨 形聲。從日，乍聲。

金  篆 所

所 suǒ (so; place)

Pictophonetic character. In the Bronze Inscriptions and Seal Script, 所 consists of the radical 斤 (jīn, ax; unit of weight) and the phonetic component 戶 (hù, door; household). The original meaning of 所 was the sound of wood being cut. Later it came to mean "place" or "so." In the Oracle-Bone Inscriptions, 斤 looks like an ax with a crooked handle and 戶 a door with one panel (as opposed to a door with two panels, represented by 門/门).

所 形聲。從斤，戶聲，本義為伐木的聲音。引申義為處所、助詞等。斤 象形。上像斧頭，下像斧柄。戶，指單扇的門。一扇為戶，兩扇為門。

甲 ϟ 金 以 篆 以

以 yǐ (with)

Associative compound. In the Bronze Inscriptions, the right side of 以 is a person 人 and the left side is a fetus, therefore meaning "rely on." 以 can also mean "according to," "by means of," "with," or "because of."

以 象形兼會意。金文字形像頭朝下、快要降生的胎兒，旁邊站著一人。本義指已成形的胎兒，引申為憑藉、原因等。

篆

久 jiǔ (long time)

Pictograph. In Seal Script, 久 looks like a person lying down with a long moxa cone* burning on her or his back. The original meaning of 久 was "moxibustion." Later the character 火 (huǒ, fire) was added under 久 to form a new character 灸 (jiǔ, meaning moxibustion). 久 then came to mean "a long time."

久 象形。篆文久字從人，背後一橫像以燃著的艾草在人背後薰灸之形，是灸的初文。

篆 錯 昔 甲 ☰ 金 ☰ 篆 𦮺

錯/错 cuò (wrong; error)

Pictophonetic character. The character 錯 consists of the radical 金 (jīn, gold; metal) and the phonetic element 昔 (xī, the past). The original meaning of 錯 was "gold inlay." Later it came to mean "interlocked," "jagged," "grind," "alternate," or "wrong." In the Oracle-Bone and Bronze Inscriptions, the upper part of 昔 looks like a flood and the lower part resembles the sun 日, referring to prehistoric times when there was an extraordinarily big flood. Hence 昔 means "the past" or "former times." The gold/metal radical is in simplified form in the character 错. (See 鐘/钟 in **Lesson 3**.)

錯 形聲。從金，昔聲，本義為用金塗飾。昔，會意。甲骨文下是日，上像洪水泛濫、遮天蔽日狀，指古代大洪水時期。簡體字错的部首由金 簡化為钅。

---

* A moxa cone is a cylinder of cotton wool or other combustible material, placed on the skin and ignited in order to treat diseases or produce analgesia. This practice is one of the Chinese traditional treatments called moxibustion.

Lesson 4

篆

想 xiǎng (to think)

Pictophonetic character. The character 想 is comprised of the radical 心 （xīn, heart） and the phonetic element 相 (xiàng, appearance), meaning "to think," "ponder," "recall," or "to want to." The character 相 combines 木 (mù, wood; tree) with 目 (mù, eye), indicating the act of looking closely at a tree. Hence the primary meaning of 相 is "to look at and appraise." Extended meanings include "appearance," "posture," "photograph," etc.

想 形聲。從心，相聲，本義為思考。相 會意。從目，從木，表示用眼睛觀察樹木。

篆 覺 草 觉

覺/觉 jué; jiào (to feel; to reckon; to sleep)

Associative and pictophonetic compound. In Seal Script, 覺 consists of the radical 見 (jiàn, to see) and the signifying and phonetic element 學 (xué, to study), indicating someone studying with open eyes. 覺 means "awake," "sense," "feel," "reckon," (jué) "sleep" (the process from falling asleep to awakening, pronounced jiào), etc. Both 覺 and 學 have the same upper component, but their lower parts are 見 and 子, respectively. The simplified character 觉 developed from the cursive form of 覺. The simplification of the top of 觉 (覺) is the same as that of 学 (學).

覺 會意兼形聲。篆文從見，學聲， 表示睜大眼睛、聚精會神來學習領悟。本義為明白、醒悟。簡體字觉是繁體字覺的草書楷化字，上半部的簡化法與學字相同，下半部與見同。

甲  金 得 篆

得 dé (to obtain; to get)

Associative compound. In the Oracle-Bone Inscriptions, the character 得 resembles a hand holding a cowry shell, suggesting obtaining money or something valuable. In the Bronze Inscription, the radical 彳 (left step; walk slowly) was added, implying that one acquires valuable things while traveling. In Regular Script the 彳 part of the character 得 remains the same; 寸 depicts the hand, but 貝 (bèi, shell) becomes 曰 with 一 underneath.

得 會意。甲骨文從又（手）持貝（錢幣），意指有所得。金文又加彳（街道），以示行有所獲。

篆

意 yì (meaning)

Associative compound. The character 意 consists of 音 (yīn, sound; music) and 心 (xīn, heart), signifying the sound of one's heart beating. 意 can also mean "desire," "intention," "will," "thought," "meaning," "expect," etc.

意 會意。從心，從音；音亦聲。用心音指心裏的想法。

篆

思 sī (to think)

Associative compound. In Seal Script, 思 is a combination of 囟 (xìn, fontanel) and 心 (xīn, heart), implying that thinking is done with one's mind and heart. 思 means "to think," "consider," "think of," or "long for." In Regular Script, the upper part 囟 has changed into 田 (tián, field; see **Radicals**), which is unrelated to the original meaning.

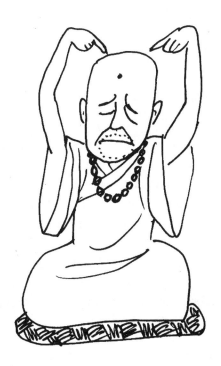

思 會意。篆文從心，從囟。囟指人的腦門。古人以為大腦與心都有思考的功能 故以二者來表示思考，思想，思念等意。

篆

只 zhǐ (only)

Explicit character. 只 is comprised of 口 (kǒu, mouth) with two strokes underneath, suggesting the action of breathing out of one's mouth. 只 originally functioned as an auxiliary word to indicate mood. Later it came to mean "only," "just," or "merely."

只 指事。從口，下有兩道，像人口說話時氣呼出狀。本義是語氣助詞。

篆

睡 shuì (to sleep)

Associative and pictophonetic compound. The character 睡 consists of the eye radical 目 and the character 垂 (chuí, hang down; droop), representing a person with his or her head bowed and eyes closed. The original meaning of 睡 was "to doze while seated." Today 睡 means "to sleep." The lower part of 垂 is 土 (tǔ, earth; soil). The upper part represents a plant with drooping branches and blossoms.

睡 會意兼形聲。從目從垂；垂亦聲。本義為坐寐。

篆

算 suàn (to calculate; to figure)

Associative compound. In Seal Script, 算 is a combination of the bamboo radical ⺮ and the character 具 (jù, utensil; tool), signifying the use of a bamboo tool, such as an abacus, which is used to make calculations. In its ancient form, the character 竹 (zhú) is a pictograph of two bamboo branches with leaves (note the difference

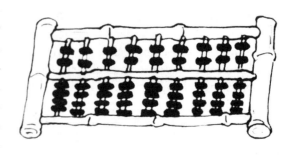

between the bamboo character 竹 and the bamboo radical ⺮). 具 resembles two hands holding a three-legged vessel (commonly used for wine). In Regular Script, the upper part of 算 is ⺮, and the bottom part is 廾 (gǒng, two hands holding something), but the middle part changes to 目.

算 會意。從竹，從具，表示計算時使用的竹制器具，即算盤。具，會意。甲骨文從雙手，從鼎（食具），指雙手舉鼎以供酒食。

找 zhǎo (to look for; to seek)

Associative compound. The character 找 consists of the hand radical 扌 and the character 戈 (gē, dagger-ax), which may suggest searching for a dagger-ax with one's hand. The primary meaning of 找 is "look for" or "seek." 找 can also mean "to give (a customer) change."

找　形聲。從扌，戈聲，像用手找戈。

甲 〳〵　篆 〱〱

別/别 bié (other)

Associative compound. In the Oracle-Bone Inscriptions, the left part of 别 represents a knife and the right part resembles bone fragments, signifying the action of separating bones from flesh. The primary meaning of 别 is "to separate" or "part." Its extended meanings include "distinguish," "other," "another," and "do not." In the simplified character 别，the right part is the knife radical 刂, just as in the traditional version, but the left bottom part is 力, which differs slightly from the traditional character 別.

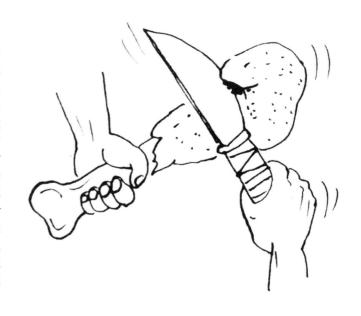

別　會意。甲骨文從刀，從咼 (guǎ)，本義指以刀剔下骨頭上肉。另，象形，与咼本為一字，甲骨文中像剔乾淨用來占卜的牛骨。簡體字別的左下方寫作力，與繁體字別稍有不同。

LESSON 5

牙 金  篆

呀 ya (exclamation)

Pictophonetic character. 呀 consists of the mouth
radical 口 and the phonetic element 牙 (yá, tooth),
suggesting a person with an open mouth. 呀 can be
used as an exclamation, onomatopoeic word, or an
auxiliary. The character 牙 is a pictograph; in Seal
Script, 牙 looks like a pair of jaws with two large
teeth in the upper part.

呀 從口，牙聲。本義指張口狀，　引申為嘆詞、象
聲詞等。牙 象形。像口中牙齒上下相錯形。

甲 金 篆 雑

進/进 jìn (to enter)

Associative compound. The character 進
consists of the walk radical 辶 and the
short-tailed bird character 隹 (zhuī).
Since birds can only walk forwards, 進
means "move forward," "enter," or "into."
In the simplified character 进, 井 (jǐng,
well) replaces 隹 since the
pronunciations of 井 and 進 (jìn) are
similar.

進 會意兼形聲。從辶，佳聲。甲骨文從止（腳趾）從佳（短尾鳥）。因佳趾只能
前進不能後退，本義為向前進。簡體字进用井替代佳，因井與進聲音相近。

篆

快 kuài (fast; quick)

Associative and pictophonetic character. 快 is comprised of the vertical heart radical 忄 and the signifying and phonetic element 夬 (guài, archery), meaning "fast," "swift," "hurry up," or "soon." In the Oracle-Bone Inscriptions, 夬 resembles a hand and a bow, signifying the act of using a bow and arrow.

快 會意兼形聲。篆文從心 從夬(guài 鈎弦射箭)，夬亦聲。本義指心情順暢，痛快高興，如射出之箭。夬，會意。甲骨文像手拉射箭時所用的鈎弦器。

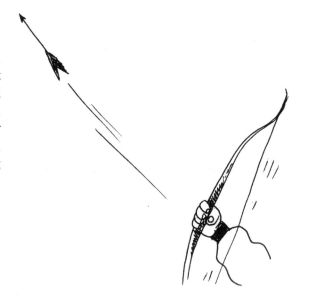

甲 来 金 来 篆 来 草 来

來/来 lái (come)

Phonetic loan character. In its ancient form, 來 looks like a wheat plant. The original meaning of 來 was "wheat," but later it came to mean "come." In Regular Script, 來 is the combination of 木 (mù, wood; tree) and two 人 (rén, man; person), suggesting two people coming together beneath a tree. The simplified character 来 derives from the cursive style of the traditional version 來.

來 象形。甲骨文中像一株有根杆葉穗的麥苗。本義為麥，後借用為來去的來，本義遂失。簡體字来是繁體字來的草書楷化字。

甲  金  篆

介 jiè (between)

Associative compound. In the Oracle-Bone Inscriptions, the character 介 resembles a man (人) wearing armor, as it originally meant "armor." Since this figure is shown between two pieces of a suit of armor, 介 extends to mean "between" or "interpose."

介 會意。從八，從人。甲骨文字形從人，四短畫表示由一片片皮革串成的甲衣，本義指人穿甲衣，引申為介於中間等。

甲 篆 紹 草

紹/绍 shào (carry on)

Pictophonetic character. 紹 consists of the silk radical 糹 and the phonetic element 召 (zhāo; summon), meaning "continue" or "carry on." The character 召 is the combination of 刀 (dāo, knife) and 口 (kǒu, mouth). You learned 召 in the character 照 (see zhào, shine, in **Lesson 2**). The simplified silk radical 纟 is derived from the cursive of the traditional radical 糹. Only this radical is simplified in the character 绍.

紹 會意兼形聲。從糹，召聲。本義為繼續、繼承，引申為介紹、引薦等。簡體字部首纟是由糹的草書楷化而來。绍字的部首纟簡化。

甲 = 金 = 篆

下 xià (below; under)

Explicit character. The character 下 is formed following the same principle that governs the formation of 上. In the Oracle-Bone and Bronze Inscriptions, 下 consists of two horizontal lines. The longer line on the top represents the horizon and the shorter one underneath refers to something below the horizon. In Regular Script, a vertical line is added beneath the longer horizontal line. The primary meaning of 下 is "below," "under," or "lower." Its extended meanings include "downward," "fall," "next," and "a short while."

下 指事。古文為指示符號，表示一物在另一物之下。

甲 金 篆 草

興/兴 xìng (mood; interest)

Associative compound. In the Oracle-Bone and Bronze Inscriptions, the character 興 depicts four hands lifting a mold, and meant "to lift" or "raise" (pronounced xīng). The extended meanings of 興 include "start," "prosper" (xīng), "mood," and "interest" (xìng). In Regular Script, the four hands are still visible in the character 興, though the two in the lower part have been simplified. The part the four hands are lifting is 同. You learned the character 同 (tóng, same) in **Lesson 3**. 同 refers to castings made out of the same mold. The simplified character 兴 is developed from the cursive style of the traditional version 興. Notice that the top parts of the two characters are different.

興 會意。甲骨文字形像四只手同力共舉一幅模具。簡體字兴是由繁體字興的草書楷化而來。

Lesson 5

漂 piào (pretty)

Pictophonetic character. The character 漂 consists of the water radical 氵 and the phonetic element 票 (piào, ticket). The primary meanings of 漂 include "float," "drift" (pronounced piāo), and "bleach" (pronounced piǎo). Since cloth looks nice after being bleached, 漂 extends to mean "pretty" (pronounced piào). In Regular Script, the lower part of 票 is the character 示 (shì, show); see **Radicals**.

漂 形聲。從水，票聲，漂浮，沖洗，漂白之意。票，會意。篆文下部從火，本義是火焰騰起。

亮 liàng (bright)

Associative compound. In Seal Script, 亮 consists of 高 (gāo, tall; high) in the upper part and 人 in the lower part, suggesting a person standing in a high place, where it is presumably also bright. Take care to distinguish 亮 from 高 (see **Lesson 2**).

亮 會意。篆文從高，從儿（人），表示人在高処則明亮。

坐 zuò (to sit)

Associative compound. The character 坐 consists of two 人 (rén, person) on top and 土 (tǔ, earth) at the bottom, representing two people sitting on the ground. In addition to "sit," 坐 also means "to travel by" some kind of vehicle (which one sits in), such as a bus, train, or airplane.

坐 會意。古文像兩人在土地上面對面而坐。

哪 nǎ/něi (which)

Pictophonetic character. 哪 is made up of the radical 口 and the phonetic 那 (see nà/nèi, that, in **Lesson 2**). As mentioned before, interrogatives often have the mouth radical 口, as in 嗎 and 呢.

哪 形聲。從口，那聲，用作疑問代詞。

---

*古文 refers to Ancient Inscriptions, a writing system used in the Warring States Period (475–221 B.C.)

甲 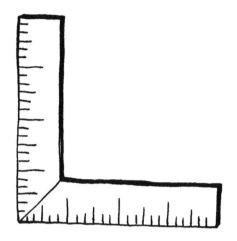 金 工 篆 工

工 gōng (tool; work; labor)

Pictograph. In the ancient writing systems, the character 工 looks like a carpenter's square or ruler. The original meaning of 工 was "tool," from which derived the meanings "work," "labor," "skill," "craftsmanship," and "construction project." You learned 工 in **Radicals**.

工 象形。像工匠用的曲尺。

甲 止 金 止 篆 𣥂

作 zuò (work; to do)

Associative compound. In the Oracle-Bone and Bronze Inscriptions, the character 作 is written as 乍, which represents stitching a collar, therefore meaning "to do" or "to make" something. In Seal Script, the person radical 亻 was added to the left of 乍 to form 作. You have encountered 乍 in the characters 怎 (zěn, how, **Lesson 3**) and 昨 (zuó, yesterday, **Lesson 4**). When 作 is used as a verb, it can often be replaced by 做, a character which was developed later. However, in certain combinations, such as 工作, 做 cannot be substituted for 作.

作 會意兼形聲。從人，從乍，乍亦聲。

校 xiào (school)

Associative and pictophonetic compound. 校 contains the radical 木 (mù, wood) and 交 (jiāo, cross) as both the phonetic and semantic component. 校 originally referred to the crossbar that latched the neck and hands of a criminal together. Today, 校 is used to mean "school." In its ancient form, 交 is a pictograph of a figure with crossed legs.

校 會意兼形聲。從木，從交；交亦聲。指用兩木相交製作的刑具。交 象形。像兩腿相交的正面人形。

喝 hē (to drink)

Pictophonetic character. The character 喝 combines the mouth radical 口 and the phonetic component 曷 (hé, how; why; when). 曷 is a pictophonetic character that consists of the radical 曰 (yuē; say) and the phonetic symbol 匃 (gài, beg; beggar).

喝 形聲。從口，曷聲，有呼喊，吸食液體等意。曷，形聲。從曰（説話），從匃（乞求），表示喝止、疑問等。

篆 茶

茶 chá (tea)

Associative compound. The character 茶 consists of 艹 (the grass or herb radical), 人 (rén, man; person), and 木 (mù, wood; tree), resembling a person harvesting tea leaves.

茶 形聲。茶与荼本為一字，從艸，余聲，本義為一種苦菜。唐代時將"荼"減去一筆而成為"茶"。

加 金 右 篆 加

咖 kā (coffee)

Pictophonetic character. 咖 is comprised of the mouth radical 口 and the phonetic component 加 (jiā; plus). Originally 咖 was an onomatopoeic word for laughter. Later it came to mean "coffee" because it sounds similar to the English word "coffee." 加 consists of 力 (lì, power; strength) and 口 (kǒu, mouth), meaning "slander" or "calumniate." Today 加 means "add" or "plus."

咖 象聲詞。加，會意。從力，從口，本義指以語言誣陷他人。

非 甲  篆 非

啡 fēi (coffee)

Pictophonetic character. The character 啡 was created to translate some English words, such as coffee (咖啡) and morphine (嗎啡). 啡 consists of the mouth radical 口 and the phonetic component 非 (fēi). In its ancient form, 非 resembles the two wings of a flying bird. Since these two wings are opposite each other, 非 originally meant "run counter to," and came to mean "not conform with," "wrong," "non-," etc.

啡　譯音用字。非，象形，甲骨文、金文像鳥展開雙翅飛翔狀。由於兩翅相背，本義為違背，引申為不正確等。

卑 金 篆

啤 pí (beer)

Pictophonetic character. The character 啤 consists of the mouth radical 口 and the phonetic symbol 卑 (bēi, contemptible). 啤 is a new character, created to translate the word "beer" (啤酒 píjiǔ). In the Bronze Inscriptions, 卑 depicted a serving container held in the left hand, and meant "low," "inferior," "contemptible," "mean," etc.

啤　形聲。從口，卑聲。卑，會意。金文從又（手），從申（指酒器），表示以手托酒器伺奉人，意為卑賤。啤酒。德文的音譯及意譯。

114　　　　　　　　　　　　　　　　　　　　　*Lesson 5*

甲 酒 篆 酒

酉 甲 金 酉 篆 酉

酒 jiǔ (wine)

Associative and pictophonetic compound. 酒 is comprised of the water radical 氵 and the signifying and phonetic element 酉 (yǒu; wine jar), thereby meaning "alcoholic drink," "wine," "liquor," or "spirits." In its ancient form, 酉 is a pictograph of a wine jar. Later it was also borrowed to mean "the tenth of the twelve Earthly Branches."

酒　會意兼形聲。從氵，從酉；酉亦聲。指從酒壇中舀酒。酉，象形。像酒壇子之形。后借為地支的第十位。

巴 篆 巴

吧 ba (question indicator, onomatopoeic)

Pictophonetic character. 吧 has the mouth radical 口 and the phonetic element 巴 (bā). 吧 can be used as a question indicator, onomatopoeic word, or particle for making a suggestion. In Seal Script, 巴 resembles a snake with a large, open mouth. Today's meanings of 巴 are still related to the characteristics of a snake, such as "cling to," "stick to," and "wait anxiously" (as a snake waiting for prey).

吧　象聲詞、語氣詞。巴，象形。篆文像嘴大能吞象的蛇形。本義為蛇，引申為依附、靠近、巴結等。

金  篆

要 yào (to want)

Associative compound. In its ancient form, the character 要 delineates a woman placing both hands on her waist. The original meaning of 要 was "waist," and its meanings now include "coerce," "demand," "must," "want," "ask for," and "important." People often stand with their arms akimbo when demanding something of someone. Later, a flesh radical 月 was added to the left of 要 to mean waist 腰.

要 會意。像一人雙手叉腰形，是腰的本字。

篆 杤

杯 bēi (cup; glass)

Pictophonetic character. 杯 consists of the wood radical 木 and the phonetic element 不 (bù), which may have referred to a wooden cup.

杯 形聲。從木，不聲，意為裝飲料的器皿或指木做的杯子。

篆

起 qǐ (to rise)

Pictophonetic character. 起 is the combination of the walk radical 走 (zǒu) and the phonetic element 己 (jǐ, oneself), meaning "up," "rise," "get up," "start" or "establish." In its ancient form, 己 resembles the large belly of a person and means "oneself."

起　形聲。從走，己聲。意為立起。走，象形兼會意。金文上像一人甩開雙臂跑步狀，下從止（腳），意指奔跑。己，象形。甲骨文像人腹之形。

篆

給/给 gěi (to give)

Pictophonetic character. 給 consists of the silk radical 糸 and the phonetic symbol 合 (hé, close). Since silk is considered a good gift, 給 is used to mean: "to provide," "give," "grant," and "for the benefit of." In its ancient form, the character 合 resembled a container with a lid, meaning "to close," "shut," "get together," and "match." The simplified character 给 contains the simplified form of the silk radical (see the character 绍 in this lesson).

給　形聲。從糸，合聲。本義為豐足，引申為供給、給與等。合，上像容器的蓋子，下像容器本身。蓋子蓋在容器上，意指合攏。簡體字给的部首簡化。

甲 〰 金 〰 篆 〰

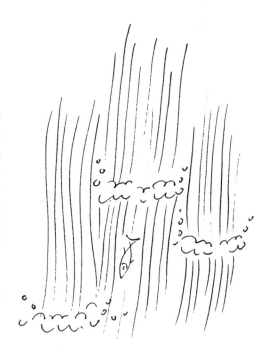

水 shuǐ (water)

Pictograph. In its ancient form, the character 水 looks like a flowing body of water. The line in the middle represents the main stream and the dots on the sides look like the spray or waves of the water. In Regular Script, the dots extend into lines, resembling the tributaries of a river. The original meaning of 水 was "river," but later came to mean "water." You learned 水 in **Radicals**.

水 象形。甲骨文中間像流水，旁似浪花 或水的支流。

篆 玩

玩 wán (to play; to visit)

Pictophonetic character. 玩 has the jade radical 王 (as a radical, the meaning of 王 is not "king," but "jade") and the phonetic component 元 (yuán), suggesting jade or something like jade for people to enjoy and play with. The primary meaning of 玩 is "play," "have fun," or "enjoy." "To visit" is one of its extended meanings. In its ancient form, the character 元 depicts two horizontal strokes on top of a person, meaning "head" (of a person). The extended meanings of 元 include "primary," "first," "chief," and "fundamental."

玩 從玉，元聲，指供玩賞之物或玩耍。玉 作為偏旁時寫作王。元，指事。從一，從兀。 本義為人頭，引申為第一。

118 *Lesson 5*

金 ▢ 篆 ▢ 草 ▢

圖/图 tú (drawing)

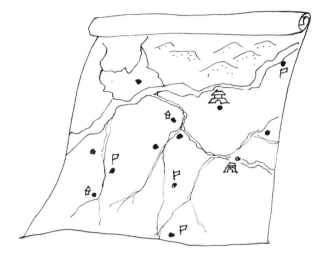

Associative compound. The character 圖 looks like a drawing of a map in which 囗 (wéi; enclosure) represents the border, while 啚 (bǐ) refers to a small administrative district (a unit of 500 households). In Regular Script, the character 啚 is comprised of 口, 十, and 回. The simplified version 图 derives from the cursive of the traditional character 圖; the character 冬 (dōng, winter) is inside 囗.

圖 會意。從囗，從啚（bǐ）。囗像一張紙，啚指城邑都鄙。將城邑繪在紙上，即是地圖。图是由圖字的草書楷化而來，內為冬字。

甲 ▢ 金 ▢ 篆 ▢

館 / 馆 guǎn (accommodation)

Associative and pictophonetic compound. 館 consists of the food radical 食 and the phonetic and signifying element 官 (guān, official), and means "accommodation for guests." In its ancient form, 官 is the combination of the roof radical 宀 and 𠂤 (duī, hill). Its original meaning was "government office," with the extended meanings of "public," "official," etc. In the simplified character 馆, the food radical is simplified (see 饭 in **Lesson 3**).

館 會意兼形聲。從食，官聲，意指供人飲食住宿娛樂的地方。官，會意。從宀，從𠂤，本義為官府。簡體字馆的部首簡化。

金 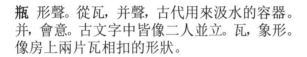 篆

瓶 **píng (bottle)**

Pictophonetic character. 瓶 is comprised of the radical 瓦 (wǎ, tile) and the phonetic element 并 (bìng, side by side; merge), meaning "bottle," "vase," "jar," or "flask." In Seal Script, the character 瓦 resembles two roof tiles. In the Oracle-Bone Inscriptions, 并 consists of two people 人人 and the character 二 (èr, two), indicating two people standing side by side.

瓶 形聲。從瓦，并聲，古代用來汲水的容器。
并，會意。古文字中皆像二人並立。瓦，象形。
像房上兩片瓦相扣的形狀。

甲 中 金 北 篆 卯

聊 **liáo (to chat)**

Associative and pictophonetic compound. The character 聊 is comprised of the ear radical 耳 (See ěr in **Radicals**) and the phonetic and signifying element 卯 (mǎo, mortise and tenon joint), suggesting that chatter and small talk can bring people closer to each other (like a mortise and tenon). In its ancient form, 卯 looks like an animal cut in half. The original meaning of 卯 was "slaughter" or "kill"; "mortise and tenon" is its extended meaning.

聊 會意兼形聲。從耳，卯聲，意為依賴、閒談等。卯，象形。甲骨文中像將一
物從中間分開。本義為剖分，引申為榫眼等。

 甲  金 篆

才 cái (just; not until; only)

Explicit character. The character 才 looks like a seedling just breaking through the ground. The horizontal stroke represents the ground and the part underneath is the root of the seedling. The meanings of 才 include "just," "only," "not until," "ability," etc.

才 指事。甲骨文中一橫畫象徵土地，表示種子已生根發芽、破土而出。本義為草木初生，引申為剛剛。

甲 金 篆

回 huí (to return)

Pictograph. In its ancient form, the character 回 represents a whirlpool or an eddy. The original meaning of 回 was "whirl" or "circle." Today it means "return," "go back," "turn around," "reply," "refuse," etc.

回 象形。甲骨文像水的漩渦。

LESSON 6

篆

話/话 huà (speech)

Associative compound. The character 話 consists of the word radical 言 and the character 舌 (shé, tongue), meaning "talk," or "spoken language." In the Oracle-Bone Inscriptions, 舌 is a pictograph of a tongue sticking out of a mouth. The speech radical in the simplified version of the character (话) is in its simplified form.

話 會意。從言，從舌，意指交談、話語等。舌，象形。下部像口，上部像舌，表示舌頭伸出口外。簡體字话的部首簡化。

畏 甲 金 篆

喂 wèi (hello; hey)

Pictophonetic character. The character 喂 consists of the mouth radical 口 and the phonetic element 畏 (wèi, fear). 喂 means: "feed," "hello," or "hey." In the Oracle-Bone and Bronze Inscriptions, 畏 looks like a large-headed monster holding a stick in its hands, ready to attack. The primary meanings of 畏 are "fear" or "frightening," but it can also mean "respect with awe."

喂 形聲。從口，畏聲，意為喂養或用於打招呼。畏，會意。甲骨文中像大頭鬼持杖欲打人狀，意為可畏。

篆

就 jiù (just)

Associative compound. The character 就 is made up of 京 (jīng, capital) and 尤 (yóu, outstanding). The original meaning of 就 was "to reach the pinnacle," and extended meanings include "accomplish," "undertake," and "come near." 就 is also used as an adverb, meaning "just," "only," "right away," "as early as," "simply," "exactly," or "then." In the Oracle-Bone and Bronze Inscriptions, 京 (jīng, capital) resembles a building at the top of a hill or mountain. You may compare 京 with 高 (see gāo, tall, in **Lesson 2**) and 亮 (see liàng, bright, in **Lesson 5**). In the Oracle-Bone and Bronze Inscriptions, 尤 looks like a wart on a hand. Thus, its original meaning was "wart." Today, 尤 is used to mean "fault," "particularly," "especially," and "outstanding."

就 會意。從京，從尤。"京"為建于高丘之上的宮殿。"尤"為突出。"就"本義指達到至高處，引申為趨向、就要、隨即等。尤，象形。甲骨文從又（右手），一斜畫表示手上的贅疣，引申為突出、特別。

位 wèi (a polite MW for a person)

Associative compound. 位 combines the person radical 亻 and the character 立 (lì, stand), to mean the location, position, or place, where a person stands. 位 is also used as the polite measure word for people. In the Oracle-Bone and Bronze Inscriptions, the upper part of 立 is the front view of a person (大), while the bottom stroke (一) stands for the ground, meaning "stand," "erect," or "upright."

位 會意。從人，從立，指人站立的位置，也用作量詞。立 會意。甲骨文、金文從大（正面人形），從一（地），表示人站立于地上。

124   *Lesson 6*

甲 金 篆

午 wǔ (noon)

Pictograph. In the Oracle-Bone and Bronze Inscriptions, 午 resembles a wooden pestle, hence "pestle" was the original meaning. Later, 午 came to mean "disobedient," "offend," etc. Today 午 is used to mark the period of time between 11:00 a.m. and 1:00 p.m.*

午 象形。像舂米用的棒杵，　是杵的初文，引申為抵觸、違逆等。後借用為午時，相當於白天十一時至十三時。

金  篆

間/间 jiān (between; MW for rooms)

Associative compound. In the Bronze Inscriptions and Seal Script 間 is the combination of 門 (mén, door) and 月 (yuè, moon), representing a sliver of moonlight seen through the door panels. In Regular Script, 月 is replaced with 日 (rì, sun). Meanings of 間 include "space in between," "opening," "separate," "between," "middle," "among," "space," and it is also used as a measure word for rooms. The door radical in the character 间 is in simplified form.

間 會意。金文從門，從月，用門中可看見月光表示空隙之意。楷書門中改月為日。簡體字間的部首簡化。

---

* In the West, "noon" is typically thought of as starting after 12:00 p.m, while in China, the "noon" period starts at 11:00 a.m.

篆 題

頁 甲 金 篆 草 頁

題/题 tí (topic; question)

Associative and pictophonetic compound. The character
題 consists of the radical 頁 (yè, head; page) and the
signifying and phonetic element 是 (shì, to be), meaning:
"headline," "topic," "title," "subject," "inscribe," or
"question." In the Oracle-Bone Inscriptions, 頁 depicts a
person with an oversized head. Its original meaning was
"head." Today it is used to mean "page." In the character
題, the component 頁 is in its simplified form.

題 會意兼形聲。從頁（頭），從是，是亦聲。本義為
額頭，引申為物體的前端、題目、書寫有特殊意义的
文字等。頁，象形。甲骨文中像一個頭部極為突出的
人形。本義為頭，引申為書頁的一張等。簡體字題右
部的页字简化。

古 開 篆 開

開/开 kāi (to open)

Associative compound. In the Ancient
Inscriptions, 開 looks like two hands
removing a door bar. Its original meaning is
"to open a door." Extended meanings include:
"open," "start," "operate," etc. The simplified
character 开 retains the hands part of the
traditional character 開 but is without the
door part.

開 會意。古文字形像雙手拿掉門閂開門
狀。簡體字开僅保留繁體字開門的那部分。

126

會/会 huì (to meet)

Associative compound. In its ancient form, 會 is made up of three parts: the lower part represents a container; the middle is the food; the top is the container's lid, meaning, "to join together," "converge," and "assemble." Extended meanings of 會 include: "to meet," "meeting," "gathering," "association," "to be able to," "to be likely to," etc. The simplified character 会 derives from the cursive style of the traditional character 會.

會 會意。甲骨文、金文字形下像容器，上像容器的蓋子，中間像盛放的食物。蓋上容器的蓋子，表示會合，引申為開會等。簡體字会是繁體字會的草書楷化字。

節/节 jié (MW for classes)

Pictophonetic character. The character 節 consists of the bamboo radical 𥫗 and the phonetic element 即 (jí), meaning "bamboo joint," "node," or "knot." Extended meanings of 節 are: "division," "part," "section," and "length." It is also used as the measure word for classes. In the Oracle-Bone Inscriptions, the left part of 即 represents a food container, and the right part shows a person kneeling to eat the food. Hence the meanings of 即 are: "in the immediate future," "to approach," "reach," "be near," etc. The simplified character 节 contains the grass radical 艹 instead of the bamboo radical 𥫗 and keeps only the right bottom part of 節.

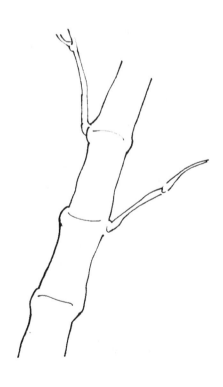

節 形聲。從竹，即聲。本義為竹節，引申為量詞、節日等。即，會意。甲骨文、金文中左邊像食器，右邊像一人跪坐，準備進食。本義為即將就食。簡體字节上部把竹字頭改為草字頭，下部保留即字的右部，十分近似節字的草體。

篆 課　果 甲 金 果 篆 果

課/课 kè (class; lesson)

Pictophonetic character. The character 課
consists of the word radical 言 and the
phonetic element 果 (guǒ, fruit), and means:
"class," "lesson," or "course." In the
Oracle-Bone Inscriptions, 果 is a
pictograph of a tree with three fruits. In the
Bronze Inscriptions, these three fruits
become one large one. In Seal Script, this
large fruit is replaced with the character 田
(tián, field), which deviates somewhat from
the original meaning. A class or course
should be fruitful, not fruitless! The speech
radical in the character 课 is in its simplified form.

課 形聲。從言，果聲，意為考試，課時等。果 象形。像樹上結出的果實。簡體
字课的部首簡化。

篆 級　及 甲 金 篆 及

級/级 jí (grade; level)

Pictophonetic character. The character 級
consists of the silk radical 糸 and the phonetic
element 及 (jí, to reach). The original meaning
of 級 referred to the grade of silk specifically. Its
extended meanings include: "grade," "level,"
"rank," and "step." In the Oracle-Bone and
Bronze Inscriptions, 及 resembles a hand
touching someone on the back, therefore meaning
"to reach" or "come up to." The silk radical in the
character 级 is in simplified form.

級 形聲。從糸，及聲。本義為絲的优劣次第，
引申為等級。及 會意。甲骨文、金文從又（右
手），從人，像一只手從後抓住一個人狀。本義
為逮捕，引申為趕上、追上、到達。级字部首
簡化。

考 kǎo (test)

Pictograph. In the Oracle-Bone and Bronze Inscriptions, 考 is written as 老, which looks like an elderly person with a walking stick in hand. The original meaning of 考 was "old" or "aged," but later came to mean "examine," "test," "inspect," "verify," etc. In ancient Chinese society, elders were considered more knowledgeable, and therefore in a position to test younger people. They might even have had the authority to use sticks to punish those who failed their tests!

考 形聲。從老，丂(kāo)聲。本義為老，引申為考試。甲骨文、金文老、考是同字，都像老人長髮弓背，扶着拐杖形。

篆

試/试 shì (to try)

Pictophonetic character. The character 試 is comprised of the word radical 言 and the phonetic 式 (shì), meaning: "to try," "test," or "examination." 式 combines 弋 (yì, arrow with rope) and 工 (gōng, tool; work). Its original meaning was "rule" or "regulation." Today it is used to mean "style," "type," or "ceremony." The speech radical in 试 is in simplified form.

試 形聲。從言，式聲，意指任用、嘗試、考試等。式，形聲。從工，弋聲，本義為建築有規則法度。簡體字试的部首簡化。

甲  金 篆

後/后 **hòu (after; behind)**

Associative compound. The character 後 consists of 彳 (walk slowly; left step), 幺 (yāo, string; tiny), and 夊 (suī, left foot), suggesting someone walking behind another with one's left foot tied by a string or rope. The meanings of 後 include "behind," "back," "after," "later," and "last." Originally 后 (hòu) was used to mean empress. In simplified form, the meaning of 后 is the same as 後.

後 會意。從彳（半條街），從幺（繩），從夊（suī 腳）。表示足被繩系住，走在後面。簡體字用后（皇后的后）替代後，屬同音替代字。

金  篆

空 **kòng (free time)**

Pictophonetic compound. The character 空 consists of the radical 穴 (xué, cave) and the phonetic symbol 工 (gōng, work). The original meaning of 空 was "hole." It is used today to mean "empty," "hollow," "in vain," "sky" (pronounced kōng), "unoccupied," "vacant," and "free time" (pronounced kòng). In Seal Script, 穴 is a pictograph of a cave dwelling.

空 形聲。從穴，工聲，本義為窟窿。穴，象形。像洞穴形。

130 *Lesson 6*

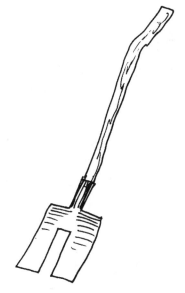

甲 金 方 篆

方 fāng (square; side)

Pictograph. In the Oracle-Bone Inscriptions, 方 looks like a shovel or spade. Its original meaning was "shovel," but today it means "to dig a hole," "cubic meter," "square," "upright," "place," "region," "side," etc.

方 象形。像剷土的工具。甲骨文上短橫像手握的橫柄，中間一長橫是腳踩的地方，下為分叉的鍤。本義為土鍤，引申義正方形、方面、正、才等。

金 篆

更 甲 金 篆

便 biàn; pián (convenient; inexpensive)

Associative compound. The character 便 combines the person radical 亻 with the character 更 (gēng, change), referring to the ways in which people create shortcuts to make things easier. Meanings of 便 include: "suitable," "beneficial," "convenient," "informal," (biàn) and "inexpensive." (pián). In the Oracle-Bone Inscriptions, 更 resembles a hand holding a spatula to turn a pancake on a griddle. Hence its meanings: "change" or "alternate."

便 會意。篆文從人、從更。人有不便時，更改方能使之安妥方便。更，會意兼形聲。甲骨文字形像手持鏟翻餅狀，引申為更改。

金 到 篆 勁

到 dào (to go to; to arrive)

Pictophonetic character. The character 到 has the signifying element 至 (zhì, arrive) on the left, and the knife radical and phonetic symbol 刂 (dāo) on the right, meaning "arrive," "reach," "go to," or "leave for." In its ancient form, 至 depicts an arrow reaching its target, and meant "arrive," "reach," "extremely," and "most."

到 形聲。篆文從至，刀聲。至，象形，像箭頭射中地面或箭靶狀。

篆 辡 辛 甲 ∀ 金 ∀ 篆 辛

辦/办 bàn (to manage)

Pictophonetic character. The character 辦 consists of the signifying element 力 (lì; power) and the phonetic symbol 辡 (biàn, to debate), meaning "handle," "manage," "do," or "punish." 辡 is made up of two 辛 (xīn). In the Oracle-Bone and Bronze Inscriptions, 辛 is a pictograph of a chiseled instrument used to tattoo the faces of prisoners. Extended meanings of 辛 are "pungent," "laborious," "suffering," and "hot" (in flavor). The simplified character 办 uses two short strokes to replace the two 辛 of the traditional form 辦.

辦 形聲。從力，辡 (biàn 剖分、爭辯) 聲。辛，象形。像在犯人臉上刺字的刑具。簡體字办用一撇一點代替兩個辛字，舊時已見。

甲 ム　金 凸　篆

公 gōng (public)

Associative compound. In the Oracle-Bone and Bronze Inscriptions, the upper part of 公 is 八 and the lower part resembles a container. The original meaning of 八 was to divide something into two parts. Therefore, 公 means to evenly divide things in a container. The extended meanings of 公 are "fair," "impartial," "public," "collective," etc.

公 會意。篆文從八（分），從厶（sī 私）。甲骨文從八，從口（指容器口），表示平均分配容器中的東西。

甲 　金 室　篆 宝

室 shì (room)

Associative and pictophonetic compound. The character 室 consists of the roof radical 宀 and the signifying and phonetic element 至 (zhì, to arrive), meaning "room." You learned 至 with the character 到 (see dào, arrive, in **Lesson 6**).

室 會意兼形聲。從宀，從至；至亦聲。指人歇息居住的地方。

行 xíng (all right; okay)

Pictograph. In the Oracle-Bone and Bronze Inscriptions, the character 行 delineates two streets intersecting. The original meaning of 行 was "intersection," and extended meanings include "road," "go," "walk," "carry out," "all right," and "will do." In Regular Script, 行 is comprised of 彳 (walk slowly; left step) and 亍 (chù, small step). You have seen 彳 in the characters 律 (see lǜ, law; rule, in **Lesson 2**) and 後 (see hòu, after, in **Lesson 6**).

行 象形。甲骨文、金文像四通八達的道路。本義指十字路，引申為行走、走得通、可以等。

篆 𤼲

等 děng (to wait)

Associative compound. The character 等 consists of the bamboo radical ⺮ and the character 寺 (sì, to manage; temple), meaning "to tidy bamboo pieces." Extended meanings of 等 include "sort," "equal," and "rank." After the Tang Dynasty, 等 came to mean "wait." In the Bronze Inscriptions, 寺 consists of stop (止) and a hand (又), meaning "hold," "handle," or "manage." Later 寺 came to mean "temple" or "monastery." See the character 時 in **Lesson 4**.

等 會意。從竹，從寺。寺，會意兼形聲。金文從又（手），從止。手之所止為持，本以為持有、操持，是持的本字。后借用為寺廟的寺。

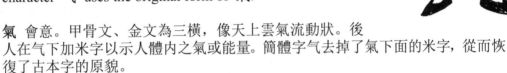

气 甲 三 金 乀 篆 气

米 甲 ⁂ 金 𣎳 篆 米

氣/气 qì (air)

Associative compound. The character 氣 combines 气 (qì, air) and 米 (mǐ, rice). In the Oracle-Bone and Bronze Inscriptions, 气 looks like three thin clouds in the sky, meaning "air," "gas," or "weather." 米 was added under 气 later. In the Oracle-Bone Inscriptions, 米 resembles grains scattered around a rack. 米 and 气 were combined to form 氣, meaning "mood," "breath," and "human energy/spirit," in addition to "air," "gas," and "weather." The simplified character 气 uses the original form of 氣.

氣 會意。甲骨文、金文為三橫，像天上雲氣流動狀。後人在气下加米字以示人體內之氣或能量。簡體字气去掉了氣下面的米字，從而恢復了古本字的原貌。

幫/帮 bāng (to help)

Pictophonetic character. The character 幫 consists of the signifying element 帛 (bó, silk) and the phonetic symbol 封 (fēng, seal). The original meaning of 幫 was "the upper part of a shoe" while extended meanings include "side" (of a boat, cart, etc.), "assist," "aid," and "help." The character 帛 combines 白 (bái, white) and 巾 (jīn, scarf), referring to un-dyed silk. 巾 is a pictograph of a hanging scarf. In Regular Script, 封 is comprised of

two 土 (tǔ, soil) and one 寸 (cùn, inch). 幇 is a variant form of 幫, and the middle part 白 was deleted from 幫 to form the simplified version 帮.

幫 從帛，封聲。本義為鞋幫，引申為輔助等意。封，會意。甲骨文、金文像在土堆上植樹，以此來劃定邊界。帛，從巾，從白；白亦聲。本義指未經染色的素白絲織物，引申為絲織品的總稱。巾 象形。像垂下的佩巾。繁體字幫的另一寫法是幇。簡體字帮去掉了幫字中間的白字。

篆 練 草 练

練/练 liàn (to drill)

Pictophonetic character. The character 練 is comprised of the silk radical 糸 and the phonetic element 柬 (jiǎn). 練 originally meant "to boil and scour raw silk," and extends to mean "practice," "drill," or "train." In its ancient form, 柬 consists of 束 (shù, a bunch of bamboo pieces; firewood) and 八 (bā, to divide; eight). The original meaning of 柬 was "to choose" or "select." Later it came to mean: "note" or "card." The silk radical is simplified to form 练, while the right part derives from the cursive style of the character 柬.

練 形聲。從糸，柬聲。本義指把生絲煮得柔軟潔白，引申為反復練習。柬，從束（一捆東西），從八（分別），意指打開一捆東西從中挑選，引申為信札書簡。簡體字练字左邊的部首由糸 簡化為纟，右邊一半是柬字的草書楷化字。

甲 習 篆 習

習 / 习 xí (to practice)

Associative compound. In its ancient form, the character 習 combined 羽 (yǔ, feather) and 日 (rì, sun), to symbolize birds practicing flying during the day. Meanings of 習 include "to practice," "exercise," "review," "habit," etc. In Regular Script, the 日 in the lower part of 習 is replaced with 白 (bái, white), which also refers to daytime. In the Oracle-Bone Inscriptions, 羽 is a pictograph of the two wings of a bird. The simplified character 习 uses only one part of the traditional character 習.

習 會意。甲骨文、金文從羽，從日，表示小鳥在陽光中展翅學習飛翔。簡體字习僅保留了繁體字習的上半部分。

兌 甲  金 篆

說 / 说 shuō (to speak)

Associative compound. The character 說 combines the word radical 言 and the character 兌 (duì, exchange), meaning "to speak," "talk," "say," or "explain." In the Oracle-Bone Inscriptions, 兌 combines 人 (rén, person), 口 (kǒu, mouth), and 八 (bā, divide), symbolizing a grinning person. The original meaning of 兌 was "joyous," while extended meanings include "exchange," "convert," and "add." The speech radical in 说 is in its simplified form.

說 會意。從言，從兌(duì)。本義為言語中有喜悅之情，引申為言辭、陳述、勸說等。兌，從人，從口，從八（分開）。人笑則口開，本義為喜悅。说字部首簡化。

啊 a (exclamation)

Pictophonetic character. The character 啊 is used as an exclamation, and consists of the mouth radical 口 and the phonetic component 阿 (ā/ē). 阿 contains the mound radical 阝 and the phonetic 可 (kě), meaning "large mound."

啊 形聲。從口，阿聲。用作嘆詞。阿，形聲。金文從阜（腳坑；土山），可聲，本意指為山的彎曲処。

但 dàn (but)

Pictophonetic character. 但 consists of the person radical 亻 and the phonetic symbol 旦 (dàn). Its original meaning was "to be stripped to the waist." It later came to mean "but," "yet," and "nevertheless." A new character 袒 was created to convey the original meaning of 但. 旦 is comprised of 日 with a horizontal stroke underneath, symbolizing the sun rising above the horizon. 旦, therefore, means "daybreak" or "dawn."

但 形聲。從人，旦聲。本義為袒露，
是袒的古字，今用為副詞或連詞。
旦，指事。一代表地平綫，表示太陽剛從地平綫上升起。

篆 知

知 zhī (to know)

Associative compound. The character 知 combines 矢 (shǐ, arrow) and 口 (kǒu, mouth), suggesting one speaking as fast as an arrow flies. Extended meanings of 知 include "realize," "know," and "knowledge." In the Oracle-Bone and Bronze Inscriptions, 矢 depicts an arrow. You have seen 矢 in the character 醫 (see yī, medicine, in **Lesson 2**).

知 會意。從矢（箭），從口，表示開
口講話的速度如射箭一般快。本義為言
詞敏捷，引申為了解知道等。

古  金 篆

道 dào (road; way)

Associative compound. The character 道 consists of the walk radical 辶 and the character 首 (shǒu, head), meaning "road," "way," or "line." 道 is also used to mean "method," "doctrine," "the (natural) way (of things)," and "Taoism." In the Oracle-Bone Inscriptions, 首 looks like a head with hair on top. The primary meaning of 首 is "head," and extended meanings include "leader," "chief," and "first."

道 會意。從辶，從首，表示一人頭在前面引導前行，意為指明道路或道路。首，象形。甲骨文、金文像有髮的人頭。

隼 甲 金 篆

準 篆

準 / 准 zhǔn (standard; criterion; allow; accurate)

Pictophonetic character. The character 準 consists of the water radical 氵 and the phonetic component 隼 (sǔn), meaning "standard," "criterion," etc. Since people used the level of a liquid in a container or the water in a lake/river as standard to judge the height of its surroundings, the character 準 contains the water radical. In its ancient form, the character 隼 depicts a bird with a person, meaning "hunting eagle."

準 形聲。從氵，隼(sǔn)聲。本義為水準，準則。隼，會意。金文從佳，從人。像人訓獵鷹狩獵，本義為獵鷹。簡體字准是準字的俗體字，漢代已有。

 甲  金 篆

備/备 **bèi** (prepare)

Associative compound. In the Oracle-Bone inscriptions and Bronze Inscriptions, the character 備 looks like an arrow in the quiver, signaling ready for a battle. Hence, the meanings of 備 are "cautious," "prepare," or "ready." 俻 is a variant form of 備, and the simplified character 备 remains only the right part of 俻.

備　會意。甲骨文、金文皆像箭在箭匣中，意指準備，防備，預備，裝備等。俻是備字的異體字，簡體字备去掉了俻字的部首亻。

甲 篆

面　**miàn** (face)

Pictograph. In the Oracle-Bone Inscription, the character 面 delineates the contour of a face with an exaggerated huge eye, since eyes are the most striking part on one's face. The meanings of 面 include: "face," "to face," "said," "aspect," surface," etc.

面　象形。甲骨文像是臉形。外似面部輪廓，中是一誇大了的眼睛，因眼睛為臉部最為醒目、最為傳神之處。本義為面孔，引申為面向、方面、表面、臉面、等。

LESSON 7

篆 跟　艮 甲 金 篆

跟 gēn (with; and; follow)

Pictophonetic character. 跟 has the foot radical 足 and the phonetic component 艮 (gěn). 跟 originally referred to "heel," from which the meanings "follow," "with," and "and" derived. You have seen 艮 in the character 很 (see hěn, very, in **Lesson 3**). In the Oracle-Bone and Bronze Inscriptions, the upper part of 艮 is a big eye and the lower part is a person, indicating someone turning back to stare. The meanings of 艮 are "disobey," "tough," "blunt," and "straightforward."

跟 形聲。從足，艮聲。本義為腳後跟，引申為跟隨，还可作連詞。

篆 助

助 zhù (to assist, to aid)

Associative and pictophonetic compound. In the Oracle-Bone and Bronze Inscriptions, the character 且 resembles a memorial tablet used in ancestral worship, and originally meant "ancestor." You have seen 且 in the character 姐 (see jiě, older sister, in **Lesson 1**). 助 combines the radical 力 (lì, strength, power) and the semantic and phonetic symbol 且 (qiě/jū), referring to the assistance one receives from ancestral spirits.

助 形聲兼會意。從力，從且（祭祀祖先之靈所用的牌位）；且亦聲。指靠祖先之靈以力相助。

甲　　金　　篆

復/复 fù (to duplicate)

Pictophonetic character. 復 consists of the radical 彳 (walk slowly; left step) and the phonetic component 复 (fù). In the Oracle-Bone Inscriptions, 复 looks like a cave dwelling with two exits. There is a foot next to the lower exit, suggesting a person returning to the cave. The first meaning of 复, therefore, was "to return." Its extended meanings include "again," "duplicate," "recover," and "reply." Later the radical 彳 (walk slowly; left step) was added to 复, but the meaning did not change. The simplified character 复 uses the original form.

復 形聲。從彳，复聲，意為往返。复，會意。甲骨文上部像有兩個出口的洞穴，下部從止（腳），表示人出入洞穴，引申為重復。复是復字的古本字，後人加偏旁彳，簡體字恢復古本字的原貌。

篆　草　　舄金　篆

寫/写 xiě (to write)

Pictophonetic character. The character 寫 contains the roof radical 宀 and the phonetic element 舄 (xì). The original meaning of 寫 was "to move things into a room," with the extended meaning "to write." In its ancient form, 舄 is a pictograph of a chattering bird (symbolized by an open beak in the upper part, and wings and claws in the lower part). 舄 originally meant "magpie." The simplified character 写 developed from the cursive form of 寫.

寫 形聲。從宀，舄(xi)聲 。本義為移置，引申為傾吐、摹畫、書寫等。舄，象形。金文像一隻張開大嘴喳喳叫的喜鵲，本義為喜鵲。 簡體字写是繁體字寫的草書楷化字，但草書写字上面多帶一點。

慢 曼 甲 金 篆

慢 màn (slow)

Pictophonetic character. The character 慢 consists of the vertical heart radical 忄 and the phonetic component 曼 (màn), meaning "slow." In the Oracle-Bone Inscriptions, 曼 depicts two hands holding an eye open. The original meaning of 曼 was "open eyes," with the extended meanings "prolonged" and "graceful." Later, the hands in the upper part changed to 曰, forming the Regular Script form of 曼.

慢 形聲。從心，曼聲，本義為惰怠。曼，會意。甲骨文、金文像看到美妙的人或事時，以兩手把眼睛撐得大大的，目不轉睛地看。本義為張目，引申為美好、嫵媚之意。

甲 金 篆

教 jiāo/jiào (to teach)

Associative and pictophonetic compound. In its ancient forms, the left part of the character 教 consists of 爻 (yáo, counting sticks) and 子 (zǐ, child), indicating a child learning. The right part of 教 is a hand holding a stick, suggesting the tutor supervising the child. Physical forms of punishment were common practice in the past. In Regular Script, the right part of 教 is simplified into the tap/rap radical 攵, and 爻 on the top left is replaced with 耂, which you have seen in the characters 老 (lǎo, old) and 考 (kǎo, test). The lower left 子 remains the same.

教 會意兼形聲。甲骨文從攴 pū（手持棍狀），從子，從爻 yáo（算籌相交之形）。表示手持棍監督教導孩子學習計算。

篆

筆/笔 **bǐ (pen)**

Associative compound. In the Oracle-Bone and Bronze Inscriptions, 聿 (yù) shows a hand holding a brush. You have seen 聿 in the character 律 (see lǜ, law, in **Lesson 2**) and 書 (see shū, book, in **Lesson 4**). The character 筆 combines the bamboo radical ⺮ and 聿, signifying a writing brush or writing instrument. The simplified character 笔 combines the bamboo radical and the character 毛 (máo, hair; fur) since the nib of a Chinese brush is made of animal fur and bamboo shafts.

筆 會意。從聿（手持筆形），從竹，指手握竹子做的筆桿寫字。。簡體笔字保留上邊竹字頭，因毛筆筆端用獸毛之故，下邊改用毛字。屬新創的會意字。

金 篆 堇 甲

難/难 **nán (difficult; hard)** Pictophonetic
character. In its ancient form, the character 難 consists of the phonetic component 堇 (jǐn) and the radical 隹 (zhuī, short-tailed bird), originally meaning a particular species of bird. In the Oracle-Bone Inscriptions, 堇 looks like a shackled person in flames. Since 堇 contains the meanings of "suffering" and "disaster," later the character 難 came to mean "difficult," "hard" or "troublesome." Note the difference between 堇 and the left part of 難. In the simplified form 难, 又 replaces 堇.

難 形聲。金文從隹，堇(jǐn)聲，本義指一種鳥，因從"堇"（焚燒人牲祭天求雨）而借用來表示艱難困苦。堇，甲骨文像用火焚燒捆綁的人牲，意指以人牲祭祀求雨，引申為乾旱、災難等。簡體字难左邊用又替代，屬符號替代字。明清已見此字。

篆

裏/裡/里 lǐ (inside)

Pictophonetic character. In **Radicals**, you learned the character 衣 (yī, clothing) as well as the clothing radical 衤. The characters 裏/裡 consist of radicals 衣/衤 and the phonetic element 里 (lǐ). 裏/裡 originally meant "lining" (of a garment), and extends to mean "inside" or "in." 里 is the combination of 田 (tián, field) and 土 (tǔ, earth; soil), referring to "native place" or "neighborhood." To form the character 裏，里 was added to the middle of 衣, while 里 was added to the right of 衤 to form the character 裡. In simplified characters, 里 is the simplified form for both 裏 and 裡.

裏/裡 形聲。從衣，里聲。本義指衣服的裏層，引申為內部、裏面。里，會意。從田，從土。有田有土，表示人所居住的地方與長度單位，如故里、鄰里、萬里等。簡體字里的字意擴充，包含了繁體字裏的所有意思。

第 dì (ordinal prefix)

Pictophonetic character. The character 第 consists of the bamboo radical 𥫗 and the phonetic element 弟 (dì, younger brother, see 弟 in **Lesson 2**). The original meaning of 第 was "the arrangement of bamboo" and its extended meaning is "order" or "sequence." 第 is also placed before a number to form ordinal numbers. Please note the differences between 第 and 弟.

第 從竹，從弟；弟也兼表聲。本義為竹的層次，引申為次第、順序。

篆

預/预 yù (to prepare)

Pictophonetic character. The character 預 consists of the radical 頁 (yè, page; head) and the phonetic component 予 (yǔ, give; push forward), originally meaning "a head thrusting forward." Its extended meanings include "beforehand," "in advance," or "to prepare." In the Oracle-Bone Inscriptions, 頁 resembles a person with an oversized head. The original meaning of 頁 was "head" with the extended meaning "page." You have seen 頁 in the character 題 (see tí, topic, in **Lesson 6**). In Seal Script, 予 resembles a hand pushing something to others, meaning "to give" or "grant." 页, the right part of 預, derives from the cursive style of 頁.

預 會意兼形聲。篆文從頁（人頭），從予（此處有前伸意），表示把頭伸到前面，引申為預先、參預等。予，象形。篆文像以手推物給他人狀，本義為給予。簡體字预右邊的页是由繁體字頁的草書楷化而來

篆

語/语 yǔ (language)

Pictophonetic character. The character 語 combines the word radical 言 and the phonetic component 吾 (wú), meaning "words," "say," or "language." 吾 consists of the phonetic component 五 (wǔ, five) and the mouth radical 口. In classical Chinese 吾 is used to mean "I" or "my." The character 語 looks like five people opening their mouths to speak five different languages! The speech radical is simplified to form 语.

語 形聲。從言，吾聲，意為談論、談話等。吾，金文從口，五聲，用作第一人稱。簡體字语的部首簡化。

金 𤱿 篆 㳒

法 fǎ (method; way)

Associative compound. The character 法 consists of the water radical 氵 and the character 去 (qù, to go). The original meaning of 法 was "to live on a river," and extended meanings include "standard," "law," "method," and "way." Many ancient cities were built on rivers, such that this practice became almost "standard" or "law."

法 會意。金文從人，從口，從水，從廌（zhì 公牛）。指人趕著牛羊，逐水草而居。逐水草而居是遊牧民族的規矩，世界上不少古老的城市也都沿河而建，因此引申為規律、法律等。篆文簡化，從水，從去。

甲 𠔏 篆 容

容 róng (to hold; to contain; to allow)

Associative compound. The character 容 is comprised of the roof radical 宀 and the character 谷 (gǔ, valley; gorge). Since both houses and valleys have the capacity to hold people and/or things, 容 means "to contain," "hold," "allow" or "tolerate." In the Oracle-Bone Inscriptions, the upper part of 谷 looks like flowing water, while the bottom part resembles a mountain pass.

容 會意。從宀，從谷，意指房屋、山谷都有容納人或物的空間。谷，象形。甲骨文中像水從山谷中流出。

甲  金 篆

易 yì (easy)

Associative compound. In the Oracle-Bone Inscriptions, the character 易 looks like pouring water from one vessel to the other, meaning "change," "exchange," "easy," etc. In Regular Script, 易 differs greatly from its original Oracle-Bone form. The upper part of 易 is instead the vessel with the lower part representing the pouring water.

易 會意。甲骨文像把水從一個容器中倒入另一容器中。本義為給予，引申為改變、容易等。

懂 dǒng (to understand)

Pictophonetic character. 懂 consists of the vertical heart radical 忄 and the phonetic symbol 董 (dǒng, to supervise), meaning "understand" or "know." 董 combines the grass radical 艹 and the phonetic component 重 (zhòng, heavy). In the Bronze Inscriptions, 重 depicts a figure carrying a heavy sack on his or her back, meaning "heavy," "serious," or "important." Be sure to distinguish 懂 from the character 鐘 (see zhōng, o'clock, in **Lesson 3**).

懂 從忄，董聲。董，形聲。篆文從艸，童聲。童，金文像身背重物、頭上有刑具的人，指男子有罪受刑罰而變成奴隸，引申為兒童。

司 甲 乙 金 司

詞/词 cí (word)

Associative compound. The character 詞 consists of the word radical 言 and the character 司 (sī, to manage), meaning "word," "term," or "statement." In the Oracle-Bone Inscriptions, 司 resembles a hand over a mouth, symbolizing a person issuing orders. Therefore, the meanings of 司 are "to take charge of," "manage," etc. The speech radical is simplified to form the character 词.

詞 會意。從司，從言。司有主管義，表示人對語言的駕馭掌握。司，會意。甲骨文、金文像把手遮在嘴上發號施令。簡體字词的部首簡化。

篆 漢

漢/汉 hàn (Chinese)

Pictophonetic character. The character 漢 contains the water radical 氵 and the phonetic component 菫 (jǐn) which you learned in the character 難 in this lesson. Originally 漢 referred to the name of a river that is a tributary of the Yangtze River. 漢 is also the character for the Han Dynasty (206 B.C.–220 A.D.), considered a golden age in ancient Chinese history. Of China's 56 ethnic groups, the Han (漢) has the largest population. 漢 also refers to the Chinese language of this Han nationality. In the simplified character 汉, 又 replaces 菫. The same simplification can be found in the character 難, with the simplified form 难.

漢 形聲。篆文從水，難聲。本義為水名，即漢水。又有漢朝、漢族、漢語等詞。簡體字汉的簡化方法與难（難）字相同，都是以又來替代菫。明清已見此字。

金 平 篆

平 píng (level; even)

Pictograph. The character 平 looks like a balance or scale that is equally weighted on both sides, meaning "even," "flat," "impartial," "equal," "fair," etc. Some scholars believe 平 looks like floating duckweed. Since the surface of a duckweed is flat, 平 means "flat," or "even."

平 一説像天平形，義為公平、不向一方傾斜。一說平字似水面浮萍。

金 篆

早 zǎo (early)

Associative compound. 早 looks like the sun rising to the top of a crossed column, an instrument for solar observation (sun dial). The meanings of 早 include "morning," "early," "long ago," etc.

早 會意。篆文從日，從甲（原為測量日光的儀器），表示太陽升到甲之上，意為早晨。

夜 yè (night)

Pictophonetic character. In its ancient form, the character 夜 consists of the radical 夕 (xī, sunset; evening) and the phonetic element 亦 (yì). In the Oracle-Bone Inscriptions, 亦 depicts a person (大) with two dots under his or her armpits, and its original meaning is "armpit." In Regular Script, 夜 looks like a person (亻) under the roof (亠) with the lower right part symbolizing an open eye.

夜 形聲。從夕，亦聲。亦，甲骨文從大（人的正面），旁邊兩點表示人的腋窩。亦本意是腋窩。

金 篆

功 gōng (skill)

Associative and pictophonetic compound. The character 功 consists of the radical and phonetic element 工 (gōng, work) and the signifying component 力 (lì, strength; power), suggesting one working with all one's strength. The meanings of 功 include "meritorious deed," "skill," "effect," and "success."

功 會意兼形聲。從力，從工；工亦聲。力，盡力；工，工作。盡力工作必有功勞功績。

甲  金 篆

真 zhēn (true; real)

Associative compound. In the Oracle-Bone Inscriptions, the lower part of 真 is a bronze vessel on a tripod and the upper part a person, thus signifying someone savoring the delicacy in the vessel. The original meaning of 真 was delicacy, and extended meanings include "true," "real," "truly," "indeed," etc. Be sure to remember that there are *three* lines inside the middle part of 真 in Regular Script.

真 會意。甲骨文從鼎，從人，指人到鼎邊拿美食吃。本義為美食，引申為真實等。

台 甲 金 篆

始 shǐ (to begin)

Associative and pictophonetic compound. In the Oracle-Bone Inscriptions, 台 looks like a fetus with its head facing down towards the birth canal, and originally meant "pregnant." The character 始 consists of the female radical 女 and the signifying and phonetic element 台 (tái), originally referring to the beginning stages of pregnancy. Extended meanings of 始 include "to begin," "start," and "just."

始 會意兼形聲。從女，從台（胎兒）；台也兼表聲。本義為剛開始受孕懷胎，引申泛指開始。台，甲骨文像頭朝下的胎兒。

Lesson 7

念 甲  金 篆

唸/念 niàn (to read)

Pictophonetic character. The character 唸 consists of the mouth radical 口 and the phonetic component 念 (niàn), meaning "to read aloud." 念 combines the heart radical 心 and the phonetic 今 (jīn), meaning "to think of," "to miss," "thought," "idea," "study," etc. The simplified character 念 contains the meaning of 唸, "to read aloud."

唸 形聲。從口，念聲，意指誦讀。念，形聲。從心，今聲，意為想念、想法、學習等。簡體字念也包含了繁體字唸的誦讀之意。

录 甲  金 篆

錄/录 lù (to record)

Pictophonetic character. In Seal Script, 錄 is comprised of the gold radical 金 and the phonetic component 录 (lù). The original meaning of 錄 was "golden color" and extended meanings include "to write down," "record," "copy," "hire," etc. In the Oracle-Bone and Bronze Inscriptions, 录 looks like water filtering through a hanging sack. 录 originally meant "filter" and extends to mean "record" and "copy." The simplified character 录 comes from the right part of 錄, which is a variant form of 錄.

錄 形聲。從金，录聲，記載、抄寫、錄用之意。录，會意。金文字形像木架上吊了一個布袋，濾出裏面的水。录的本義為濾。繁體字錄的另一寫法是彔，簡體字录去掉錄的金字旁。

甲  金 帥 篆 帥

帥/帅 shuài (handsome)

Associative compound. In the Oracle-Bone Inscriptions, the character 帥 resembles two hands (the left part) holding a flag or scarf (the right part), and originally meaning "commander-in-chief." Since such commanders often have a commanding presence and impressive bearing, "handsome" became one of the extended meanings of 帥. Be sure to distinguish 帥 from the character 師 (shī, teacher, **Lesson 7**). *I hope you are lucky enough to have 很帥的中文老師 (a handsome Chinese teacher)!* The simplified character 帅 derives from the cursive style of the traditional character 帥. The same simplification can be found in the character 師, with the simplified form 师.

帥 形聲。甲骨文字形右似佩巾，左為伸出的雙手，像用兩手展開佩巾狀。本義為佩巾，借用為軍中統帥，引申為英俊，有風度等。簡體字帅是繁體字帥的草書楷化字，簡化方法與師字相同。

篆 枝

枝 zhī (twig; branch; measure word for long, thin objects)

Pictophonetic character. The character 枝 consists of the wood/tree radical 木 and the phonetic element 支 (zhī). The primary meaning of 枝 is "branch," or "twig." It is also used as a measure word for something long and narrow, such as a pen, candle, rifle, etc.

枝 形聲。從木，支聲。本義為樹枝，引申為一些狹長條形物體的量詞。支，古字像手持折斷的竹枝，本義為枝條，引申為分支、支撐、支援等。

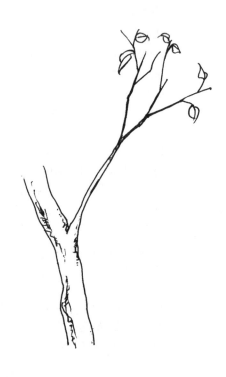

篆

紙 zhǐ (paper)

Pictophonetic character. The character 紙 is comprised of the silk radical 糸 and the phonetic element 氏 (shì), meaning "paper." Before paper was invented, rich people sometimes wrote on silk. Therefore, 紙 contains the silk radical.

紙 形聲。從糸，氏聲。本義為紙張。古時未造紙之前寫文于絲竹上，固有糸做部首。氏，古文像根在地下形，本義為根本，根柢，引申為古代貴族的分支、傳説中的人物、已婚婦女等。

篆

酷 kù (cruel; extremely)

Pictophonetic character. The character 酷 consists of the radical 酉 (wine jar) and the phonetic 告 (gào, tell). 酷 originally referred to the smell of strong alcoholic drinks and extends to mean "cruel," "extremely," etc. Since the pronunciation of 酷 is similar to "cool," it was used to translate the English word in recent years. In the Oracle-Bone Inscriptions, 告 is comprised of 牛 (niú, ox) and 口 (kǒu, mouth), originally referring to the sound an ox makes and extending to mean "inform," "tell," etc.

酷 形聲。從酉，告聲。本義為酒味濃烈，引申義有酷烈殘暴與表程度很深的意思。因音與英文 cool 相似，所以用來直譯 cool 在俚語中表達時興並有吸引力的意思。告在甲骨文從口，從牛。本義為牛叫，引申為上報、告訴、佈告等。

LESSON 8

扁 篆

篇 piān (MW for articles)

Pictophonetic character. The character 篇 is comprised of the bamboo radical 𥫗 and the phonetic component 扁 (biǎn). Since Chinese wrote on pieces of bamboo before paper was invented, 篇 means "chapter," or "a piece of writing," and also functions as a measure word for articles. In Seal Script, 扁 is the combination of 戶 (hù, household) and 冊 (cè, volume; copy), and originally referred to the horizontally inscribed board that often hung inside or outside a family's house. Today, 扁 is usually used to mean "flat." In the Oracle-Bone Inscriptions, 戶 is the pictograph of a door with one panel. In the ancient writing systems, 冊 represented a scroll of bamboo pieces bound together.

篇 形聲。篆文從竹，扁聲，意為典籍、著作、文章，也可用做文章的量詞。扁，會意。篆文從戶，從冊。本義為匾，引申為平薄物體等。

篆 記

記/记 jì (to record)

Pictophonetic character. 記 is made up of the word radical 言 and the phonetic 己 (jǐ), meaning "to record," "write down," "remember," "notes," etc. In its ancient form, 己 resembles a person with a big belly. It means "oneself," "one's own," or "personal." You have seen 己 in the character 起 (see qǐ, rise, in **Lesson 5**). The speech radical is simplified to form the character 记.

記 形聲。從言，己聲，意為記錄、記載、記憶。簡體字记的部首簡化。

甲 𠂤 篆 牀

牀/床 chuáng (bed)

Associative compound. In the Oracle-Bone Inscriptions, the character 床 depicts the outline of a bed (爿). In Seal Script, the character wood (木) is added to the right side of 爿, indicating that the bed is made of wood. 床 is a variant form of 牀, combining 广 (yǎn, shed; shelter; roof) and 木, suggesting a bed is a wooden article used inside of a house. The simplified character for bed is also 床.

牀/床 牀，從木，從爿（pán），泛指臥具。爿，象形。像床形。牀亦寫作床。床，從广，從木。牀與床是異體字，兩者通用，但舊時多用牀。簡體字為床。

篆 洗

洗 xǐ (to wash)

Associative and pictophonetic character. The character 洗 consists of the water radical 氵 and the signifying and phonetic element 先 (xiān, first; ahead of). In its ancient form, the top part of 先 represents a foot and the lower part a person. You learned 先 in **Lesson 1**. Since 先 has the foot part, the character 洗 originally meant "to wash one's feet" and later came to mean "to wash," "bathe," etc.

洗 形聲兼會意。從水，從先（人腳向前伸），本以為洗腳。先也兼表聲。

158   *Lesson 8*

澡 zǎo (bath)

Pictophonetic character. The character 澡 consists of the water radical 氵 and the phonetic element 喿 (zào). It originally meant "to wash one's hands" but now is used to mean "bath." In the Bronze Inscriptions and Seal Script, 喿 delineates a tree with three mouths, signifying birds chirping in a tree. The original meaning of 喿 was the sound of birds or insects, and "clamorous," "noisy," or "a confusion of voices" are its extended meanings.

澡 形聲。從水，喿（zào）聲。喿，會意。金文從三口，從木，指群鳥在樹上鳴叫。引申為嘈雜。

金 篆

邊/边 biān (side)

Pictophonetic character. 邊 is comprised of the walk radical 辶 and the signifying and phonetic element 臱 (biān, side), meaning "side," "edge," "border" or "next." In the Bronze Inscriptions, 臱 combines 自 (zì, nose; oneself) with 旁 (páng, side), referring to the sides of a nose. In Regular Script, 臱 is the combination of 自, 穴 (xuè, cave), and 方 (fāng, square). In the simplified character 边, 力 replaces 臱.

邊 會意兼形聲。從辶，臱（biān）聲。臱，會意。從自，從旁，金文像鼻的兩翼。自，象形。像鼻形，本義為鼻子，後引申為自己。簡體字边用力替代臱，屬符號替代字。元明時已有边字。

金  篆 草

發/发 fā (to emit; to issue)

Pictophonetic character. The character 發 consists of the radical 弓 (gōng, bow) and the phonetic element 癹 (bá), meaning "to shoot an arrow." The extended meanings of 發 include "to shoot," "issue," "emit," "utter," "express," etc. The character 癹 combines 癶 (bō, two feet) with 殳 (shū, throw a weapon), meaning "to trample" or "tread on." The simplified character 发 is derived from the cursive style of the traditional character 發.

發 形聲。從弓，從癶（bō 兩隻腳相並），從殳（投擲），本義為射箭。簡體字发是繁體字發的草書楷化字。

篆

腦/脑 nǎo (brain)

Pictograph. The right part of the character 腦 is the pictograph of a baby's head with a few hairs on the fontanel. The left part contains the flesh radical 月, which also serves to indicate the meaning of the character. Current meanings of 腦 include "brain," "mind," "head," and "essence." In the simplified character 脑, the right part is simplified, but still retains the flesh radical 月 of the traditional character.

腦 象形。左為肉月旁，右部像囟門與頭髮。簡體字脑的右邊簡化，但保留了繁體字腦的輪廓。舊時已有此字。

篆

餐 cān (meal)

Pictophonetic character. The character 餐 consists of the radical 食 (shí, eat) and phonetic element 奴 (cán), meaning "to eat," "food," or "meal." You learned the character 食 in **Radicals**. In the Oracle-Bone Inscriptions, the character 奴 depicts a hand next to a skeleton or bones, meaning "remnant," "ferocious," etc.

餐 形聲。從食，奴聲，意為吞嚥、吃飯。

廳/厅 tīng (hall)

Pictophonetic character. The character 廳 consists of the radical 广 (yǎn, shed; shelter; roof) and the phonetic element 聽，referring to a hall for holding meetings and/or receiving guests. In the Oracle-Bone Inscriptions, the character 聽 consists of an ear and a mouth only. Later the character becomes more complex. In Regular Script, one can find 耳 (ěr, ear), 王 (wáng, king), 十 (shí, ten), 目 (mù, eye), 一 (yī, one), and 心 (xīn, heart), all in the character 聽. You learned 聽 in **Lesson 4.** In the simplified character 厅, 广 changes to 厂 (hǎn, cliff) and 聽 (tīng) is replaced with 丁 (dīng), as the two are similarly pronounced.

廳 會意兼形聲。從广（yǎn, 敞屋，）聽聲。聽，會意。甲骨文從耳，從口，指用耳聽別人説話。後加悳(dé)。悳，從直，從心，表示心地正直，引申為真誠、認真。聽字表明人在聽時要用心用耳，全神貫注。簡體字厅將广改為厂，聽改為丁，因聽丁聲音近似。古時已有此字。

甲  金 篆 草

報/报 **bào** (newspaper)

Associative compound. In the Bronze Inscriptions, the character 報 depicts a hand pressing the head of a handcuffed person onto his or her knees, signifying that the prisoner will be punished. The original meaning of 報 was "to sentence someone according to law." Since a judge needs to report the conviction to the appropriate authorities and make it public, 報 extends to mean "report," "announce," "declare," and "newspaper." The simplified character 报 is developed from the cursive style of 報, with a hand radical 扌 replacing 幸.

報 會意。金文中像一隻手從後按住一個像帶手銬跪著的人，表示行將處決犯人。報的本義是判決犯人。因這類事情要通報，引申為報告。簡體字报是繁體字報的草書楷化字，左邊以扌替換幸字。

甲 金 篆

宿 **sù** (to stay)

Associative compound. In the Oracle-Bone Inscriptions, the character 宿 consists of a person lying on a mat beneath the roof radical 宀, meaning "to stay overnight." In Regular Script, the character 百 (bǎi, hundred) replaces the mat part of 宿, which could suggest a lot of people lodging in a guesthouse.

宿 會意。甲骨文從宀，從人，從茵（tiàn 席），像人在屋裏的席子上休息。

162

金  篆 舍

舍 shè (house)

Pictograph. In the character 舍, 亼 represents the roof, 十 the pillar, and 口 the wall, creating a combined meaning of "hut," "shed," or "house." 舍 is also used as a verb (pronounced shě) meaning "give alms," "dispense charity," "give up," "abandon," etc.

舍 象形。舍字上部亼像房頂，中間是支撐房屋的柱子，下面的口代表牆。

甲  金 篆 正

正 zhèng (just; straight)

Associative compound. In the Oracle-Bone Inscriptions, the character 正 is the combination of a 口 (wéi, enclosure, here standing for a city) on the top and a foot 止 underneath, suggesting people marching towards enemy territory. The extended meanings of 正 are "righteous" "correct," "upright," "straight," "precisely," "just now," etc. In Regular Script, the 口 in the upper part of 正 has been simplified into 一, and the foot in the lower part has become 止 (zhǐ, foot; stop).

正 會意。從一，從止（足）。甲骨文、金文中像人足抵達一城邑，與"征"本為同一字。引申為端正、正面、正義等。

篆

前 qián (front; before)

Associative compound. In its ancient form, the character 前 combines 止 (zhǐ, foot) in the upper part and 舟 (zhōu, boat) in the lower part, suggesting the action of moving forward by boat. Meanings of 前 include "forward," "ahead," "front," "before," "formerly," etc. In Regular Script, the upper part of 前 resembles two feet on a horizontal line, 月 replaces 舟, and a knife radical 刂 is added to the right.

前 會意。金文從止（足），從舟，表示人乘船而行。

甲 金 篆

告 gào (to tell; to inform)

Associative compound. In the Oracle-Bone Inscriptions, 告 is comprised of 牛 (niú, ox) and 口 (kǒu, mouth), referring to the sound an ox makes. Extended meanings include "inform," "tell," "notify," "declare," "sue," etc. In its ancient form, the character 牛 depicts an ox head as viewed from the front.

告 會意。甲骨文從口，從牛。本義為牛叫，引申為上報、告訴、佈告等。

篆

訴/诉 sù (to tell; to relate)

Pictophonetic character. The character 訴 consists of the word radical 言 and the phonetic component 斥 (chì), meaning "tell," "relate," "complain," "accuse," and "appeal to." You have seen 斤 (jīn, ax; unit of weight) in the character 所 (suǒ, so, in **Lesson 4**). In the Oracle-Bone Inscriptions, 斤 looks like an ax with a crooked handle. When you add a short stroke to the middle of 斤, it becomes the character 斥 (chì, oust; reprimand). The speech radical is simplified to form the character 诉.

訴 形聲。從言，斥聲，告訴、控訴之意。斥，斤字加一點，意為指責、責備。簡體字诉的部首簡化。

甲 𗁣 金 𗁣 篆 𗁣

已 yǐ (already)

Pictograph. In the Oracle-Bone Inscriptions, 已 looks like a fetus in a head-down position, meaning "stop," "cease," "end," and "already." 已, 台, and 以 are cognate characters; in the Oracle-Bone Inscriptions the same character was used to mean 已, 台, and 以, and the three different characters evolved later.

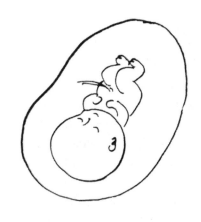

已 象形。甲骨文、金文、篆文均像頭朝下要出生的胎兒形，引申為已經。

金  篆 草

經/经 jīng (to pass through)

Associative and pictophonetic compound. In the Bronze Inscriptions, 巠 (jīng) is a pictograph of a loom with vertical strands of fabric, known as the "warp" (as opposed to the horizontal strands, called the "weft"). The character 經 consists of the silk radical 糸 and the signifying and phonetic element 巠 (jīng), meaning "warp," "through," "pass through," "undergo," "endure," etc. The simplified character 经 derives from the cursive of the traditional character 經.

經 會意兼形聲。從糸，從巠（像繃在織布機上的三根經線；一說像水流與地面）；巠也兼表聲。經的本意是織物的縱綫，引申為經過、經歷。簡體字经是繁體字經的草書楷化字。

甲 金 篆

封 fēng (MW for letters)

Associative compound In the Oracle-Bone and Bronze Inscriptions, the right part of the character 封 is a hand (cùn, 寸) and left part depicts a tree on the ground, suggesting the act of planting trees to define a boundary. Extended meanings of 封 are "boundary," "limit," "seal," "envelope," and it is also used as a measure word for letters (as in mail). In Regular Script, the tree part of 封 is replaced with two 土. You have seen 封 in the character 幫 (see bāng, to help, in **Lesson 6**).

封 會意。甲骨文、金文中像用手在土地上植樹，用種樹木來劃定疆界。引申為封閉，書信的量詞等。

金  篆 信

信 xìn (letter)

Associative compound. The character 信 consists of the vertical person radical 亻 and the character 言 (yán, word; speak), implying that a person's words should be trustworthy. Therefore, the meanings of 信 are "true," "trust," "faith," and "believe." 信 is also used to mean "message" or "letter," which also might connote that one's written word should be true.

信 會意。從人，從言，本義指人要言而有信，引申為書信。

篆

最 zuì (most)

Associative compound. In Seal Script, 最 is made up of 冃 (mào, headgear) and 取 (qǔ, get; take). In the Oracle-Bone Inscriptions, 取 depicts a right hand holding an ear. In ancient times, soldiers cut off the ears of their enemies as evidence of military victories. 取, therefore, means to "capture," "get," "take," or "fetch." The character 最 consists of the headgear, ear, and hand parts. It originally meant "gather," "total," and "the highest military merit," from which is derived its usage as a superlative degree marker. In Regular Script, 曰 replaces the 冃 part of 最, but the bottom part still combines ear 耳 and right hand 又.

最 會意。篆文從冃（帽子、頭盔），從取（以手割下戰俘耳朵為立軍功的證據）。本義指以士兵殲敵的數目來判斷誰立下頭等戰功，引申為總計、極度等。

近 jìn (near)

Pictophonetic character. The character 近 consists of the walk radical 辶 and the phonetic 斤 (jīn), meaning "near," "close," "intimate," and "approximately." In the Oracle-Bone Inscriptions, 斤 (jīn, ax; unit of weight) looks like an ax with a crooked handle.

近 形聲。從辶，斤聲。斤，象形。甲骨文中上像斧頭，下像斧柄。

除 chú (except)

Associative and pictophonetic compound. The character 除 is comprised of the mound radical 阝 and the signifying and phonetic element 余 (yú, hut). Its original meaning was "doorstep," and later came to mean "leave," "remove," "get rid of," "except," etc. The character 余 combines 亼 (jí, top) and 木 (mù, wood), signifying "hut." In classical Chinese 余 means "I."

除 會意兼形聲。篆文從阜（土山），從余；余亦聲。本義為階梯，引申為除去等。余，形聲。甲骨文、金文上像屋頂，下像支撐的木頭。本義為茅屋，引申為剩下、多出來等。

甲  篆 專 草 专

專/专 zhuān (special)

Associative and pictophonetic compound. In the Oracle-Bone Inscriptions, 專 consists of a hand (寸 cùn) and a spindle (叀 zhuān), signifying the act of winding thread on a spindle. Early meanings of 專 were "spindle" and "revolve." Later it came to mean: "concentrate," "focus," or "special." The simplified character 专 derives from the cursive style of the traditional character 專.

專 形聲。從寸，叀聲，甲骨文像用一手轉動紡錘形。本義為紡錘，後為專一，專心等。簡體字专是繁體字專的草書楷化字。

金 業 篆 業

業/业 yè (occupation)

Pictograph. In the Bronze Inscriptions, the character 業 resembles a wooden frame with bars on top from which musical instruments, such as bells or drums, are hung. Since playing musical instruments is a type of profession, extended meanings of 業 include "profession," "career," "course of study," "occupation," "line of business," etc. In Regular Script, the top of 業 still looks like the bars of the frame and the bottom contains the wood part. The simplified character 业 retains only the top part of the traditional 業.

業 象形。金文中像懸掛鐘鼓樂器帶齒的木架，引申為事業、家業、學業等。簡體字业僅取業字的上半部。

貫　篆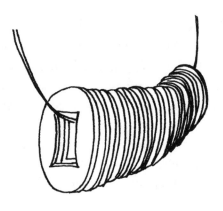

慣/惯 guàn (to be used to)

Pictophonetic character. The character 慣 consists of the vertical heart radical 忄 and the phonetic component 貫 (guàn), meaning "to be used to," or "indulge." 貫 combines 毌 (guàn, string; pierce) with 貝 (bèi, cowry shell), meaning "pass through," "link together," or "a string of 1,000 copper coins." In the simplified character 惯, only the shell part 贝 has been simplified.

慣 從忄，貫聲，意為習慣。貫，會意兼形聲。從毌（貫穿），從貝，表示把錢幣穿成一串。簡體字惯中的貝簡化為贝。

篆

清 qīng (clear; clean)

Pictophonetic character. The character 清 consists of the water radical 氵 and the phonetic 青 (qīng). Originally 清 refers to "clear water" and extends to mean "clear," "pure," "clean," "clarified," etc. 青 is the character for "green." In the Bronze Inscriptions, the upper part of 青 is 生 (shēng, to grow) and the lower part is 丹 (dān, color), referring to the green color of growing plants. You learned 青 in the character 請 (see qǐng, please, in **Lesson 1**). 青 is used as a phonetic symbol in numerous characters, such as 情 (qíng, feeling; affection), 晴 (qíng, clear up; sunny day), 精 (jīng, spirit; energy), and 睛 (jīng, eyeball).

清 形聲。篆文從水，青聲，本義指水清澈透明。

甲 金 篆

楚 chǔ (clear; neat)

Pictophonetic character. In its ancient form, the character 楚 combined the signifying part 林 (lín, grove; forest) and the phonetic element 足 (zú; foot), meaning the Judas tree. Since the branches of this tree were used to beat criminals, 楚 extends to mean "pain" or "suffering." 楚 can also mean "neat" and "clear." In Regular Script, 疋 (shū, foot) replaces the 足 part of 楚. 足 and 疋 were the same character in their ancient forms.

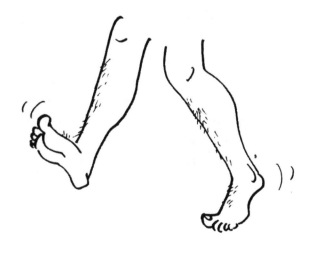

楚 形聲。從林，疋(shū)聲。甲骨文、金文從足，從林。本義為灌木，也叫荊，引申為杖刑、整齊等。

甲 金 篆

步 bù (to step)

Associative compound. In its ancient form, the character 步 consists of two footprints, one in front of the other, indicating the act of walking. The original meaning of 步 is "walk" or "go on foot," with extended meanings: "step," "pace," and "pace out." 步 may be seen in the character 歲 (see suì, year of age, in **Lesson 3**), separated into two parts.

步 會意。古文皆從二止，像一前一後的向前邁步行走的兩只腳。

希 xī (to hope)

Associative compound. In Seal Script, 希 consists of 木 (mù, wood), 爻 (yáo, a wooden or bamboo fence) and 布 (bù, cloth), representing loosely woven cloth. The original meanings of 希 were: "sparse," "scarce," while "hope" is its extended meaning. In its ancient form, 乂 is shaped like a pair of scissors and 布 resembles a hand holding a scarf (巾 jīn). You learned 巾 in the character 帥 (see shuài, handsome, in **Lesson 7**).

希 會意。篆文從爻（籬笆交織狀），從巾，指織得像籬笆一樣稀疏的布或網，是"稀"的本字，引申為企求、希望。

金  篆

望 wàng (to look into the distance; to hope; to wish)

Associative compound. In the Bronze Inscriptions, the character 望 looks like a person with large eyes looking up at the moon, and it means "gaze into the distance." Extended meanings of 望 include "wish," "hope," "call on," "reputation," etc. In Regular Script, 望 combines the signifying part 月 (yuè, moon) and the phonetic elements 亡 (wáng, run away) and 王 (wáng, king).

望 會意。金文像人睜大眼睛望月狀。後加王字以表聲。

Lesson 8

能 néng (to be able)

Pictograph. In the Bronze Inscriptions, 能 depicts a bear, complete with head, claws, body, and tail. Originally 能 referred to a "bear." Since bears are strong and can withstand low temperatures, 能 extends to mean "ability," "capability," and "to be able." Later, the fire radical 灬 was added under 能 to make the character 熊 (xióng) for "bear."

能 象形。甲骨文像有頭、背、尾、掌的熊形。本義為熊，因熊兇猛力大，後被借為能字。

用 yòng (to use)

Pictograph. In its ancient form, the character 用 resembles a wooden tub or bucket. Since tubs and buckets are often used in daily life, 用 extends to mean "use," "operate," "need," and "with."

用 象形。甲骨文、金文均像木桶形狀。因古人日常生活中常使用木桶，引申為使用。

篆 笑　夭 甲 夫 金 夫 篆 夭

笑 xiào (to laugh)

Associative compound. The character 笑 consists of the bamboo radical ⺮ and the character 夭 (yāo). In the Oracle-Bone and Bronze Inscriptions, 夭 resembles a person dancing with one arm up and one arm down, suggesting lithe and graceful movement. 夭 is also used to describe luxuriant and gorgeous plants. A person's laughter may be compared to bamboo dancing in the wind, so the character 笑 means "laugh," "smile" or "laugh at." In Seal Script, the character 夭 resembles a person with her or his head tilted to one side, meaning "die young."

笑　會意。從竹，從夭（彎曲）。李陽冰勘定《說文》中解釋說"竹得風，其體夭曲，如人之笑。"夭，像人兩手搖擺起舞狀。有嬌媚、艷麗、茂盛、夭折等意。

甲 祝 金 祝 篆 祝

祝 zhù (to wish)

Associative compound. In the Oracle-Bone and Bronze Inscriptions, the character 祝 delineates a person on his or her knees praying next to an altar, meaning "pray" and "prayer." 祝 also extends to mean "express good wishes" or "wish." In **Radicals**, you learned 示/礻 (shì, show), a pictograph of a stone table upon which sacrificial offerings to gods or ancestors are placed. The radical 礻 is often found in characters related to religious rituals.

祝　會意。從示/礻（用石塊搭起的祭臺），從人，從口。甲骨文中像人跪在祭臺邊向神靈或祖先祈禱。

篆

累 lèi (tired; fatigued)

Pictophonetic character. In the Seal Script, the character 累 is comprised of the semantic component 糸 (mì, silk thread) and the phonetic element 畾 (léi), originally meaning "rope." The extended meanings of 累 include "tie up," "bind," "detain," "get somebody into trouble," "toil," "tired," etc. In the Regular Script, the character 累 is made up of 田 (tián, field) and 糸 (mì, silk string). In the past men worked in the field and women made silk. Both jobs were laborious and made people exhausted.

累 會意兼形聲。篆文從糸，畾聲，有纏繞、捆綁、牽連、拖累、勞累等意。正體字上為田，下為糸(束絲)，可想為男耕女織都是使人勞累之事.

甲  金 篆

網/网 wǎng (net)

Pictograph. In its ancient form, the character 網 resembles the contour of a net. In the Regular Script, the silk radical 糸 is added to indicate a net is made from ropes and 亡 (wáng) suggests the pronunciation. The simplified character 网 restores the original form.

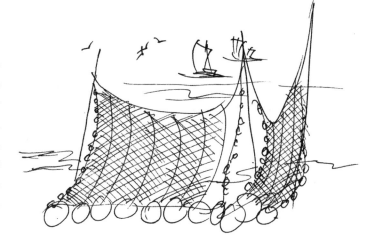

網 象形。甲骨文、金文、篆文皆像一張網形。楷書加糸 字旁表意，加亡字表聲。簡體字网恢復了古體字的本來形狀。

LESSON 9

甲 金 篆 草

買/买 mǎi (to buy)

Associative compound. In the Oracle-Bone and Bronze Inscriptions, 買 is the combination of 网 (wǎng, net) and 貝 (bèi, cowry shell). These shells were used as money in ancient times. In the Oracle-Bone Inscriptions, the character 网 is the pictograph of a net. In Regular Script, the net radical is written as 罒. The character 買 contains 罒 and 貝. The simplified form 买 is developed from the cursive style of 買.

買 會意。甲骨文、金文從网，從貝，像用網撈貝。古時以貝殼做為貨幣換取物品，意為購買。簡體字买是繁體字買的草書楷化字。

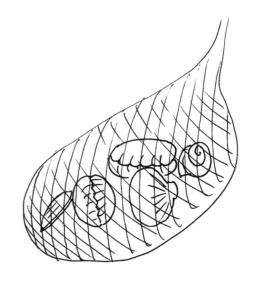

甲 金 篆 草

東/东 dōng (east)

Associative compound. The character 東 consists of 日 (rì, sun) and 木 (mù, tree; wood), representing the sun rising behind a tree. Given that this scene may be observed in the east at dawn, the meaning of 東 is "east." The simplified character 东 derives from the cursive style of 東.

東 會意。從木，從日，以示太陽剛從東方升起，以此來表示東邊。簡體字东是繁體字東的草書楷化字。

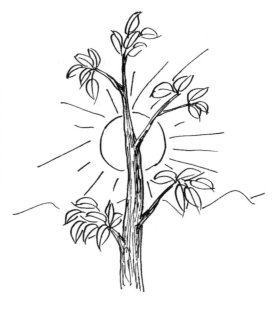

甲  金　篆

西 xī (west)

Associative compound. In the Oracle-Bone and Bronze Inscriptions, 西 resembles a bird's nest. In Seal Script, a bird is drawn at the top of the nest. Since birds return to their nests at dusk while the sun sets in the west, 西 means "west." Note the similarities and differences between 西 and 四 (sì, four).

西 會意。甲骨文、金文像鳥巢形，篆字則進一步在鳥巢上添一只鳥。鳥類多半在日落時回巢，而日在西邊落下，故引申為西。造字方法與東相同。

篆　售

售 shòu (to sell)

Associative compound. The character 售 consists of 隹 (zhuī, short-tailed bird) and 口 (kǒu, mouth), referring to the shouting of peddlers, as it resembles the chirping of birds.

售 會意。從口，隹聲，指像鳥鳴一樣的叫賣聲。

篆 偵 化 甲 ⺨⺨

貨/货 huò (merchandise)

Associative and pictophonetic compound. In Seal Script, the character 貨 is comprised of the radical 貝 (bèi, cowry shell) and the signifying and phonetic element 化 (huà, change). Since shells were used as money in ancient times, 貨 means "goods," "merchandise," "commodity," or "money." In the Oracle-Bone Inscriptions, the character 化 depicts two people heading in different directions, meaning "change," "turn," "convert," etc. The shell part 貝 is simplified to form the character 货.

貨 會意兼形聲。從化（變化），從貝（古時錢幣）；化亦聲。指用錢購買貨物。 化，會意。甲骨文中像一正立人形，一倒立人形，意為變化。簡體字货中的贝是繁體字貝的草書楷化字。

甲 員 金 員 篆 員

員/员 yuán (personnel)

Pictograph. In its ancient form, 員 resembles a tripod with a round mouth on top, meaning "round" or "circular." Later 員 was used to mean "member," "personnel," or, "a person engaged in some field of activity," and 圓 was created to mean "round" or "circle." In Regular Script, 員 combines 口 (kǒu, mouth) and 貝 (bèi, cowry shell), suggesting a person conducting business by talking with others. 贝 is simplified to form the character 员.

員 指事。甲骨文、金文中貝像鼎形，口是鼎口。本義指圓形，引申為人的數額以及從事某種職業的人。簡體字员中的贝字簡化。

甲 ⑂ 金 ⑁ 篆 ⑁

衣 yī (clothing)

Pictograph. In its ancient forms, the character 衣 outlines a garment with the collar and sleeves in the upper part, and the hemline in the lower part. In Regular Script, 衣 resembles a garment on a clothes hanger. Characters with the radical 衤 often relate to clothing or cloth, e.g. 襯衫 (chènshān, shirt), and 褲 (kù, pants).

衣 象形。像衣領、衣袖、衣襟形。

甲 𦚣 金 𦜖 篆 𦝠

服 fú (clothing)

Associative compound. In the Oracle-Bone Inscriptions, the right part of 服 consists of a person on his or her knees, and a hand, with a plate comprising the left part, signifying a person with a serving plate. The original meaning of 服 is "to serve" or "wait upon," and the extended meanings include "to take," "to wear," "clothing," etc. In Regular Script, the flesh radical 月 replaces the left part of 服, while the right part is the same as the right part of the character 報 (see bào, newspaper, in **Lesson 8**).

服 會意。甲骨文從凡（盤），從跪人，從手，表示人跪着端盤服侍。衣服為其引申義。

牛 甲 金 篆

件 jiàn (MW for items)

Associative compound. The character 件 consists of the person radical 亻 and the character 牛 (niú, ox), signifying a person butchering an ox. The original meaning of 件 therefore was "to cut apart" or "divide." Later, 件 came to mean "single item" and is used as a measure word for "matter," "clothing worn on top," "furniture," "luggage," etc. In the Oracle-Bone Inscriptions, 牛 depicts an ox head from the front.

件 會意。篆文從人，從牛，指人把牛分解成部分。本義為分解、分割，引申為量詞。牛，象形。像带角的牛頭正面。

襯 /衬 chèn (lining)

Pictophonetic character. The character 襯 consists of the clothing radical 衤 and the phonetic component 親 (qīn), meaning "lining." 襯 also extends to mean "place something underneath," "provide a background for," or "set off." In the Bronze Inscriptions, 親 contains the radical 見 and the phonetic component 辛 (xīn), meaning "close" or "intimate." In the simplified character 衬, 寸 replaces 親, since the pronunciation of 寸 (cùn) is similar to that of 襯 (chèn).

襯 形聲。從衣/衤，親聲。意指內衣、襯裏。親，形聲。從見，亲聲。本義為常見，引申為親近。簡體字衬右邊以寸代替親，因寸與襯聲音相近。

篆

衫 shān (shirt)

Pictophonetic character. The character 衫 is comprised of the clothes radical 衤 and the phonetic element 彡 (shān), meaning "unlined upper garment" or "short-sleeved shirt." 彡 may also refer to a decorative pattern, tassel, ribbon, hair, beard, carving, or shadow. You encountered 彡 in the character 影 (see yǐng, shadow, in **Lesson 4**).

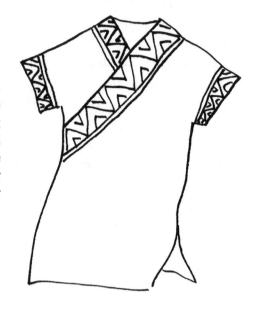

衫 形聲。篆文從衣，三聲，意為單衣。

篆 颜 彦金 彦 篆 彡

顏 yán (face; countenance)

Pictophonetic character. The character 顏 consists of the radical 頁 (yè, originally meaning "head," rather than "page") and the phonetic component 彥 (yàn), meaning "forehead." Extended meanings of 顏 include "face," "countenance," and "color." In the Oracle-Bone Inscriptions, 頁 resembles a person with a large head. You have seen 頁 in 題 (see tí, topic; question, in **Lesson 6**) and 預 (see yù, prepare, in **Lesson 7**). In the Bronze Inscriptions, the character 彥 combines 文 (wén, writing; language) and 弓 (gōng, bow), referring to those who are skilled at both literary and martial arts. In Regular Script, 彡 replaces the lower part of 彥 (弓). 頁 is simplified to form the character 颜. See also 预 in **Lesson 7.**

顏 形聲。篆文從頁，彥聲。意指額頭、面容、色彩等。頁像人頭形。彥，會意兼形聲。金文從文，從弓，指文武雙全、德才兼備的人。簡體字颜中的页字簡化。

篆

色 sè (color)

Associative compound. In Seal Script, the upper part of 色 is a standing person, and the lower part is a kneeling person, suggesting someone angrily rebuking another. The original meaning of 色 was "an angry look," and later came to mean: "color," "look," "expression," "appearance," "feminine charms," etc. In Regular Script, the lower part of 色 has changed to 巴, which you have seen in the character 吧 (see ba, a particle, in **Lesson 5**).

色 會意。篆文上是站立之人，下為下跪之人，前者訓斥後者。本義為怒色，引申為顏色、姿色、臉色、景色等。

甲 金 篆

黃/黄 huáng (yellow)

Pictograph. In the Oracle-Bone Inscriptions, the character 黃 looks like a pendant with a knot above and tassels underneath, meaning "annular jade pendant." Since this kind of ornament was usually made with yellow jade, "yellow" is the extended meaning of 黃. The simplified version of 黃 is the variant form 黄.

黃 甲骨文、金文像佩璜形。上為系帶，中為佩璜，下為垂穗，本義為佩玉。因這種佩玉多為黃色，引申為黃顏色。黄是黃的異體字，後也用為黃的簡體字。

篆

紅/红 **hóng (red)**

Pictophonetic character. The character 紅 consists of the silk radical 糸 and the phonetic element 工 (gōng). The original meaning of 紅 was "pink silk," and later came to mean "red." You learned the character 工 (gōng, labor; work; craft) in **Radicals**. The silk radical is simplified to form the character 红.

紅 形聲。從糸，工聲。本義為粉紅色的絲綢，後泛指紅色。顏色常用絲帛表示，故從糸 。簡體字红的偏旁纟 是由繁體糸簡化而來。

篆

穿 **chuān (to wear)**

Associative compound. The character 穿 consists of the radical 穴 (xué, cave; hole) and the character 牙 (yá, tooth), referring to animals creating holes with their sharp teeth. The primary meaning of 穿 is "pierce through," and extended meanings include "pass though," "cross," "string together" and "wear." You learned the cave radical in the character 空 (see kòng, free time, in **Lesson 6**) and 牙 in 呀 (see ya, a grammatical particle, in **Lesson 5**).

穿 會意。從穴，從牙，表示用牙咬穿或掘洞。本義為穿透，引申為穿戴。

篆

條 /条 tiáo (MW for long objects)

Pictophonetic compound. The character 條 consists of the signifying part 木 (mù, wood) and the phonetic component 攸 (yōu), meaning "twig." 條 is also used as a measure word for long, narrow, or thin objects. In the Bronze Inscriptions, 攸 resembles a person paddling a boat in a river, meaning: "flowing water," "long," etc. The simplified character 条 retains only the right part of 條.

條 形聲。從木，攸(yōu)聲。本義為小樹枝，引申為量詞。簡體字条僅採用繁體字條的右邊。元明已有此字。

草 车

褲/裤 kù (pants)

Pictophonetic character. 褲 consists of the clothing radical 衤 and the phonetic part 庫 (kù), meaning "pants" or "trousers." The character 庫 is comprised of 广 (yǎn, shed; shelter) and 車 (chē, vehicle), originally meaning "garage," and later "warehouse." In the Oracle-Bone and Bronze Inscriptions, 車 depicts a chariot. In Seal Script, 車 is simplified to one wheel and its axle. Only the vehicle part 车 is simplified to form the simplified character 裤. The simplified character 车 derives from the cursive style of the traditional character 車.

褲 形聲。從衣，庫聲。庫，會意。從車，從广。广指大棚，本義指放兵車的大棚，引申為倉庫。簡體字庫下部的车是繁體字車的草書楷化字。

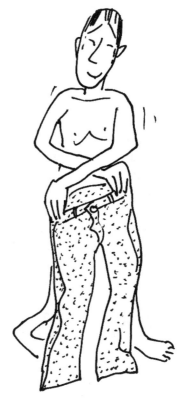

宜 yí (suitable)

Associative compound. In the Oracle-Bone and Bronze Inscriptions, the character 且 (qiě) looks like a memorial tablet used in ancestral worship, originally meaning "ancestor." You have seen 且 in the character 姐 (see jiě, elder sister, in **Lesson 1**) and 助 (see zhù, to assist, in **Lesson 7**). The character 宜 consists of the roof radical 宀 and the character 且, referring to the act of placing ancestral offerings on the memorial tablet in a room. The original meaning of 宜 is "to offer sacrifices to ancestors or gods." Since this ritual was considered obligatory, 宜 extends to mean "should," "ought to," "suitable," and "appropriate."

宜 會意。從宀，從且（祖宗的牌位）。把祖宗的牌位放在室內，本義為祭祀，引申為合適、應當。

金 廾 篆 閂

付 fù (to pay)

Associative compound. In the Bronze Inscriptions, the character 付 consists of a person and a hand, signifying a person passing something to another. Therefore, 付 means "hand over," "turn over," or "pay." In Regular Script, 付 is comprised of the person radical 亻 and the character 寸 (cùn, inch). In Seal Script, 寸 combines 又 with 一. 又 means "right hand." 一 symbolizes the place on one's forearm an inch from the wrist, where a traditional Chinese doctor would feel a patient's pulse and diagnose ailments. Like 又, 寸 often signifies a hand when used within a character.

付 會意。篆文從寸（手），從人，意指用手把物交與他人。

篆

錢 / 钱 qián (money)

Pictophonetic character. 錢 contains the gold/metal radical 金 and the phonetic element 戔 (jiān), meaning "metal currency," "money," "cash," or "fund." Since the character 戔 consists of two dagger-axes, meaning "to kill" or "murder," 錢 possibly refers to the fact that disputes involving money can generate jealousy and strife. The left part has simplified from 金 to 钅, and the right part from 戔 to 戋, to form the simplified character 钱.

錢 形聲。從金，戔聲。戔，會意。從二戈，本義為殘殺，是殘的古字。簡體字钱左邊部首由金 簡化為钅， 右邊戔簡化為戋。

甲 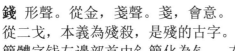 金 篆

共 gòng (altogether)

Associative compound. In the Oracle-Bone and Bronze Inscriptions, the character 共 represents two hands holding a piece of jade, meaning to "present jade or offerings." Since one uses both hands to present a gift, 共 extends to mean "together," "altogether," "in company," "common," "share," etc.

共 會意。金文像用雙手捧一塊碧玉形。本義為供奉，共給，引申義有拱手、環繞、合計、共同等。

甲 ⺍　金 少　篆 ⺙

少 shǎo (few; little)

Pictograph. The character 少 (shǎo, few; little; less; be short) derives from 小 (xiǎo, small; petty; minor; young). In the Oracle-Bone Inscriptions, both 小 and 少 depict a few grains of sand. In Regular Script, a downward left stroke is added under 小 to become 少. 少 is often used for the quantity of things, whereas 小 is for size or age.

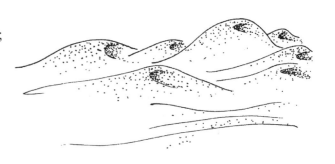

少　象形。少是由小字分化而來，古時小、少常通用。小在甲骨文、金文中為三點，像是細小的沙粒。少為四點。

篆 甶　鬼 甲 　金 　篆 鬼

塊/块 kuài (piece; dollar)

Pictophonetic character. 塊 consists of the earth/soil radical 土 and the phonetic element 鬼 (guǐ), originally meaning "lump of soil." Extended meanings of 塊 are "lump," "piece," "chunk," "gold or sliver dollar," and "dollar." In the Oracle-Bone Inscriptions, the character 鬼 resembles a monster with a huge head, meaning: "ghost," "spirit," "spooky," "sinister," etc. In Seal Script, a tail is added to the monster. 夬 replaces 鬼 to form the simplified character 块, as the pronunciation of 夬 (guài, archery) is similar to that of 塊 (kuài).

塊　形聲。從土，鬼聲。本義為土塊，引申為量詞。鬼，象形。在甲骨文、金文中均像大頭鬼。簡體字块用夬 (guài; archery) 替代鬼，因夬與塊聲音相似。

金 ㄓ 篆 乇

毛 máo (hair; dime)

Pictograph. In the Bronze Inscriptions, the character 毛 looks like a tuft of hair, originally meaning "fur." Extended meanings of 毛 are "hair," "wool," "rough," "mao" (a fractional unit of money in China), or "dime." Be sure to distinguish 毛 from 手 (see shǒu, hand, in **Radicals**).

毛 象形。金文像皮上叢生的毛。

甲 ㄍㄍ 金 分 篆 分

分 fēn (penny; minute)

Associative compound. 分 consists of 八 (bā, divide; eight) and 刀 (dāo, knife), conveying the act of cutting something in half. The primary meanings of 分 are "separate," "divide," "part," while extended meanings include "share," "distribute," "distinguish," "branch," "minute," "fen" (the smallest unit of Chinese currency), etc.

分 會意。上從八，下從刀，指用刀將一物體切為兩半。八的本義是分，後加刀以強化此意。

甲 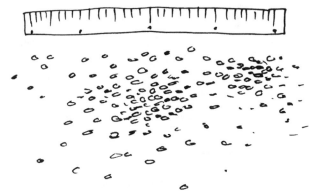 金 篆

百 bǎi (hundred)

Associative compound. In the Oracle-Bone Inscriptions, the upper part of 百 may represent a ruler and lower part a grain of white rice 白, suggesting a long line of rice grains. Meanings of 百 are "hundred," "numerous," and "all kinds of."

百 會意。一說甲骨文字形上像一把尺子，下像白米粒，表示擺下一尺長的米粒，引申為一百。白，象形。像一粒白米。

篆 雙

雙/双 shuāng (pair)

Associative compound. In Seal Script, 雙 resembles a person holding a pair of birds in one hand. Consequently, meanings of 雙 include "pair," "two," "twin," "both," and "dual." In Regular Script, 雙 consists of two short-tailed birds 隹隹 and a right hand 又. Two hands replace the one hand holding two birds to form the simplified character 双.

雙 會意。從又（右手），從雙隹（短尾鳥），表示一隻手抓兩隻鳥。簡體字双把繁體字雙該為兩個又字，意為雙手，屬會意詞。宋元時期已見双字。

革 甲 𠦪 金 𩈌 篆 革

鞋 xié (shoes)

Associative compound. The character 鞋 consists of 革 (gé, leather) and two 土 (tǔ, earth; soil), referring to shoes – (being leather products which touch the ground). In the Bronze Inscriptions, the character 革 looks like an animal skin, meaning "leather," "hide," "remove," etc.

鞋 從革，從雙土。革，本義為剝去動物的皮毛，引申為皮革。

篆 𢸬 草 换

換/换 huàn (to change)

Pictophonetic character. The character 換 is comprised of the hand radical 扌 and the phonetic component 奐 (huàn), meaning "exchange," "barter," "change," and "convert." In Seal Script, 奐 depicts a person on top, a cave dwelling in the middle, and two hands at the bottom, possibly referring to people building a large dwelling with their hands. Meanings of 奐 include "magnificent," "abundant," and "bright-colored." The simplified character 换 derives from the cursive style of 換 and differs only slightly from the traditional form.

換 形聲。從手，奐聲，意為對換、變換等。奐，會意。篆文下有雙手，上有人站在高大的洞穴之上，本義指用手建造高大洞穴以為居所，引申為盛大。簡體字换是繁體字換的草書楷化字，字右部稍有改動。

金 篆

黑 hēi (black)

Associative compound. In the Bronze Inscriptions, the character 黑 depicts a sweaty person with a smoke-blackened face. In Regular Script, the top part of 黑 resembles the blackened face, while the middle part is 土, which stands for the ground, and the bottom part is the fire radical 灬. You have seen 黑 in the character 點 (see diǎn, dot; o'clock, in **Lesson 3**).

黑 會意。金文字形像被煙熏火烤，大汗淋漓、滿面污垢的人。

虫 甲 金 篆

雖/虽 suī (though; while)

Pictophonetic character. The character 雖 consists of 口 (kǒu, mouth), 虫 (chóng; worm, insect), and 隹 (zhuī, short-tailed bird), originally referring to a particular kind of reptile, similar to a lizard. Today 雖 is used as conjunction, meaning "although," and "even if." In its ancient form, the character 虫 looks like a kind of snake, meaning "venomous snake." Its extended meanings are "insect," "worm," and "reptile." The simplified character 虽 retains only the left part of the traditional character 雖.

雖 形聲。從虫，唯聲。本義指一種似蜥蜴的爬蟲，今用作連詞，表示轉折。唯，甲骨文從口，從隹（短尾鳥），意指恭敬的應答。簡體字虽僅取繁體字雖的右部，舊時已有此字。

 金 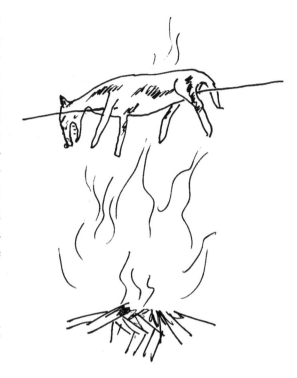 篆 然

然 rán (like that; so)

Associative and pictophonetic compound. In the Bronze Inscriptions, the character 然 consists of the fire radical 灬 on the bottom and the signifying and phonetic part 肰 (rán, dog meat) on the top, referring to the roasting of a dog over fire*. The original meaning of 然 was "burn" or "ignite." Later a fire radical 火 was added to the left of 然 (燃) to mean "burn" or "ignite." Now 然 is used to mean "right," "so," "like that," "but," "nevertheless," etc. In Seal Script, 肰 combines the flesh radical 月 with the character 犬 (quǎn, dog). 犬 depicts a large dog in the Oracle-Bone and Bronze Inscriptions, meaning "big dog."

然 會意兼形聲。金文從火，從肰（狗肉）；肰亦聲。意指用火烤狗肉。犬，象形。甲骨文中像一條大狗形，本義為大狗。

 甲 金 篆 合

合 hé (to suit; to agree)

Associative compound. In its ancient forms, the character 合 has a lid 亼 (jí) on top of a container, with 口 in the lower part, meaning "to close" or "shut." Extended meanings include "combine," "join," "suit," "agree," etc. You learned 合 in the character 給 (see gěi, to give, in **Lesson 5**).

合 會意。下像盒子，上像盒蓋，合在一起表示合攏。

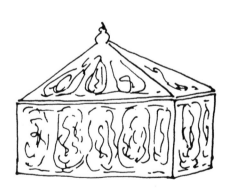

* Traditionally, in the eyes of some Chinese, dog meat was delicious and had the special function of helping to guard against cold weather. Nowadays this practice is much less popular, as people are more aware of protecting animals.

適/适 shì (to suit; to fit)

Pictophonetic character. The character 適 consists of the walk radical 辶 and the phonetic element 啇 (dì, screech; scream). The primary meanings of 適 are: "to go to" (a place), "follow," and "pursue." Extended meanings include "right," "well," "comfortable," "fit," "suitable," "proper," etc. In Regular Script, 啇 shows ten mouths screaming inside a building. In the simplified character 适, 舌 (shé, tongue) replaces 啇, as the pronunciation of 舌 is similar to 適 (shì).

適 形聲。從辶，商聲。本義指前往、來到，引申為舒適、適合、適宜等。
商，甲骨文、金文、篆文中從口，從帝，意為高聲。簡體字适以舌代替商，因舌與適聲音相似，屬同音替代字。

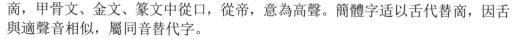

甲　金　篆

商 shāng (commerce; business)

Pictograph. In its ancient form, the character 商 looks like a wine container, which was its original meaning. The wine container had a measuring function, so 商 extended to mean "measurement," "consult," "discuss," "negotiate." Since business involves a lot of negotiation, 商 came to mean "commerce," "business," and "trade."

商 象形。甲骨文、金文像古代盛酒的容器。酒器有量度，故引申為估量、商量。做生意重在雙方商議，因此又引申為經商、做買賣。

194　　　　　　　　　　　　　　　　　　　　　*Lesson 9*

篆

店 diàn (shop; store)

Pictophonetic character. In the Seal Script, the character 店 consists of the soil/earth radical 土 and the phonetic element 占(zhàn), originally referring to a clay stand designed for storing things in the main room of a house. Later it extended to mean "store," "shop," "inn," etc. In Regular Script, the shed/shelter radical 广 is used to replace the soil/earth radical 土. It shows the progress of selling things inside a shed instead of on a stage made of soil.

店 形聲。篆文從土，占聲。本義為置放物品的土臺子。后改土字旁為广（敞屋），有商店、旅店等意。店字展示了由在土臺上售貨到在大房內售貨的演變過程。

甲 𡆥 金 𠱾 篆 如

如 rú (as; if)

Associative compound. The character 如 consist of 女 (nǚ, female) and 口 (kǒu, mouth), meaning "obey," or "in compliance with" because women should listen to men's words according to the traditional concept. One of the Confucian classics lists the three rules women must obey: obeying her father before marriage, her husband after marriage, and her son if her husband dies. The extended meaning of 如 includes "according to," "as if," "as," "if," etc.

如 會意。從女，從口。按照傳統的價值觀念，女人應該柔順，聽從男人的話。《儀禮 喪服 子夏傳》道"未嫁從父，既嫁從夫，夫死從子"。如本義為順從、遵照。引申為如同、例如、假如等。

甲 金 篆

果 guǒ (fruit; result)

Pictograph.   In the Oracle-Bone Inscriptions,
果 is a pictograph of a tree with three fruits. In
the Bronze Inscriptions, these three fruits become
one large one. In Seal Script, this large fruit is
replaced with the character 田 (tián, field),
which deviates somewhat from the original
meaning.

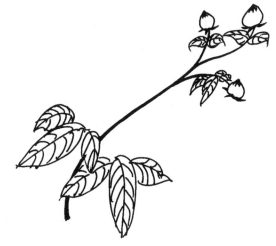

果 象形。像樹上結出的果實。甲骨文樹上有三
個果子，金文變成一個大果子。在楷書中方形
化則變成了田字。

甲 金 篆 草

長/长 cháng (long)

Pictograph. In its ancient form, the
character 長 looks like an old man
with long hair and a walking stick. The
original meaning of 長 was "long
hair," and the extended meanings
include "long," "length," "strong
point," "be good at," etc.

長 象形。古字像一長髮拄杖之老
人。本義為髮長，引申義有長度、長
久、長處、擅長等。

篆 短

短 duǎn (short; brief)

Pictophonetic character. The character 短
is comprised of the arrow radical 矢 and
the phonetic 豆 (dòu, beans) meaning
"short". In the Oracle-Bone Inscriptions
and Bronze Inscriptions, 矢 is the
pictograph of an arrow. In ancient times
people could use an arrow to measure the
length of other things, therefore the
character 短 has the arrow radical.

短 形聲。從矢，豆聲。意為不長。矢
即是箭，古人可用矢量長度，故短從矢
部。豆，象形。像一種古代食器。豆本
義為食器，后借用為豆類植物。

篆 種 種

種/种 zhǒng (species; kind; sort)
zhòng (grow; plant)

Pictophonetic character. The character 種
consists of the growing grain radical 禾
and the phonetic element 重 (zhòng,
heavy), meaning "plant," or "grow." The
extended meanings of 種 are "seed,"
"breed," "species," "kind," "type," etc. In
the Bronze Inscriptions, 重 is the sketch
of a man carrying a heavy sack on his
back, meaning "heavy," or "serious." In
the simplified character 种, the right part
of 種 is replaced by 中 **because** the
pronunciation of 中 (zhōng) is similar to
重 (zhòng).

種 形聲。從禾，重聲。本義指種植，引申為種子、種族、種類等。重，象形。
像人身負重物。簡體字种把種字的聲旁重用中替代。

篆

挺 tǐng (erect; straighten up; very; rather)

Pictophonetic character. The character 挺 consists of the hand radical 扌 and the phonetic element 廷, and it originally meant "pull out," "pull up," or "draw." Its extended meanings include "straight," "erect," "stick out," "straighten up," "quite," "very," etc. In the Bronze Inscriptions, the character 廷 looks like a man standing in front of the steps of a court, and means "royal court."

挺 形聲。從扌，廷聲。本義為拔出，引申為
挺立、挺拔、筆挺、突出、相當等。
廷，象形。金文像一人立於宮廷臺階前，本義為朝廷。

甲  金　篆

它 tā (it)

Pictograph. In its ancient form, the character 它 looks like a snake moving in a zigzag way, and its original meaning was "snake." Later 它 was borrowed to mean "other," or "it," and a worm radical 虫 was added the left of 它 to make a new character 蛇 (snake).

它 象形。古字像一頭部突出、身體彎曲
的蛇形。本義為蛇，后借為別的、另外等意。近代用它來指代事物、動物。而蛇
的意思則由它字左邊加部首虫來表示。

篆

刷 **shuā (scrub; brush; swipe)**

Pictophonetic character. The character 刷 consists of the phonetic element shuā on the left and the knife radical 刂 on the right. Its original meaning was "scrape," extended to mean "scrub," "brush," "daub," "remove," etc.

刷 形聲。左半邊為聲, 右從 刂。本義為用刀刮, 引申為用刷子清洗、梳理、塗抹、划過、刷子等。

卡 **qiǎ (wedge; get stuck; be jammed)**
kǎ (card)

Associative compound. The character 卡 is the combination of 上 (up) and 下 (down), signifying something is stuck in a particular position and cannot move upward or downward. The meanings of 卡 include "wedge," "block," "clip," "outpost," etc. 卡 is also used to transliterate some English words because of the similar pronunciation, such as "card," (卡 kǎ), "calorie" (卡路里 kǎlùlǐ), "cartoon" (卡通 kǎtōng), etc.

卡 會意。無古字。由上下二字合併而成, 意指不上不下, 卡在中間。也用作關卡, 卡子等。因聲音近似, 還用來音譯一些英文詞彙, 如卡片(card), 卡路里 (calorie), 卡通 (cartoon) 等。

篆

收　**shōu (receive; accept)**

Pictophonetic character. In the Seal Script, the character 收 consists of the signifying element 攴 (pō, hit with stick) on the right and the phonetic element 丩 (jiū) on the left, originally meaning "arrest." The extended meanings are "take in," "collect," "receive," "gather in," "harvest," etc. In Regular Script, in the character 收, 攴 is replaced by the tap/rap radical 攵, for the meaning of 攵 is the same as 攴. You have seen 攵 in the character 教 (jiāo, to teach) in **Lesson 7**.

收　形聲。篆文從攴(pō 手持杖擊打)，丩聲。本義為逮捕，收監，引申為收容、收集、收到、收復、收獲等。部首攵與攴意思相同。

LESSON 10

甲 〳〵 金 ⼁⼁ 篆 ⼁⼁

比 bǐ (compare)

Associative compound. The ancient form of 比 depicts two people standing side by side, meaning "juxtapose." Extended meanings of 比 include "close together," "next to," "cling to," "compare," "compete," "model after," etc. Can you tell what the differences are between the left and right part of 比?

比 會意。古文的比字像一前一後靠在一起的兩個人。本義為並列，引申為靠近、親近、比較等。

甲 ⼎ 金 冊 篆 雨

雨 yǔ (rain)

Pictograph. In its ancient form, the character 雨 looks like big raindrops falling from the sky. You learned 雨 in the **Radicals** Section.

雨 象形。像天上落下的雨滴。

甲 金 篆

更 gèng (even more)

Associative compound. In the Oracle-Bone Inscriptions, the character 更 resembles a hand holding a spatula to turn a pancake over on a griddle, meaning "to change" or "alternate" (pronounced gēng). 更 can be used as an adverb meaning "even more" and "furthermore" (pronounced gèng). You encountered 更 in the character 便 (see biàn, convenient, in **Lesson 6**).

更 會意兼形聲。甲骨文從攴（手持鏟）從丙（餅鐺），意指持鏟翻餅。引申為更改、更加等。

甲 金 篆

而 ér (and; in addition)

Pictograph. In the Oracle-Bone Inscriptions, 而 resembles a long beard on someone's chin, originally meaning "beard." Today 而 is used as a conjunction, meaning "and," "but," "moreover," "so that," etc.

而 象形。甲骨文像下巴上幾縷下垂的髯鬚，本義為髯鬚。

甲  金 且 篆 且

且 qiě (for the time being)

Pictograph. In the Oracle-Bone and Bronze Inscriptions, the character 且 looks like a memorial tablet used in ancestral worship, originally meaning "ancestor." Later, the meaning of "ancestor" became expressed with the new character 祖, and 且 became used as an adverb or conjunction to mean: "just," "for the time being," "even," "both…and…," etc. You encountered 且 in 姐 (see jiě, elder sister, in **Lesson 1**), 助 (see zhù, to assist, in **Lesson 7**), and 宜 (see yí, suitable, in **Lesson 9**).

且 象形。甲骨文、金文均像用來祭祀祖先的牌位。

篆 煖 爰 甲 爰 金 爰 篆 爰

暖 nuǎn (warm)

Pictophonetic character. 暖 consists of the sun radical 日 and the phonetic element 爰 (yuán), meaning "warm," "genial," and "warm up." In the Oracle-Bone Inscriptions, 爰 depicts a hand extending a stick to another hand, meaning "pull by hand" or "hand over."

暖 形聲。篆文從火，爰聲，本義為暖和。爰，會意。甲骨文上方像一只手持物，讓下方的另一只手（又）抓住，本義為援助。

約/约 yuē (make an appointment)

Pictophonetic character. The character 約 is composed of the silk radical 糸 and the phonetic symbol 勺 (sháo), meaning "to tie" or "bundle up." The extended meanings of 約 include: "keep within bounds," "restrain," "agreement," "make an appointment," "ask or invite in advance," etc. In the Bronze Inscriptions, 勺 is the pictograph of a ladle. You have seen 勺 in the character 的 (see de, a possessive or modifying particle, in **Lesson 2**). The silk radical is simplified to form the character 约.

約 形聲。從糸，勺聲。本義為捆縛，引申為約束、預先約定等。勺，象形，像勺瓢形。簡體字约的部首簡化。

園/园 yuán (garden)

Pictophonetic character. The character 園 consists of the enclosure radical 囗 and the phonetic element 袁 (yuán), meaning "garden" or "park." In Seal Script, the bottom part of 袁 is a garment 衣 (yī); the middle part resembles a ring，and the top part the ring's band, meaning "quartz ring" or "long garment." In the simplified character 园, 元 (yuán, first, basic) replaces 袁 (yuán), as the two have the same pronunciation.

園 形聲。從囗，袁聲。袁，會意。篆文上像系帶，中為玉佩，下乃衣服，意指胸前挂玉。本義為環玉，引申為環繞、長袍等。簡體字园以元代替袁，屬同音替代字。元明已有此字。

Lesson 10

葉/叶 **yè (leaf)**

Pictograph. In the Oracle-Bone Inscriptions, the character 葉 depicts a tree with three large leaves on its branches. In Regular Script, 葉 consists of the grass/plant radical 艹 on top, 世 in the middle, and 木 (mù, wood; tree) at the bottom. In its ancient form, 世 (shì) looks like leaves, meaning "lifetime" or "the world." The character 叶 (the original pronunciation was xié, originally meaning "harmonious") became used as the simplified character for 葉 (yè), because they are similarly pronounced.

葉 象形。甲骨文中像長着三片樹葉的樹枝。楷書加草字頭。叶字本讀作 xié，是協的異體字，現用來作為葉的簡體字，屬近音替代。

像 **xiàng (image)**

Pictophonetic character. The character 像 is composed of the person radical 亻 and the phonetic element 象 (xiàng), meaning "to resemble," "take after," "seem," "portrait," "picture," "image," etc. In the Oracle-Bone Inscriptions, the character 象 represents an elephant. In Regular Script, the upper part of 象 depicts the elephant's head and trunk, while the lower part delineates the body, legs, and tail.

像 形聲。從人，象聲，意指肖像、相像、好像等。象，象形。甲骨文簡要勾畫出大象的輪廓。

金  篆

海 hǎi (sea)

Pictophonetic character. 海 consists of the water radical 氵 and the phonetic 每 (měi), meaning "sea," "a great number of people or things coming together," "countless," "great capacity," etc. In the Oracle-Bone Inscriptions, the character 每 depicts a woman 女 with featherlike ornaments on her head, originally referring to female beauty.

海 形聲。金文從水，每聲。每，會意。甲骨文、金文均像婦女頭戴裝飾物，表示女子之美，後借用為每天的每。

篆 糟

糟 zāo (messy)

Pictophonetic character. The character 糟 is comprised of the rice radical 米 and the phonetic 曹 (cáo), meaning "distiller's grains," or "pickled with grains or wine." Extended meanings of 糟 are "rotten," and "messy." You encountered 米 in the character 氣 (see qì, air, in **Lesson 6**). In its ancient form, 曹 looks like two lanterns hanging over a doorway, originally meaning "pair" or "twin."

糟 形聲。從米，曹聲，意為酒渣、酒糟。米，象形。像散落的米粒。曹，會意。甲骨文從兩個東，從口，像門口挂著兩個燈籠。本義為雙、偶。

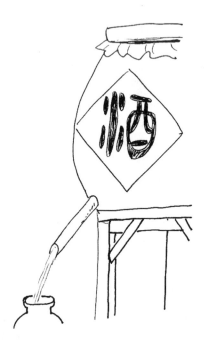

篆 糕 羔 甲  金 篆 美

糕 gāo (cake)

Pictophonetic character. 糕 consists of the rice radical 米 and the phonetic 羔 (gāo, lamb), meaning "cake." The character 羔 contains the goat/sheep radical (羊 yáng) on top and the fire radical (灬) underneath, referring to a lamb being roasted over fire. Compare 羔 with the character 美 (see měi, beautiful, in **Lesson 1**).

糕 形聲。從食，羔聲，意指糕餅。羔，甲骨文、金文上從羊，下從火，表示烤小羊。本義為小羊羔。

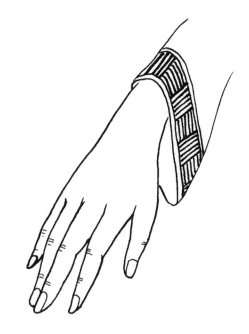

甲 金 篆

又 yòu (again)

Pictograph. In its ancient form, the character 又 was shaped like a right hand, meaning "right hand." Today 又 is used to mean "again," "also," "in addition," "both…and…," etc.

又 象形。甲骨文像右手形。

甲  金 篆

剛/刚 gāng (just now)

Associative and pictophonetic compound. In the Oracle-Bone Inscriptions, the character 剛 depicts a knife next to a net, indicating the act of cutting a net. Its original meaning was "sharp and solid," and extended meanings are: "indomitable," "firm," and "strong." 剛 may also be used as an adverb, meaning "just," "just now," "only," "barely," etc. In Regular Script, 剛 consists of the phonetic component 岡 (gāng, ridge) and the knife radical 刂. The simplified version of 岡 is 冈, which is used to form the simplified character 刚.

剛 會意兼形聲。甲骨文以刀斷網來表示物體堅硬，岡也兼表聲。岡，形聲兼會意。篆文從山從网，指山梁如網狀。意為山脊、山嶺、山坡等。繁體字岡的簡體字為冈。簡體字刚字左邊的冈簡化，右邊不變。

甲 金 篆

出 chū (go out)

Associative compound. In the Oracle-Bone and Bronze Inscriptions, the character 出 resembles a foot on top of a cave dwelling, meaning "to go or come out." Extended meanings of 出 include "to appear," "happen," "issue," "produce," etc. In Regular Script, 出 looks quite different from its earlier forms.

出 會意。甲骨文中本字上部從止，下部像洞穴，表示人從穴居走出。

金 𣥂 篆 𤎼 草 热　執 甲 𡎚 金 𡎚 篆 𡎚

熱/热 **rè (hot)**

Pictophonetic character. 熱 consists of the fire radical 灬 and the phonetic symbol 埶 (yì), meaning "heat," "hot," "to heat up," "to warm up," "fever," "craze," "ardent," etc. In the Oracle-Bone Inscriptions, 埶 resembles a person planting a sapling with her or his hands, meaning "to plant." In the Bronze Inscriptions, 土 (tǔ, earth; soil) is added under the sapling. The simplified character 热 derives from the cursive style of the character 熱, with 扌 on the top left instead of 坴 (lù).

熱 形聲。從火，埶聲。埶，會義。甲骨文中像一人手持樹苗栽種狀，本義為種植。簡體字热是繁體字熱的草書楷化字，左上方以扌代替。

篆 𨤖

舒 **shū (to stretch)**

Associative compound. The character 舒 consists of 舍 (shè, house; shě, give alms) and 予 (yǔ, give, grant, bestow). Since both 舍 and 予 carry the meaning of "open and give," 舒 means: "unfold," "spread," "stretch," "smooth out," "leisurely," etc. You learned the character 舍 in **Lesson 8**. In Seal Script, 予 looks like a hand pushing something towards others.

舒 會意兼形聲。從舍，從予；予亦聲。舍和予都有給與、放開之意，故舒本義為伸展，緩解。舍，象形。像房舍形，引申為施与，放棄等。予，像以手把物推給他人。

金  篆

夏 xià (summer)

Pictograph. In the Bronze Inscriptions, the character 夏 represents a robust man with strong arms akimbo. 夏 is the name of the first dynasty in recorded Chinese history (ca. 2100 B.C.–ca. 1600 B.C.) as well as an ancient name for China. Today, 夏 is used to mean "summer." Some scholars believe the character refers to a man with limbs exposed in hot summer weather.

夏 象形。金文中像人形，有頭（頁）、身、手、足，像個四肢發達、高大強壯的人。一説像夏天天熱，人的手足都露在外面。

篆

涼/凉 liáng (cool)

Pictophonetic character. The character 涼 consists of the water radical 氵 and the phonetic symbol 京 (jīng), meaning "cool," "cold," "chilly," and "discouraged." In the Oracle-Bone and Bronze Inscriptions, 京 (capital) looks like a palace at the top of a hill. You have seen 京 in 就 (see jiù, just, in **Lesson 6**). In the simplified character 凉, the ice radical 冫 replaces the water radical 氵.

涼 形聲。從水，京聲。京，象形。甲骨文、金文字形像在高丘上建造的宮殿，引申為京城。凉過去為涼的俗寫字，現用作涼的簡體字。冫 的意思是冰，例如用在冰、冷等字中。

金 篆

春 chūn (spring)

Associative and pictophonetic compound. In the Bronze Inscriptions, the character 春 consists of grass 艸 (cǎo), bud 屯 (tún), and sun 日 (rì), representing the thriving and lively "spring." In Regular Script, the upper part of 春 resembles grass or plants growing from the soil while 日 in the lower part remains unchanged.

春 會意兼形聲。甲骨文從日，從艸，從屯（tún 植物發芽）；屯亦聲。春字是春天陽光普照，草木萌發，生機勃勃的寫照。

甲 金 篆

冬 dōng (winter)

Associative compound. The character 冬 consists of "end" (zhōng) on top and "ice" (bīng) at the bottom, referring to winter—the cold period at the end of a year. In its ancient form, the word ice 仌 (bīng) looks like frost. 仌 is written as 冫 when it functions as a radical. Take care to distinguish between the ice radical 冫 and the water radical 氵.

冬 會意。上部為古文終字，下部兩點水代表冰，意指冬天是年終天寒結冰的日子。

篆 令 甲 金 篆

冷 lěng (cold)

Pictophonetic character. The character 冷 is comprised of the ice radical 冫 and the phonetic element 令 (lìng), meaning "cold," "frosty," "deserted," etc. In the Oracle-Bone Inscriptions, 令 resembles a person sitting under a roof, "issuing instructions" (this is the original meaning of 令). Be sure to distinguish between 令 and 今. (See also jīn, today; now, in **Lesson 3** and 唸 niàn, to read, in **Lesson 7**).

冷 從冫，令聲。令，甲骨文上像屋頂，下像一跪坐人形，指人于室內發號施令。

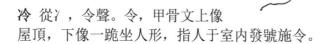

篆

悶/闷 mēn (stuffy)

Associative and pictophonetic compound. The character 悶 is composed of the radical and phonetic element 門 (mén, door) and the signifying component 心 (xīn, heart), meaning "shut oneself or somebody else indoors," "cover tightly," "stuffy," "muggy," "keep silent," etc. The radical 門 is simplified to form the character 闷.

悶 會意兼形聲。從心，從門（表示關閉），意指人關在屋內，心中憋悶。門也兼表聲。簡體字闷的部首簡化。

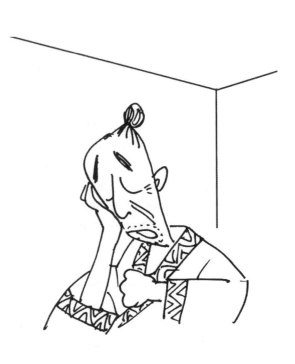

甲  金 篆 後

次 cì (MW for occurrence)

Associative compound. In the Oracle-Bone Inscriptions, the character 次 combines 二 (èr, two) and 欠 (qiān, yawn), referring to a person yawning multiple times. The meanings of 次 include: "next," "second," "time," "order," "position in a series," and the measure word for "occurrence." In the Oracle-Bone Inscriptions, 欠 looks like a man breathing or yawning, originally meaning "yawn." Extended meanings of 欠 include "not enough," "owe," etc. You encountered 欠 in the characters 歡 /欢 (see huān, joyful, in **Lesson 3**) and 歌 (see gē, song, in **Lesson 4**). In Regular Script, the ice radical 冫 replaces the 二 part of 次, even though ice has nothing to do with the original meaning of 次.

次 象形。從二，從欠（張口打呵欠），像人連連打呵欠狀。引申為前後順序以及動作的次數。

篆 烞

秋 qiū (autumn; fall)

Associative compound. The character 秋 combines 禾 (hé, standing grain) and 火 (huǒ, fire), indicating the fire-like colors of crops when they are ripe in the fall. 秋 originally meant "harvest time," and extends to mean  "autumn." In the Oracle-Bone and Bronze Inscriptions, 禾 resembles a ripe rice plant with hanging leaves. You learned 禾 in the character 和 (see hé, and, in **Lesson 2**).

秋 會意。從禾，從火。秋天穀物成熟顏色變深，高粱變紅，故加義符火。禾，象形。甲骨文中像禾苗形。

臺/台 tái (platform)

Associative compound. In Seal Script, 臺 looks like a platform built up high, meaning "platform," "stage" or "terrace." In the Oracle-Bone Inscriptions, 台 resembles a fetus with its head down, as in the womb, and originally meant "pregnant." Before the official simplification of Chinese characters, 台 (tái) had been used as a simplified version of 臺 (tái) since they are pronounced the same. You have seen 台 in the character 始 (see shǐ, begin, in **Lesson 7**).

臺/台 會意。篆字整體像是高臺：上部像高臺上的建築，中間是高字的省略，下部為至（到達），意指人可到高臺上眺望四方。早在金元時期台已在作為臺字的簡化字而使用。

北 běi (north)

Associative compound. In the Oracle-Bone Inscriptions, the character 北 depicts two people standing back-to-back, meaning "contrary," "deviate from," or "back." Since traditional Chinese houses usually face south (with their backs towards the north), 北 means "north."

北 會意。甲骨文中像二人背對背站着，本義為違背，引申為脊背。後來加肉月旁作"背"，表示脊背之義，而"北"則借用為方位名詞。

篆

灣/湾 wān (strait; bay)

Associative and pictophonetic compound. The character 灣 consists of the water radical 氵 and the signifying and phonetic element 彎 (wān, bend; tortuous), meaning "a bend in a stream," "gulf," or "bay." The top part of 彎 contains 言 between two 糹, and 弓 in the lower part, originally meaning "to draw a bow." "Curved," "tortuous," "bend," and "turn" are the extended meanings of 彎. The simplified character 湾 developed from the cursive style of 灣.

灣 會意兼形聲。從水，從彎（彎曲）；彎亦聲。意為水流彎曲之処、港灣、海灣等。彎，形聲。從弓，䜌 (luán)聲。本義為拉開弓，引申為彎曲。簡體字湾是繁體字灣的草書楷化字。

篆

郵/邮 yóu (post; mail; postal)

Associative compound. In the Seal Script, the character 郵 is the combination of 垂 (chuí, hang down; border area; frontier) and 邑 (yì, living area; town; city), originally referring to the inns for couriers who carried mail on horseback and extending to mean "post," "mail," "postal," "postman," etc.

郵 會意。從阝（阝 指邑，即居住區域），從垂（義為邊陲）。郵本義指古代供信差食宿的驛站。引申義為郵遞、郵差等。

金  篆 城

城 chéng (wall; city wall; city)

Pictophonetic character. The character 城 is comprised of the soil/earth radical 土 and the phonetic element 成 (chéng; succeed), originally meaning "wall." Since all cities had walls in ancient times, 城 extended to mean "city." The character 成 originally meant "cease-fire", and extended to mean "succeed," "accomplish," "achievement," "become," etc. The right part of 成 is 戈 (ge, dagger-ax), which you have learned in the **Radicals** section.

城 形聲。從土，成聲。本義指城牆。古代城市皆有牆，因而引申為城市。成，形聲。從戊（古代一種斧型兵器），丁聲，本義為休兵言和結盟，引申成功，完成、成為、成全、成就等。

甲 肖 金 宁 篆 肖

市 shì (market; city)

Associative and pictophonetic compound. In its ancient form, the character 市 has 之 (zhī; go) on the top and 冂 (jiǒng, designed market area) at the bottom, meaning "go to the market". Since every city had a market, 市 extended to mean "city." In the ancient form of character 市, 之 also functions as the phonetic element.

市 會意兼形聲。甲骨文從之（去，前往），從冂（jiǒng，劃出的集市範圍），之亦表聲。本義指集市，市場。因有城即有市場，引申為城市。

古 特 篆 特

特 tè (special; unusual)

Pictophonetic characters. The character 特 consists of the ox radical 牛 and the phonetic element 寺 (sì, temple), and it originally meant "bull," "ox," "calf" or "small livestock." Since ox horns are striking, 特 extended to mean "outstanding," "special," "unusual," "exceptional," etc. In its ancient form, 牛 is the front view of an ox head. You have seen 寺 in the character 時 in **Lesson 4**.

特 形聲。從牛，寺聲。本義指公牛。因牛角突出醒目，引申為獨特、特別、特點、特色等。

LESSON 11

寒 hán (cold)

Associative compound. In the Bronze Inscriptions, the character 寒 looks like a person hiding in the straw inside a house, and the two strokes at the bottom stand for ice. The original meaning of 寒 is "cold," and extended meanings are "tremble," "poor," and "needy."

寒 會意。金文、篆文中像人躲在屋内草中取暖，下面兩橫代表冰，表示屋内極為寒冷。

段 金 𦥑 篆 𠬝

假 jià (vacation)

Pictophonetic character. The character 假 consists of the person radical 亻 and the phonetic component 叚 (jiǎ/jià), meaning "borrow," "in case," "assume," "false" (pronounced jiǎ), "holiday," or "vacation" (pronounced jià). In the Bronze Inscriptions, the left part 叚 represents a cliff and the right part represents two hands, suggesting a person climbing up a cliff. 叚 originally meant "lean against," or "rely on," but is only used as a part within characters.

假 形聲。從人，叚聲，意為假期。叚，會意。金文左邊是山崖，右邊是兩只手，意指用雙手攀崖。叚本義為憑借、借助。

篆

飛/飞 fēi (to fly)

Pictograph. In Seal Script, 飛 resembles a flying bird flapping its wings, meaning "to fly," "flit," "hover," or when used as an adjective, "swiftly." In Regular Script, the character 飛 combines 升 (shēng, ascend; go up) and two 飞, which look like the two wings of a bird. In the simplified character 飞, only the top part of 飛 remains, still resembling a flying bird.

飛 象形。篆文中上像鳥頭，下像鳥身與展開的雙翅，意為飛翔。簡體字飞僅沿用了飛字的一部分，但仍像一只飛鳥的輪廓。

金  篆

機/机 jī (machine)

Pictophonetic character. The character 機 is composed of the wood radical 木 and the phonetic element 幾 (jǐ), meaning "machine," "plane," or "chance." The character 幾 consists of two wisps of silk 幺 (yāo, tiny; small) on the top, and a person with a dagger-ax 戍 (shù, guard; defend) at the bottom. Originally 幾 referred to dangerous signs to ward against, and later came to mean "a few" and "how many." You learned 幾 in **Lesson 2**. The simplified form of 幾 is 几, which also forms the simplified character 机.

機 形聲。從木，幾聲，指機器、機會、重要事務等。簡體字机的右部以几替代繁體的幾，屬同音替代。

票 piào (ticket)

Associative compound. In Seal Script, the upper part of 票 means "to rise," or "leap up," and the lower part is a fire radical, referring to "flame" or "blaze." Today 票 means "ticket," "ballot," "bank note," etc. In Regular Script, 票 is rather different from its earlier form. The upper part is similar to 西 (xī, west) while the character 示 comprises the lower part (see 示 in **Radicals**). You learned 票 in the character 漂 (see piào, pretty, in **Lesson 5**).

票 會意。篆文中下部從火，上部意指升高，本義指火焰騰起。

篆 場　草 **场**　易 甲 ☒　金 ☒　篆 易

場/场 chǎng (field)

Pictophonetic character. The character 場 is comprised of the earth radical 土 and the phonetic element 易 (yáng), meaning "field," "stage," or "a large place used for a specific purpose." In the Oracle-Bone Inscriptions, the upper part of 易 is 日 (rì, sun), while the lower part resembles sunlight piercing through the clouds. 易 means "sun" or "sunshine." When comparing 易 with 易 (see yì, easy, in **Lesson 7**), note that 易 has a horizontal line under the sun part. The simplified character 场 derives from the cursive style of the traditional character 場.

場 形聲。從土，易聲。古代祭神用的平地，引申為場地、處所等。易，會意。從日，從勿 (像陽光穿過雲層射出狀)，意指日出。簡體字场是由繁體字場的草書楷化而來。

篆

汽 qì (steam)

Associative and pictophonetic compound. The character 汽 combines the water radical 氵 and the signifying and phonetic element 气 (qì), meaning "vapor" or "steam." In the Oracle-Bone and Bronze Inscriptions, 气 looks like three thin clouds in the sky, meaning "air," "gas," or "weather." Try to compare 汽 with 氣/气 (see qì, air, in **Lesson 6**) and 吃 (see chī, eat, in **Lesson 3**).

汽 會意兼形聲。從水，從气；气亦聲。意為水蒸氣、氣體。气，象形。甲骨文像雲气升騰浮動狀。

甲 　　金 　　篆 　車 草

車/车 chē (car)

Pictograph. In the Oracle-Bone and Bronze Inscriptions, the character 車 depicts a chariot, complete with frame, axle, wheels, and yokes. In Seal Script, 車 is simplified to one wheel on its axle. You learned 車 in 褲/裤 (see kù, pants, in **Lesson 9**). The simplified character 车 developed from the cursive style of 車.

車 象形。篆文像簡化了的車形，只有車架、一個輪子與軸 簡體字车是繁體字車的草書楷化字。

甲 ㅂ 金 或 篆 或 域

或 huò (or)

Associative compound. In the character 或, 囗
(wéi, enclose) stands for the boundary or moat of
a city, 一 the land, and 戈 (gē, dagger-ax) the
weapon used to protect the country. The original
meaning of 或 was "country" or "nation."
However, "country" later became expressed with
國, while 或 means "or," "either," "perhaps,"
"maybe," etc.

或 會意。甲骨文從戈，從囗（囗像城的圍牆），
表示以武器（戈）保衛城池。金文、篆文下部
加一橫以示國土疆界。本義為邦國，假借義為
或者。

甲 ㅂ 金 ㅂ 篆 ㅂ

者 zhě (auxiliary to indicate a class of persons and things)

Associative compound. In the Oracle-Bone
and Bronze Inscriptions, the character 者
represents the food cooking in a wok, and
meant "burn" or "kindle." Later 者 became
primarily used as an auxiliary word after a
verb, or adjective to indicate a class of persons
or things, such as 讀/读者(dúzhě, reader), 老
者 (lǎozhě, old person). In Regular Script, the
upper part of 者 is the same as that of 老,
and the bottom part is 曰. You have seen 者
in 都 (see dōu, all, in **Lesson 2**).

者 會意。甲骨文中上像架起的木架與水蒸
汽，下從火。本義為燒、煮，後常用在形容
詞、動詞後以表示某類人或事物。

篆

地 dì (earth)

Pictophonetic character. The character 地 consists of the earth radical 土 and the phonetic symbol 也 (yě, also), meaning "earth," "land," "soil," "ground," "floor," etc. You learned 也 in **Lesson 1**.

地 形聲。從土，也聲。本義指土地，引申為地區、領域等。

篆

鐵/铁 tiě (iron)

Pictophonetic character. The character 鐵 consists of the gold/metal radical 金 on the left and the phonetic symbol 䥫 (zhì) on the right, meaning "iron." Extended meanings of 鐵 include: "arms," "weapon," "hard and strong as iron," "indisputable," "unalterable," etc. In Regular Script 鐵 is comprised of five components: 金，土，口，王, and 戈. In the simplified character 铁, 失 (shī) replaces 䥫 (zhì), because of their similar pronunciations.

鐵 形聲。從金，䥫（zhì）聲，意為鐵製的用具。簡體字铁左邊部首簡化，右邊以失（shī）代替䥫（zhì），屬近音替代。元明時已見簡化了的鉄字。

金 走 篆 走

走 zǒu (to walk)

Associative compound. In the Bronze Inscriptions, the upper part of 走 looks like a person walking rapidly with arms swinging, while the lower part depicts a human foot. In Regular Script, the lower part resembles a person striding forward with one arm swinging high, and the upper part becomes 土 (tǔ, earth), the surface upon which we walk. You learned 走 in **Radicals**.

走 會意。金文上像人擺動雙臂，下從止（腳），表示人用腳快步前行。

站 zhàn (stand; station)

Pictophonetic character. 站 combines the radical 立 (lì, stand) and the phonetic element 占 (zhàn, divination), meaning "stand," "halt," "stop," "station," etc. In the Oracle-Bone and Bronze Inscriptions, the upper part of 立 is the front view of a person (大), while the bottom stroke represents the ground. You learned 立 in 位 (see wèi, a polite measure word for people, in **Lesson 6**). The character 占 consists of 卜 (bǔ, a crack on an oracle-bone) and 口 (kǒu, mouth), referring to the interpretation of oracle-bone cracks used in divination. 占 is also the right part of 點 (see diǎn, dot; o'clock, in **Lesson 3**).

站 形聲。從立，占聲。立，會意。甲骨文、金文從大（正面人形），從一(指地面)，表示人站在地上。占，會意。上從卜（龜甲燒裂后之兆紋），下從口，意指觀察兆紋解説兇吉。

篆

綠/绿 lǜ (green)

Pictophonetic character. The character 綠 is composed of the silk radical 糹 and the phonetic component 彔 (lù), meaning "green." In the Oracle-Bone and Bronze Inscriptions, the character 彔 looks like water filtering through a hanging sack. 彔 originally meant "filter" and extends to mean "record," or "copy." You learned 彔 in 錄 (see lù, to record, in **Lesson 7**). 绿 is a variant form of 綠, of which the silk radical is simplified to 纟, to form the simplified character 绿.

綠 形聲。從糹，彔聲，本義為綠色。绿是綠的異體字，部首簡化後變為簡體字。

泉 甲 篆

線/线 xiàn (line)

Pictophonetic character. The character 線 consists of the silk radical 糹 and the phonetic element 泉 (quán), meaning "thread," "string," "wire," "line," etc. In the Oracle-Bone Inscriptions, 泉 (spring), looks like water gushing out of a mountain springhead. In Regular Script, 泉 combines 白 (bái, white) and 水 (shuǐ, water). 綫 is a variant form of 線. In the simplified character 线, both 糹 and 戔 are simplified. See the character 钱 (錢) in **Lesson 9**.

線 形聲。從糹，泉聲。泉，象形。甲骨文像水從泉眼流出。綫是線的異體字。簡體字线是將繁體字綫左邊的部首簡化為纟，右邊戔簡化為戋。參見 L.9 錢字的簡化法。

篆 藍 草 監甲 金 篆

藍/蓝 lán (blue)

Pictophonetic character. 藍 is composed of the grass radical 艹 and the phonetic symbol 監 (jiān), meaning "indigo plant" and extending to mean "blue." In the Oracle-Bone Inscriptions, the character 監 represents a girl kneeling next to a basin and gazing at her reflection in the water, meaning "watch," "oversee," "supervise," etc. In Regular Script, 臣 (chén, a vertical eye, extends to mean "official") and 皿 (mǐn, utensil) still carry traces of the original version of 監. The simplified character 蓝 derives from the cursive style of 藍 with two vertical lines replacing the component 臣.

藍 形聲。從艸，監聲。本義指蓼藍，葉子可用來提煉藍色染料。監，象形。甲骨文、金文中本字像人睜大眼用水盆照自己的容顏 簡體字蓝是繁體字藍的草書楷化字，將臣簡化為兩豎。

金 麻 篆 麻

麻 má (hemp; numb)

Associative compound. The character 麻 combines 广 (yǎn, shed; roof; shelter) and 林 (pài; peel; hemp), referring to people working with hemp in a workshop. 麻 originally meant "hemp" or "flax." Extended meanings of 麻 include "rough," "coarse," "numb," etc.

麻 會意。篆文從广（敞屋，），從 林（pài 治麻），表示人在屋下劈麻晾麻。麻是大麻、亞麻、黃麻等植物的統稱。

篆 煩

煩/烦 fán (bother)

Associative compound. The character 煩 consists of
火 (huǒ, fire) and 頁 (yè, originally meaning
"head," now meaning "page"), implying that one has
fire in one's head. Meanings of 煩 therefore, are "to
be vexed," "irritated," "tired of," "trouble," "bother,"
etc. You learned 火 in **Radicals**, and saw 頁 in 題/
题 (see tí, topic, in **Lesson 6**), 預/预 (see yù,
prepare, in **Lesson 7**), and 顏/颜 (yán, face, in
Lesson 9). The right part 页 is simplified to form the
simplified character 烦.

煩 會意。從頁（人頭），從火，表示腦袋發熱，煩
躁不安。簡體字烦右邊的页由頁簡化而來。

篆 租

租 zū (to rent)

Pictophonetic character. The
character 租 consists of the radical
禾 (hé, standing grain), and the
phonetic element 且 (qiě/jū),
meaning "land tax," "rent," "hire,"
"lease," etc. You saw 禾 in 和 (see
hé, and, in **Lesson 2**) and 秋 (see
qiū, autumn, in **Lesson 10**). You
learned 且 in Lesson 10 and in 姐
(see jiě, elder sister, in **Lesson 1**), 助
(see zhù, to assist, in **Lesson 7**), and
宜 (see yí, suitable, in **Lesson 9**).

租 形聲，從禾，且(jū)聲。田賦、
出租、租用之意。

甲 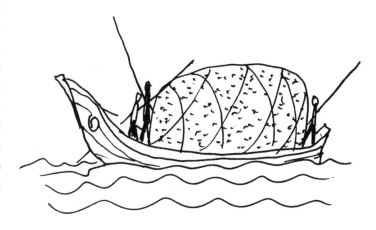 金

送 sòng (to deliver)

Associative compound. In the Oracle-Bone and Bronze Inscriptions, the character 送 depicts a boat, two hands, and a punt-pole, referring to someone poling a boat to deliver passengers or goods. Meanings of 送 include "send," "deliver," "carry," "see somebody off," "escort," and "give as a present." In Regular Script, 送 combines the walk radical 辶, with 丷 and 天.

送 會意。從辶，從关。"送"字在甲骨文、金文中左像船形，右像雙手持篙，本意指以船運送。

甲 金 篆 草

過/过 guò (to pass)

Pictophonetic character. The character 過 is composed of the walk radical 辶 and the phonetic element 咼 (guō), meaning "pass," "cross," "spend," "go beyond," "go through," etc. 咼 combines 口 (kǒu, mouth) and 冎 (guǎ, dismember; slit), meaning "mouth that goes awry." The simplified character 过 developed from the cursive style of 過 with 寸 replacing 咼.

過 形聲。從辶，咼聲。咼，形聲。從口，從冎（殘缺）；冎亦聲。咼本義指歪嘴。簡體字过用寸代替咼，是由繁體字過的草書楷化而來。

篆

讓/让 ràng (to let)

Pictophonetic character. The character 讓 consists of the word radical 言 and the phonetic element 襄 (xiāng), originally meaning "blame." Today 讓 means "yield," "let," "allow," "make," etc. In the Bronze Inscriptions, the character 襄 consists of mouths (suggesting weeping), twigs (used in funerals), and clothes, referring to the removal of mourning apparel after a funeral. Therefore, 襄 means "to get rid of," "finish," "assist," etc. The characters 襄, 裏 (see lǐ, inside, **in Lesson 7**) and 還 (see hái, still; yet, in **Lesson 3**), all contain the character/radical 衣. In the simplified character 让, the speech radical on the left is simplified while 上 (shàng) replaces 襄 (xiāng), as their pronunciations are similar.

讓 形聲。從言，襄聲，本義為責備。襄，從衣，其中兩口表示哭聲，意指辦完喪事脫去喪服去耕地。襄本義為解衣耕地，借用為升高、輔助等。簡體字让用上代替襄，屬於近音替代字。

甲 佗 金 篆

花 huā (spend; flower)

Pictophonetic character. The character 花 consists of the grass/plant 艹 radical and the phonetic 化 (huà), meaning "flower," "blossom," "flowery," "multicolored," etc. Today 花 also means "to spend." In the Oracle-Bone Inscriptions, 化 depicts two people heading in different directions, meaning "change," "turn," "convert," etc. You encountered 化 in 貨 / 货 (see huò, merchandise, in **Lesson 9**).

花 形聲。從艸，化聲。化，會意。甲骨文像兩人一正一倒形，意指變化。

甲  金 篆

每 mǎi (every)

Associative compound. In the Oracle-Bone Inscriptions, the character 每 represents a woman with featherlike ornaments on her head, originally referring to female beauty. In the Bronze Inscriptions, two dots are added to the woman's chest to indicate her breasts. You learned the character 美 (see měi, beautiful, in **Lesson 1**) which represents a person wearing goat horns for decoration. 美 originally referred to male beauty and later came to encompass all kinds of beauty. 每 is now used to mean "every," "each," "each time," "often," etc. You have seen 每 in 海 (see hǎi, sea, in **Lesson 10**).

每 會意。甲骨文、金文像婦女頭上戴有裝飾物。本義表示女子之美，後借用為每天的每。

甲 金 篆

速 sù (speed)

Pictophonetic character. The character 速 is comprised of the walk radical 辶 and the phonetic element 束 (shù), meaning "swift," "rapid," "speedy," "speed," or "velocity." In the Oracle-Bone Inscriptions, the character 束 looks like a sack tied on both ends with cord, meaning: "tie," "bind," "control," "restrain," "bundle," "bunch," etc. Some scholars think 束 looks like a bunch of bamboo pieces or firewood.

速 形聲。從辶，束聲，本義指迅速。束，會意。金文從口從木，像袋子的兩端被捆扎起來。本義為束縛。

金 路　篆 路

路 lù (road; way)

Pictophonetic character. The character 路 is the combination of the foot radical 𧾷 and the phonetic symbol 各 (gè), meaning "road," "path," "way," "route," etc. In the Oracle-Bone and Bronze Inscriptions, 各 combines 夂 (an approaching foot) and 口 (the entrance of a cave-dwelling). The original meaning of 各 was "to arrive" and later came to mean "each" or "every." You have seen 各 in 客 (see kè, guest, in **Lesson 4**).

路 形聲。從足，從各（到來），各亦聲。意指道路。

篆 緊　草 緊

緊/紧 jǐn (tight)

Associative compound. The character 緊 combines the vertical eye 臣, right hand 又, and silk 糸, referring to the tightening of a silk string. 緊 originally means "tighten," or "tight," and extends to mean "tense," "urgent," "strict," "short of money," etc. The simplified character 紧 derives from the cursive style of 緊. Just as in the character 蓝/藍 in this lesson, two vertical lines replace the eye part 臣.

緊 會意。上部左為豎著的眼睛，右是手，下部從絲（省為糸），本義指眼睛盯着，用手將絲弦調緊。　簡體字紧是繁體字緊的草書楷化字。如同本課的藍字，將臣簡化為兩豎。

甲  金 篆

自 zì (self)

Pictograph. In the Oracle-Bone Inscriptions, 自 represents the shape of a nose. 自 originally meant "nose," and came to mean "self," "one's own," "from," "since," etc. 自 no longer carries its original meaning, as the character 鼻 now indicates "nose."

自 象形。甲骨文像鼻形。本義為鼻子，後引申為自己，而鼻子則寫作 "鼻"。

甲 己 金 己 篆

己 jǐ (oneself)

Pictograph. In its ancient form, 己 resembled a large belly, meaning "oneself," "personal," etc. You learned 己 in 起 (see qǐ, rise, in **Lesson 5**) and 記 (see jì, to record, in **Lesson 8**). Note the slight difference between 己 and 已 (see yǐ, already, in **Lesson 8**).

己 象形。古文字中像人腹形，用作人稱代詞、自己、本身等。注意己（jǐ）和已（yǐ）的區別。（已 yǐ 象形。甲骨文、金文、篆文中本字像頭朝下的胎兒，引申為已經）。

甲  金 新 篆 新

新 xīn (new)

Associative and pictophonetic compound. The character 新 consists of the signifying parts 木 (mù, wood) and 斤 (jīn, axe), and the phonetic component 辛 (xīn), originally meaning "cut firewood" or "firewood." Since people in primitive societies made fire by creating friction on wood, 新 extends to mean "new," "fresh," "newly," "recently," "unused," etc. In the Oracle-Bone Inscriptions, 斤 looks like an ax with a crooked handle, meaning "ax," and later became used as a unit of weight in traditional Chinese measurements. You encountered 斤 in 所 (see suǒ, place, in **Lesson 4**), and 近 (see jìn, near, in **Lesson 8**). In the Oracle-Bone and Bronze Inscriptions, the character 辛 is the pictograph of a chisel-like instrument used to tattoo prisoners. Extended meanings of 辛 are: "pungent," "laborious," "suffering," and "hot" (in flavor). You saw 辛 in 辦/办 (see bàn, to manage, in **Lesson 6**).

新 會意兼形聲。從木，從斤(斧)，辛聲。本義為用斧頭砍柴，是薪的本字，後用作新舊的新。辛，象形。甲骨文中像鑿子一類的刑具，用來在犯人臉上刺字。

APPENDIX
Explanations in Simplified Characters

Key: 甲 refers to the Oracle-Bone Inscriptions,
金 the Bronze Inscriptions, 篆 the Seal Script, and
草 the Cursive Script. See the Preface for more information.

Radicals

人 象形。甲骨文、金文像有头、背、臂、腿的侧面人形。

刀 象形。像刀形。上像刀柄，下像刀刃及刀背。

力 象形。甲骨文、金文均像耕田用具。因耕田要有力，引申为力气。

又 象形。像右手形。

口 象形。像人口形状。

篆

口 象形。像环围形。从口的字多有外围或边界。

土 象形。像一土块状，下方 "一" 字意指大地。

夕 象形。像半个月亮，傍晚或夜晚之意。

大 象形。像伸展双臂的正面人形。天地万物中以人为大为贵，故用人形表示"大"意。

女 象形。甲骨文像女子俯首，双臂交叉下跪形。

子 象形。像襁褓之中的婴儿。

篆

寸 指事。从又，从一。"又"为右手，"一"指手后一寸之处。中医所言寸口。

小 会意。甲骨文、金文作三点，表示沙粒微小的意思。

工　象形。像工匠用的曲尺。

幺　象形。像一小把细丝。甲骨文么、糸　（mì）、丝为同源字。糸、丝都像丝束形，不同的是糸为一束丝，　丝为两束丝。系(xì) 字在甲骨文中为一只手握两束丝。

弓　象形。甲骨文像有弓弦弓背的完整弓形。金文简化。

心　象形。像人的心脏。

戈　象形。戈是古代常用的一种长柄横刃的兵器。

手　象形。像五指伸开的手掌。

日　象形。甲骨文、金文像太阳的轮廓。日字写成方形则出于汉字书写的习惯

月 象形。像弯月形。

木 象形。像一棵树。上像树枝，中像树干，下像树根。

水 象形。甲骨文字形中间像流水，旁似浪花或水的支流。

火 象形。像火焰形。

田 象形。像阡陌纵横的田地。

目 象形。甲骨文、金文像人眼形。为书写方便，小篆将横目改为竖目。

示 象形。甲骨文中像用石块搭起的简单祭台。

糸 象形。像丝束形。

甲　　金　　篆

耳　象形。像耳朵的形状。

甲　　金　　篆

衣　象形。像有领、袖、长襟的衣服。

甲　　金　　篆

言　会意。甲骨文字形下像嘴，上像伸出的舌头。意指言乃是从舌上发出的声音。

甲　　金　　篆　　草

貝/贝　象形。像贝壳形。简体字贝是由繁体字贝的草书楷化而来。

金　　篆

走　会意。金文上像人摆动双臂，下从止（脚），表示人用脚快步前行。

甲　　金　　篆

足　象形。从口、从止。口像小腿；止是脚。合起来表示人足。

金　　篆

金　象形兼会意。金文左边像两块青铜块，右边上是箭头下是斧，指可用来制作箭、斧等器具的金属。本义为金属，引申为黄金。

門/门 象形。像两扇门之形。门是門字的草书楷化字。

隹 象形。意指短尾巴鸟。

雨 象形。像水滴从天上落下形。

食 会意。甲骨文中"食"字上边像是向下张开的嘴，下边像是盛满了食物的容器，表示张口向下吃容器中的食物。一说下像装满食物的容器，上则为盖子。

馬/马 象形。上像马头与鬃毛，下像身、腿、尾。简体的马字保留了繁体馬字的大体轮廓，十分接近馬字的草书。

Numerals

一 二 三 指事。以一至三画表示数字一到三，是原始的记数符号。

四 在甲骨文中是四横。金文"四"像脸部的口鼻。本义为喘息，是呬的本字，因读音相近而借用为四字。

五 在西安半坡仰韶文化遗址出土的陶器上，X 即五。 甲骨文、金文在 X 上下各加一横。

六 在甲骨文、金文中为茅棚状，本义为庐。由于读音相近的关系，借用为六字。

七 在半坡陶器上以及甲骨文、金文中，十的意思皆是七。小篆将十的意思改为十，而将十的一竖弯曲，另造七字，以区别于十。

八 甲骨文中用两划来表示将一物分开，是分字的初文，后借用位数字。

九 甲骨文像是兽类臀部上长出的尾巴，是尻（kāo 屁股）的初文。后借为数目字。

十 指事。在半坡陶器上，十字为一竖画，甲骨文同。金文中间加一点，篆文又由一点延长为一横。一说在一根绳上打一个结表示一个十。

LESSON 1

先 会意。甲骨文从之（足）在儿（人）前，本义为走在他人前面。

生 会意。像地面上刚长出的一株幼苗，本义指草木生长。

你 古时写作爾，像蚕吐丝结茧。一说像花枝垂下之形。假借为第二人称的代词。楷书加人字旁。

好 会意。从女、从子，以能生儿育女使家族兴旺的妇女为好。

小 会意。甲骨问及金文作三点，像细小的沙粒形，表示微小的意思。

姐 形声。从女，且声。且在甲骨文金文中像代表祖先之灵的牌位，供祭祀时用。

王 象形。甲金文中像斧形，上像其柄，下像其圆弧形的锋刃。王是一种斧状的的兵器，后来成为执法的刑具，是权威的象征。引申意指以武力征服天下者为王。

李 会意兼形声。从木，子声。本义为果木。孩子站在树下看树上的李子，考虑如何摘下。

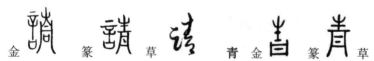

請/请 形声。从言，青声。青，会意兼形声。金文从生，从丹，丹为颜色。用植物生长的颜色来表示绿色之意。后楷书写作青。丹，象形。四周像丹砂井，中间一点像丹砂形。简体字请的部首讠是由繁体部首言的草书楷化而来。

問/问 形声。从口，门声。像人到门下张口问事。简体字问的部首门是繁体字門的草书楷化字。

您 会意。你的敬称。

貴/贵 会意。篆文上像双手捧物，下从贝。贝代表钱，凸显出手捧之物十分贵重。简体字贵下部的贝是繁体貝的草书楷化字。

姓 会意兼形声。从女，从生；生亦声。姓是母系社会的反应。上古姓是族号，随母系。

我 甲骨文像兵器之形。后借为第一人称，遂失本义。从手，像手执戈以自卫。

呢 语气词。会意兼形声。从口，尼声。尼，像二人从后相近之形，意为二人亲昵，后作"昵"。

叫 形声。从口，丩声。丩意为纠缠，像藤蔓纠结状。一说像丝线缠绕。

什 会意。从人，从十。古代户籍十家为什，兵制十人为什。"什"后借用为疑问代词。

麼/么 助词，语气词。从么，麻声。么同幺，像一把细丝。麻，像在敞屋下（或屋檐下）劈麻晾麻。简体字么取繁体字麼的下半部。

名 会意。从口，从夕。夕，夜里。夜里色昏暗，相互看不见，只好叫名字。

字 会意兼形声。从宝盖头，从子；子亦声。用房屋中有子意指生养孩子。现可想象为孩子在屋中写字。

朋 象形。甲骨文、金文像两串贝壳形，本义为为古代货币单位，后引申为朋友。楷书写作朋。

友 会意。甲骨文以两人右手握在一起来指志同道合的朋友。

是 会意。金文从日，从正，表示日正当午。本义为正、直，引申意有正确、是非、肯定等。

老 象形。像长发长须老人弓腰扶拐杖之形。

師/师 会意。師字左边 **自** (duī)意为小土山，右部帀（zā）是环绕的意思，意指众人环绕在土山旁。本义指众人，军队，都邑，引申为学习、老师等。师是師字的草书楷化字。

嗎/吗 形声。部首"口"用于疑问词或象声词。马，象形字。简体字右边用了简化的马字。

不 像种子萌芽即将破土而出时的形状，是胚的本字。后多借为否定词，本意遂不用。

學/学 会义。金文像屋里一个孩子双手摆布小木棍，学习计算。简体字学是繁体字學的草书楷化字。

也 在金文中"也"是一条拖着尾巴、头部突出的蛇形。本义为蛇，后被借为语气词、助词与副词。

中 会意。甲骨文、金文像树立在场地中央迎风飞舞的旗帜。本义为旗帜，引申为中央。

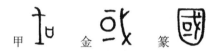

國/国 会意。囗像城池，一为土地，口指人口，戈用以守卫。简体字将國字中间部分改为玉字。国有玉玺，是会意字。

人 象形。甲骨文、金文像人侧立之形。

美 会意。从羊，从大。男子头戴羊角作装饰，是男性健美的表现。一说是羊肥大则肉鲜美。

京 象形。像建于高丘之上的华屋大厦，引申为京城，首都。

紐/纽 会意兼形声。从糸，丑声。本义为打结，钮扣为其引申义。丑，古字像以手用力扭曲一物，本义为拧扭，后借用表示地支的第二位而另造"扭"字表示拧扭之意。丑现也是繁体字醜的简化字。

LESSON 2

那 会意兼形声。篆文从邑（城邑），冄 rǎn 声，本义指留有长发长须的西夷国人。楷书写作那。

張/张 形声。从弓，长声。本义指把弦绷在弓上，引申为拉开弓。引申义有张开、扩张等。长，象形。甲骨文中像一长发长须的老人弓腰拄拐形。简体字张的右部长是由繁体字长的草书楷化而来。

照 会意兼形声。金文左边像手持火把状，右边召是声旁。篆文改为火字旁，昭声，昭也有日光明亮之意。

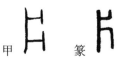

片 指事。从半木，是树木劈开后右边的一半。

的 形声。篆文从日，勺声，楷书写作"的"。白 象形。像日出光芒射出状。一说像白米粒。勺 象形。像用勺舀物。

這/这 本义为迎接。从辶，表示前去；从言，表示以言语相迎。简体字这以文取代言，属符号替代字。清代已见此字。

爸 从父、巴声。父 象形。甲骨文、金文字形像手持石斧工作状。巴，象形。篆文中像一条张着大嘴的蛇。

媽/妈 形声。从女，马声。简体字妈右边的馬简化为马。

篆

個/个 象形。竹像两根并生的竹子，个为一根竹子，本用以指竹子的数量，扩大范围以后用作量词。后另造"個"字。個，从人，固声，简化后仍为"个"。固，从口，从古，指城四周有墙保护，便可永固不破，引申为坚硬，牢固等。古，从十从口，十代表众多，意指在有文字记载以前，众口相传远古之事。

甲　金　篆

男 会意。从田，从力(甲骨文像犁形)，借用犁耕田来代表男子。"男耕女织"，在田里耕种主要是男人的事。

亥 甲　金

孩 形声。从子，亥声。本义为小儿笑声，引申为儿童，孩子。亥，象形。甲骨文像切掉头、蹄的猪，是"刻"的本字，本义为切割。

甲　金　篆

子 象形。像头部突出、手臂在外、裹在襁褓中的婴儿。

金　篆

誰/谁 形声。从言，佳声。简体字偏旁简化。
他 第三人称代词。人字旁加也。也，见第一课的解释。

甲　金　篆

弟 象形。像人身上背弓箭形，古时年轻人挂弓箭祭奠死去的长者。一说上像总角，下像腿形。另一说弟本意指以绳捆物的次第。

甲　金　篆

女 象形。甲骨文像女子双臂交叉，跪坐在地形。

甲   金   篆

妹 形声。从女，未声。未，甲骨文像树木生长旺盛，枝叶繁茂状。本义为繁茂，引申义为将来。

她 从女，从也。女性第三人称代词。

甲   金   篆

兒/儿 象形。像头囟未合的婴儿。简体字儿仅保存兒字的下半部。

金   篆

有 会意兼形声。金文、篆文从又（右手）持肉（肉月旁），意为持有。

篆

没 会意。从水。篆文像人淹没在漩涡中，水面上只能看见一只手状。本义为淹没，引申为没有。

甲   金   篆

高 象形。像高耸的楼台。

甲   金   篆

家 会意。从宝盖头，从豕，表示在家中养猪。农业社会中不养牲畜不像一个家。

金   篆

幾/几 会意。上部"么么"表示微小，下部"戍"意为防备。表示在发现细微迹象时就要警惕，加以防备。本义为细微迹象、先兆，后作为数词、疑问词。戍，会意。甲骨文、金文像人持戈。几字早已存在，如茶几。简体字用几代替幾，属同音替代字。

篆

哥 会意。从二可。可有欢乐的意思，表示声声相连歌不断，乐在其中，是歌的本字。后称兄为哥，遂加欠作歌。

兩/两 会意兼形声。金文像车衡上有两个轭的战车，引申为并列成双之物。简体字两去掉两字中间一竖，并把中间的两个入字改为两个人字。这种写法元代已见。

和 形声。甲骨文从龠，禾声，意指乐声和谐。引申为和谐、协调、和睦、和好等意，也可用作连词。古文简化，改龠为口。龠，像一由多条竹管做成的笙箫。禾，像一株禾形。上像禾穗，下像根部。

做/作 会意。从人，从乍。甲骨文、金文写为"乍"，意指缝制衣领。后加人字旁为"作"。"做"是后起字，在一些意思上二字相通。

英 形声。从艹，央声。本义指花，引申为美好、杰出、才能出众。央，古文像一人挑担，意为正中、中心。

文 象形。甲骨文像一正面站立、胸有刺青的人形。

律 从彳（左脚走半步为彳，一说彳为小步走走停停的样子，一说指半条街），聿声。意为法律、规则。聿，象形。甲骨文像以手持笔状，本义为笔。

都 形声。金文从邑，者声。本义为都市，引申义为全部（副词）。者，会意。甲骨文、金文中像将食物投到锅中煮。者是煮的本字。

篆

醫/医 会意。医，古时盛箭的器具。殳 shū，会意。甲骨文像一只手拿一件圆头兵器，意指一种
古代兵器。酉，象形。像一个尖底的酒坛子。酒可以用以治病。醫指受到箭伤或兵器的伤害，可
以用酒来消毒治病。简体字医仅保留繁体醫字左上方的部分。

篆　　　　　　草

愛/爱 会意兼形声。篆文上部标声兼表意(ài, love),下部从夊(suī 脚)，表示心有所爱而脚下徘徊
不忍离去，有慈爱、情爱、喜爱等意。爱是爱字的草书楷化字，去掉爱字中间的心字而将夊字改
为友。

LESSON 3

甲　　　　金　　　　篆

月 象形。像弯月形。

篆　　　　虎 甲　　　金　　　篆

號/号 会意兼形声。从号，从虎；号亦声。本义为虎叫，引申为呼叫、日期等。号像口中出气，
意指呼喊。虎，象形。像老虎之形。简体字号仅保留繁体的左边一半。

甲　　　　金　　　　篆

星 形声。从日，生声。甲骨文像光芒闪耀的群星，金文改成三颗星，下加声旁，楷书减为一颗
星。

篆

期 形声。从月，其声。其，象形。甲骨文像簸箕形，本义为簸箕。后因用为语气词，遂另造箕
字。

甲　　　　金　　　　篆

天 指事。从一、大。"大"为正面人形，"一"指头上有天。

甲　　　　金　　　　篆

日 象形。像太阳的轮廓，

今　象形。像一人正张口和下面坛子里的酒，表示此时、现在的意思。

年　形声兼会意。从禾，从人。甲骨文像人背禾形，表示五谷成熟是一年劳作的成果。引申为一年。

多　会意。多字像两块肉形。古时祭祀用肉，用两块以表示多。

大　象形。像正面人形。天地万物中以人为大为贵，故用人形来表示大。

歲/岁　会意。甲骨文、金文从戉（yuè 斧形，此处象征收割用具），从步，指在田里迈步向前用镰刀之类农具收割庄稼。戉也兼表声。歲本义为收割，引申为一年的收成、年龄等。篆文改戉为戌（xū 斧形兵器）。歲有异体字崴，简体岁字保留了繁体崴字上部的山，而下部改为夕字。

吃　形声。从口，乞声，意为进食。乞，本为气，像天上的云气浮动状。后省去一笔为乞。乞由气字分化而来，意为请求、乞讨。

晚　形声。从日，免声。免，会意。像人带着冠冕形，意为脱去，赦免等。

飯/饭　形声。从食，反声。反，会意。从厂（hǎn 山崖），从又（右手），表示以手攀崖。简体字中，作为部首的食 一律简化为饣。饣由食 的草书楷化而来。

怎　代词，表示疑问。从心，乍声。乍，像用针缝制衣领。

樣/样 形声。从木，羕声。羕，形声。从永，羊声，形容水长。永，会意。甲骨文从人，像人在水流中游泳状。本义指游泳，是泳的本字。后加水旁作泳，而以永为永久意。羊，象形。像羊头之形。简体字样把繁体右部的声旁羕改为羊。

太 指事。为强调事物过大，在大字下再加一点。

了 象形。从子，但无臂，像婴儿在襁褓中束其两臂。本义为收束，引申为完毕，了解，结束等。

謝/谢 形声。从言，射声。射，会义。甲骨文像张弓射箭形。金文加手。篆文将弓改为身，从寸。寸有手义。意指用手张弓射箭始于身而及于远。身，像人腹有身孕形。简体字中，作为字左边部首的訁 一律简化为讠 。

喜 会意。从壴（zhù 鼓），从口，意指张口笑着，欢乐击鼓。

歡/欢 形声。从欠，雚 guàn 声。雚，小雀或猫头鹰。欠，象形。甲骨文中像人张口出气状。人像鸟一般张口叽叽喳喳般说话，意为欢喜快乐。简体欢字左边以又取代雚。明清已有欢字。

還/还 形声。从辶，睘(qióng/huán)声，返回、交还之意。亦用作副词，表示持续。睘，回首惊视之意。简体字还用不取代睘。元代已有此字。

可 会意兼形声。从口，从丂(kǎo); 丂亦声。丂，气欲舒出状。本义为口中舒气以示认可，引申为许可、同意等。

們/们 形声。从人，门声。简体字中，門皆简化为门。

篆   占 甲   占 篆

點/点 形声。从黑，占声。黑 会意。甲骨文、金文中像一个被烟熏火烤、大汗淋漓、满面污垢的人。占 会意。从卜（龟壳烧裂后出现的兆纹），从口，意指观察兆纹解释凶吉。简体字点去掉黑字的上半部，把灬移到占字下。明清已有此字。

篆   草 钟   童 金   篆

鐘/钟 形声。从金，童声，意指古代钟乐。童，会意兼形声。金文从辛（刑刀），从人，从东（东西），指人头上有刀，身负重物。本义为男奴隶，引申为儿童。釒作为部首时，在简体字中简化为钅，是由草书楷化而来。钟字右边以中替代童，属近音替代。

金   篆

半 会意。上从八（分开），下从牛。表示将牛从中切为两半，意为事物的二分之一。

甲   金   篆

上 指事。表示在一物在另一物之上。

甲   金   篆   草

見/见 会意。从目从儿。儿指人，表示人看东西时要睁大眼睛。简体字见是繁体字见的草书楷化字。

甲   金   篆

再 会意。甲骨文中其上下横为二，当中像篓中的鱼形，意指提两条鱼。本义为第二次，两次。一说像两鱼相遇状。

甲   金   篆

白 象形。像太阳初升、光芒四射状。一说像一粒白米。

玉 甲

現/现 从玉，见声，本意指玉光外射，引申为显露、出现、此刻之意。玉，象形。甲骨文像一串玉。金文和篆文改为三片玉。玉作为偏旁写作王。简体字现的右部简化。

甲   金   篆

在 形声兼会意。从土，从才；才亦声。像草木从土中长出，以此表示存在。才，象形。像小苗破土而出，本义指才长出的草木。

篆

刻 形声兼会意。从刂，亥声，本义为切割，后用于计时单位。亥，甲骨文中像割了头蹄的猪形，是"刻"的本字。

甲　金　篆

明 会意。从日，从月。日月皆明亮之物，所以用来表示明亮。

忙 形声。从忄，亡声。《说文》认为亡字从人，从乚。乚为隐蔽，意指人逃亡时躲在于隐蔽之处。

艮　甲　金　篆

很 会意兼形声。从彳（走路，道路），艮(gěn)声，指人在走路时回头瞪眼怒视。本义指不顺从、凶狠，引申义为程度高。艮，会意。甲骨文从人，像人回首瞪视状。

甲　金　篆

事 会意。在甲骨文中像一手持猎叉状。因古代狩猎是经常发生的事，故以此来泛指做事。

甲　金　篆　草

為/为 会意。甲古文中像一只手牵象鼻形。因古代用大象为人做事，故本义为做。简体字为是繁体字为的草书楷化字。

甲　金　篆

因 会意。从口，从大。像人仰卧于席上。意为凭借、依靠等。

甲　金　篆

同 象形。上像模子，下像模子制出的产品。指用同一个模子制造相同的东西。

忍　金　篆

認/认 形声。从言，忍声。忍，会意兼形声，从心，刃声。忍的滋味就像一把刀插在心上。刃 指事。从刀，一点指向刀刃处。简体认字部首由訁 简化为讠，声旁由人替代忍。

　　　　　　　　　　　　　　　　　　　　　　　　　　　　　Appendix

戠甲 金 篆

識/识 形声。从言，从戠(zhī)；戠也兼表声。戠，甲骨文像戈上挂有铃、环之类的饰物，本义为标志、记住。音，会义。表示口舌发出的声音。戈，象形。是一种长柄横刃的兵器。简体字识左边部首简化，右边声旁用只替代戠，属于近音替代。

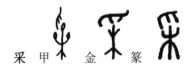

采甲 金 篆

菜 篆

菜 会意兼形声。本义为蔬菜。从艸，采声。采亦有采摘之意。采，会意。像以手采树上果实。

LESSON 4

甲 金 篆

週/周 会意。甲骨文像田地形，中间四点代表田里种的庄稼。本义为农田，引申为周围、环绕、一定循环的时段等。简体周字去掉辶。

金 篆

末 指事。从木，木上一横表示树梢所在的位置。

篆

打 会意。从手，从丁。用手钉钉子来表示敲打。

篆 求 甲

球 形声。从玉，求声，意为美玉或球形的物体。求，象形。像毛翻在外的皮裘。后求加衣字为裘。"求"引申为寻求、乞求等。

篆

看 会意。从手，从目。表示以手掌置于目上遮光向远望。

金　篆

電/电 会意。金文中从雨，从申，像雷雨时闪电划过长空状。简体字去掉上部的雨字。

甲　篆

視/视 会意兼形声字。甲骨文从示，从目，指用眼观看天象。示也兼表声。示 象形。甲骨文像用石块搭起来的祭台。视字右边简化。

昌

篆

唱 形声。从口，昌声。昌，会意。从日，从曰（说话）。本义指光明磊落的言词， 引申为美好、昌盛等。

歌 形声。从欠（人张口出气），哥声。本义为高声吟诵。

篆

跳 从足，兆声。兆，象形。古文像龟甲烧裂后出现的纹路，意为征兆。

甲　　金　篆

舞 象形。甲骨文中像一人双手持物起舞。

甲　　金　篆

聽/听 会意兼形声。甲骨文中从耳、从口，表示用耳听别人说话。后加悳 dé。悳，真诚。直，会意。甲骨文字形像用眼睛正对标杆以测量物体是否直正。聽字强调要认真用心领悟所闻之事。简体听字左边口字表意，右边斤字表声。

甲　　金　篆

音 会意。音与言同源，是由同一个甲骨文字演变来的。金文在口中加一横，表示发音时舌头的位置。

甲　　金　篆　草

樂/乐 象形。甲骨文从丝，从木。表示将丝弦绷于木上，意指琴瑟之类的乐器。简体字乐字是繁体字樂的草书楷化字。

對/对 会意。篆文左边一半是板子，右边从寸（手），本义为手持笏板回答，引申为对答，正确，面对等。简体对字左边以又替代。明代已有此字。

時/时 形声。从日，寺声。寺，形声。金文从又（手），从止。手之所止为持，本以为持有。简体字时是繁体字时的草书楷化字，右边以寸代替寺。

候 形声，篆文从人，矦声，本义是等候。矦，会意。从厂从矢（箭），厂像靶子，矢在靶上，本义为箭靶。

書/书 会意。甲骨文上是手持笔形，下为一器物，指手持笔在器物上书写。书是書字的草书楷化字。

影 形声兼会意。三撇意为饰纹、光影等。景（日光），有影子就有光，景还兼表声。景，形声。从日，从京（高）。表示太阳高照。京 指事。甲骨文、金文中像在高丘上建宫观之形，有高大、国都之意。

常 形声。篆文从巾，尚声。本义指裙子，与裳本为一字，后分开，常意为经常，常规，日常等。

去 会意。甲骨文从大（人），从口（洞穴出口），表示人离开洞穴。

外 会意。从夕，从卜。古人在早上占卜。晚上占卜，则不在常规之内了。

金　篆

客 会意兼形声。从宀，从各；各亦声。指人自外面进屋之意。各，会意。甲骨文、金文中从止（脚趾），从口（古人穴居洞口），本意指来到，引申为每个。

篆

昨 形声。从日，乍声。

金　篆

所 形声。从斤，户声，本义为伐木的声音。引申义为处所、助词等。斤 象形。上像斧头，下像斧柄。户，指单扇的门。一扇为户，两扇为门。

甲　金　篆

以 象形兼会意。金文字形像头朝下、快要降生的胎儿，旁边站着一人。本义指已成形的胎儿，引申为凭借、原因等。

篆

久 象形。篆文久字从人，背后一横像以燃着的艾草在人背后熏灸之形，是灸的初文。

篆　昔 甲　金　篆

錯/错 形声。从金，昔声，本义为用金涂饰。昔，会意。甲骨文下是日，上像洪水泛滥、遮天蔽日状，指古代大洪水时期。简体字错的部首由釒 简化为钅 。

篆

想 形声。从心，相声，本义为思考。相 会意。从目，从木，表示用眼睛观察树木。

篆　草

覺/觉 会意兼形声。篆文从见，學声， 表示睁大眼睛、聚精会神来学习领悟。本义为明白、醒悟。简体字觉是繁体字覺的草书楷化字，上半部的简化法与学字相同，下半部与见同。

甲　　　金　　　篆

得　会意。甲骨文从又（手）持贝（钱币），意指有所得。金文又加彳（街道），以示行有所获。

篆

意　会意。从心，从音；音亦声。用心音指心里的想法。

篆

思　会意。篆文从心，从囟。囟指人的脑门。古人以为大脑与心都有思考的功能，故以二者来表示思考，思想，思念等意。

篆

只　指事。从口，下有两道，像人口说话时气呼出状。本义是语气助词。

篆

睡　会意兼形声。从目从垂；垂亦声。本义为坐寐。

篆

算　会意。从竹，从具，表示计算时使用的竹制器具，即算盘。具，会意。甲骨文从双手，从鼎（餐具），指双手举鼎以供酒食。

找　形声。从扌，戈声，像用手找戈。

甲　　　篆

別/别　意。甲骨文从刀，从冎 (guǎ)，本义指以刀剔下骨头上肉。另，象形，与冎本为一字，甲骨文中像剔干净用来占卜的牛骨。简体字别的左下方写作力，与繁体字别稍有不同。

LESSON 5

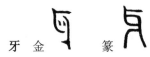

牙 金　篆

呀 从口，牙声。本义指张口状， 引申为叹词、象声词等。牙 象形。像口中牙齿上下相错形。

甲　　金　　篆

進/进 会意兼形声。从辶，隹声。甲骨文从止（脚趾）从隹（短尾鸟）。因隹趾只能前进不能后退，本义为向前进。简体字进用井替代隹，因井与进声音相近。

篆

快 会意兼形声。篆文从心，从夬（guài 钩弦射箭），夬亦声。本义指心情顺畅，痛快高兴，如射出之箭。夬，会意。甲骨文像手拉射箭时所用的钩弦器。

甲　　金　　篆　　草

来 象形。甲骨文中像一株有根杆叶穗的麦苗。本义为麦，后借用为来去的来，本义遂失。简体字来是繁体字來的草书楷化字。

甲　　金　　篆

介 会意。从八，从人。甲骨文字形从人，四短画表示由一片片皮革串成的甲衣，本义指人穿甲衣，引申为介于中间等。

甲　　篆　　草

紹/绍 会意兼形声。从糸，召声。本义为继续、继承，引申为介绍、引荐等。简体字部首纟 是由糸 的草书楷化而来。绍字的部首纟 简化。

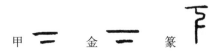

甲　　金　　篆

下 指事。古文为指示符号，表示一物在另一物之下。

興/兴 会意。甲骨文字形像四只手同力共举一幅模具。简体字兴是由繁体字興的草书楷化而来。

漂 形声。从水，票声，漂浮，冲洗，漂白之意。票，会意。篆文下部从火，本义是火焰腾起。

亮 会意。篆文从高，从儿（人），表示人在高处则明亮。

古文 (古文 refers to Ancient Inscriptions, a writing system mainly used in the Warring States Period (475-221 BC)

坐 会意。古文像两人在土地上面对面而坐。

哪 形声。从口，那声，用作疑问代词。

工 象形。像工匠用的曲尺。

作 会意兼形声。从人，从乍，乍亦声。

校 会意兼形声。从木，从交；交亦声。指用两木相交制作的刑具。交 象形。像两腿相交的正面人形。

喝 形声。从口，曷声，有呼喊，吸食液体等意。曷，形声。从曰（说话），从匃（乞求），表示喝止、疑问等。

篆

茶 形声。茶与荼本为一字，从艹，余声，本义为一种苦菜。唐代时将"荼"减去一笔而成为"茶"。

咖 象声词。加，会意。从力，从口，本义指以语言诬陷他人。

非 甲  篆

啡 译音用字。非，象形，甲骨文、金文像鸟展开双翅飞翔状。由于两翅相背，本义为违背，引申为不正确等。

卑 金 篆

啤 形声。从口，卑声。卑，会意。金文从又（手），从申（指酒器），表示以手托酒器伺奉人，意为卑贱。啤酒。德文的音译及意译。

甲  篆 酉 甲  金  篆

酒 会意兼形声。从氵，从酉；酉亦声。指从酒坛中舀酒。酉，象形。像酒坛子之形。后借为地支的第十位。

巴 篆

吧 象声词、语气词。巴，象形。篆文像嘴大能吞象的蛇形。本义为蛇，引申为依附、靠近、巴结等。

金  篆

要 会意。像一人双手叉腰形，是腰的本字。

篆

杯 形声。从木，不声，意为装饮料的器皿或指木做的杯子。

篆

起 形声。从走，己声。意为立起。走，象形兼会意。金文上像一人甩开双臂跑步状，下从止（脚），意指奔跑。己，象形。甲骨文像人腹之形。

給/给 形声。从糸，合声。本义为丰足，引申为供给、给与等。合，上像容器的盖子，下像容器本身。盖子盖在容器上，意指合拢。简体字给的部首简化。

水 象形。甲骨文中间像流水，旁似浪花或水的支流。

玩 从玉，元声，指供玩赏之物或玩耍。玉作为偏旁时写作王。元，指事。从一，从兀。本义为人头，引申为第一。

圖/图 会意。从囗，从啚（bǐ）。囗像一张纸，啚指城邑都鄙。将城邑绘在纸上，即是地图。图是由圖字的草书楷化而来，内为冬字。

舘/馆 会意兼形声。从食，官声，意指供人饮食住宿娱乐的地方。官，会意。从宀，从𠂤，本义为官府。简体字馆的部首简化。

瓶 形声。从瓦，并声，古代用来汲水的容器。并，会意。古文字中皆像二人并立。瓦，象形。像房上两片瓦相扣的形状。

聊 会意兼形声。从耳，卯声，意为依赖、闲谈等。卯，象形。甲骨文中像将一物从中间分开。本义为剖分，引申为榫眼等。

才 指事。甲骨文中一横画象征土地，表示种子已生根发芽、破土而出。本义为草木初生，引申为刚刚。

回 象形。甲骨文像水的漩涡。

LESSON 6

話/话 会意。从言，从舌，意指交谈、话语等。舌，象形。下部像口，上部像舌，表示舌头伸出口外。简体字话的部首简化。

喂 形声。从口，畏声，意为喂养或用于打招呼。畏，会意。甲骨文中像大头鬼持杖欲打人状，意为可畏。

就 会意。从京，从尤。"京"为建于高丘之上的宫殿。"尤"为突出。"就"本义指达到至高处，引申为趋向、就要、随即等。尤，象形。甲骨文从又（右手），一斜画表示手上的赘疣，引申为突出、特别。

位 会意。从人，从立，指人站立的位置，也用作量词。立 会意。甲骨文、金文从大（正面人形），从一（地），表示人站立于地上。

甲

午 象形。像舂米用的棒杵，是杵的初文，引申为抵触、违逆等。后借用为午时，相当于白天十一时至十三时。

間/间 会意。金文从門，从月，用門中可看见月光表示空隙之意。楷书门中改月为日。简体字间的部首简化。

題/题 会意兼形声。从页（头），从是，是亦声。本义为额头，引申为物体的前端、题目、书写有特殊意义的文字等。頁，象形。甲骨文中像一个头部极为突出的人形。本义为头，引申为书页的一张等。简体字题右部的页字简化。

開/开 会意。古文字形像双手拿掉门闩开门状。简体字开仅保留繁体字开门的那部分。

會/会 会意。甲骨文、金文字形下像容器，上像容器的盖子，中间像盛放的食物。盖上容器的盖子，表示会合，引申为开会等。简体字会是繁体字會的草书楷化字。

節/节 形声。从竹，即声。本义为竹节，引申为量词、节日等。即，会意。甲骨文、金文中左边像食器，右边像一人跪坐，准备进食。本义为即将就食。简体字节上部把竹字头改为草字头，下部保留即字的右部，十分近似節字的草体。

課/课 形声。从言，果声，意为考试，课时等。果 象形。像树上结出的果实。简体字课的部首简化。

級/级 形声。从糸，及声。本义为丝的优劣次第，引申为等级。及 会意。甲骨文、金文从又（右手），从人，像一只手从后抓住一个人状。本义为逮捕，引申为赶上、追上、到达。级字部首简化。

甲 　金 　篆

考 形声。从老，丂(kǎo)声。本义为老，引申为考试。甲骨文、金文老、考是同字，都像老人长发弓背，扶着拐杖形。

篆

試/试 形声。从言，式声，意指任用、尝试、考试等。式，形声。从工，弋声，本义为建筑有规则法度。简体字试的部首简化。

甲 　金 　篆

後/后 会意。从彳（半条街），从幺（绳），从夂（suī 脚）。表示足被绳系住，走在后面。简体字用后（皇后的后）替代後，属同音替代字。

金 　篆

空 形声。从穴，工声，本义为窟窿。穴，象形。像洞穴形。

甲 　金 　篆

方 象形。像铲土的工具。甲骨文上短横像手握的横柄，中间一长横是脚踩的地方，下为分叉的锸。本义为土锸，引申义正方形、方面、正、才等。

金 　篆 　更甲 　金 　篆

便 会意。篆文从人、从更。人有不便时，更改方能使之安妥方便。更，会意兼形声。甲骨文字形像手持铲翻饼状，引申为更改。

金 　篆

到 形声。篆文从至，刀声。至，象形，像箭头射中地面或箭靶状。

篆 　辛甲 　金 　篆

辦/办 形声。从力，辡 (biàn 剖分、争辩) 声。辛，象形。像在犯人脸上刺字的刑具。简体字办用一撇一点代替两个辛字，旧时已见。

公 会意。篆文从八（分），从厶（sī 私）。甲骨文从八，从口（指容器口），表示平均分配容器中的东西。

室 会意兼形声。从宀，从至；至亦声。指人歇息居住的地方。

甲  金  篆

行 象形。甲骨文、金文像四通八达的道路。本义指十字路，引申为行走、走得通、可以等。

篆

等 会意。从竹，从寺。寺，会意兼形声。金文从又（手），从止。手之所止为持，本以为持有、操持，是持的本字。后借用为寺庙的寺。

气 甲 金  篆 米 甲  金  篆

氣/气 会意。甲骨文、金文为三横，像天上云气流动状。后人在气下加米字以示人体内之气或能量。简体字气去掉了氣下面的米字，从而恢复了古本字的原貌。

幫/帮 从帛，封声。本义为鞋帮，引申为辅助等意。封，会意。甲骨文、金文像在土堆上植树，以此来划定边界。帛，从巾，从白；白亦声。本义指未经染色的素白丝织物，引申为丝织品的总称。巾 象形。像垂下的佩巾。繁体字幫的另一写法是幇。简体字帮去掉了幫字中间的白字。

篆  草

練/练 形声。从糸，柬声。本义指把生丝煮得柔软洁白，引申为反复练习。柬，从束（一捆东西），从八（分别），意指打开一捆东西从中挑选，引申为信札书简。简体字练字左边的部首由糸 简化为纟，右边一半是柬字的草书楷化字。

甲  篆

習/习 会意。甲骨文、金文从羽，从日，表示小鸟在阳光中展翅学习飞翔。简体字习仅保留了繁体字習的上半部分。

兑 甲　　金　　篆

說/说 会意。从言，从兑(duì)。本义为言语中有喜悦之情，引申为言辞、陈述、劝说等。兑，从人，从口，从八（分开）。人笑则口开，本义为喜悦。说字部首简化。

啊 形声。从口，阿声。用作叹词。阿，形声。金文从阜（脚坑；土山），可声，本意指为山的弯曲处。

但 形声。从人，旦声。本义为袒露，是袒的古字，今用为副词或连词。旦，指事。一代表地平线，表示太阳刚从地平线上升起。

篆

知 会意。从矢（箭），从口，表示开口讲话的速度如射箭一般快。本义为言词敏捷，引申为了解知道等。

古　　金　　篆

道 会意。从辶，从首，表示一人头在前面引导前行，意为指明道路或道路。首，象形。甲骨文、金文像有发的人头。

隼 甲　　金　　篆

準 篆

準/准 形声。从氵，隼(sǔn)声。本义为水準，準则。隼，会意。金文从佳，从人。像人训猎鹰狩猎，本义为猎鹰。简体字准是準字的俗体字，汉代已有。

甲　　金　　篆

備/备 会意。甲骨文、金文皆像箭在箭匣中，意指准备，防备，预备，装备等。俻是备字的异体字，简体字备去掉了俻字的部首亻。

甲　　　　　篆

面 象形。甲骨文像是脸形。外似面部轮廓，中是一夸大了的眼睛，因眼睛为脸部最为醒目、最为传神之处。本义为面孔，引申为面向、方面、表面、脸面、等。

LESSON 7

篆　　　艮甲　　　　金　　　　篆

跟 形声。从足，艮声。本义为脚后跟，引申为跟随，还可作连词。

篆

助 形声兼会意。从力，从且（祭祀祖先之灵所用的牌位）；且亦声。指靠祖先之灵以力相助。

甲　　　　金　　　　篆

復/复 形声。从彳，复声，意为往返。复，会意。甲骨文上部像有两个出口的洞穴，下部从止（脚），表示人出入洞穴，引申为重复。复是復字的古本字，后人加偏旁彳，简体字恢复古本字的原貌。

篆　　　草　　　　舄金　　　　篆

寫/写 形声。从宀，舄(xì)声。本义为移置，引申为倾吐、摹画、书写等。舄，象形。金文像一只张开大嘴喳喳叫的喜鹊，本义为喜鹊。 简体字写是繁体字寫的草书楷化字，但草书写字上面多带一点。

慢　　　曼甲　　　　金　　　　篆

慢 形声。从心，曼声，本义为惰怠。曼，会意。甲骨文、金文像看到美妙的人或事时，以两手把眼睛撑得大大的，目不转睛地看。本义为张目，引申为美好、妩媚之意。

甲　　　　金　　　篆

教 会意兼形声。甲骨文从攴 pū（手持棍状），从子，从爻 yáo（算筹相交之形）。表示手持棍监督教导孩子学习计算。

篆

筆/笔 会意。从聿（手持笔形），从竹，指手握竹子做的笔杆写字。简体笔字保留上边竹字头，因毛笔笔端用兽毛之故，下边改用毛字。属新创的会意字。

金　　篆　　堇　甲

難/难 形声。金文从佳，堇(jǐn)声，本义指一种鸟，因从"堇"（焚烧人牲祭天求雨）而借用来表示艰难困苦。堇，甲骨文像用火焚烧捆绑的人牲，意指以人牲祭祀求雨，引申为干旱、灾难等。简体字难左边用又替代，属符号替代字。明清已见此字。

篆

裏/裡/里 形声。从衣，里声。本义指衣服的里层，引申为内部、里面。里，会意。从田，从土。有田有土，表示人所居住的地方与长度单位，如故里、邻里、万里等。简体字里的字意扩充，包含了繁体字裏/裡的所有意思。

第 从竹，从弟；弟也兼表声。本义为竹的层次，引申为次第、顺序。

篆

預/预 会意兼形声。篆文从页（人头），从予（此处有前伸意），表示把头伸到前面，引申为预先、参预等。予，象形。篆文像以手推物给他人状，本义为给予。简体字预右边的页是由繁体字頁的草书楷化而来。

篆

語/语 形声。从言，吾声，意为谈论、谈话等。吾，金文从口，五声，用作第一人称。简体字语的部首简化。

金　　篆

法 会意。金文从人，从口，从水，从廌（zhì 公牛）。指人赶着牛羊，逐水草而居。逐水草而居是游牧民族的规矩，世界上不少古老的城市也都沿河而建，因此引申为规律、法律等。篆文简化，从水，从去。

容 会意。从宀，从谷，意指房屋、山谷都有容纳人或物的空间。谷，象形。甲骨文中像水从山谷中流出。

易 会意。甲骨文像把水从一个容器中倒入另一容器中。本义为给予，引申为改变、容易等。

懂 从忄，董声。董，形声。篆文从艹，童声。童，金文像身背重物、头上有刑具的人，指男子有罪受刑罚而变成奴隶，引申为儿童。

詞/词 会意。从司，从言。司有主管义，表示人对语言的驾驭掌握。司，会意。甲骨文、金文像把手遮在嘴上发号施令。简体字词的部首简化。

漢/汉 形声。篆文从水，难声。本义为水名，即汉水。又有汉朝、汉族、汉语等词。简体字汉的简化方法与难（難）字相同，都是以又来替代堇。明清已见此字。

平 一说像天平形，义为公平、不向一方倾斜。一说平字似水面浮萍。

早 会意。篆文从日，从甲（原为测量日光的仪器），表示太阳升到甲之上，意为早晨。

夜 形声。从夕，亦声。亦，甲骨文从大（人的正面），旁边两点表示人的腋窝。亦本意是腋窝。

功 会意兼形声。从力，从工；工亦声。力，尽力；工，工作。尽力工作必有功劳功绩。

真 会意。甲骨文从鼎，从人，指人到鼎边拿美食吃。本义为美食，引申为真实等。

始 会意兼形声。从女，从台（胎儿）；台也兼表声。本义为刚开始受孕怀胎，引申泛指开始。 台，甲骨文像头朝下的胎儿。

唸/念 形声。从口，念声，意指诵读。念，形声。从心，今声，意为想念、想法、学习等。简体字念也包含了繁体字唸的诵读之意。

錄/录 形声。从金，录声，记载、抄写、录用之意。录，会意。金文字形像木架上吊了一个布袋，滤出里面的水。录的本义为滤。繁体字錄的另一写法是録，简体字录去掉錄的金字旁。

帥/帅 形声。甲骨文字形右似佩巾，左为伸出的双手，像用两手展开佩巾状。本义为佩巾，借用为军中统帅，引申为英俊，有风度等。简体字帅是繁体字帥的草书楷化字，简化方法与师(師)字相同。

枝 形声。从木，支声。本义为树枝，引申为一些狭长条形物体的量词。支， 古字像手持折断的竹枝，本义为枝条，引申为分支、支撑、支援等。

紙/纸 形声。从糸 ，氏声。本义为纸张。古时未造纸之前写文于丝竹上，固有糸 做部首。氏，古文像根在地下形，本义为根本，根柢，引申为古代贵族的分支、传说中的人物、已婚妇女等。

酷 形声。从酉，告声。本义为酒味浓烈，引申义有酷烈残暴与表程度很深的意思。因音与英文 cool 相似，所以用来直译 cool 在俚语中表达时兴并有吸引力的意思。告在甲骨文从口，从牛。本义为牛叫，引申为上报、告诉、佈告等。

LESSON 8

扁　篆　

篇 形声。篆文从竹，扁声，意为典籍、著作、文章，也可用做文章的量词。扁，会意。篆文从户，从册。本义为匾，引申为平薄物体等。

記/记 形声。从言，己声，意为记录、记载、记忆。简体字记的部首简化。

甲　　篆

牀/床 牀，从爿（pán），从木，泛指卧具。爿，象形，像床形。牀亦写作床。床，从广，从木。床是牀的异体字，两者通用，但旧时多用牀。简体字为床。

篆

洗 形声兼会意。从水，从先（人脚向前伸），本以为洗脚。先也兼表声。

篆

澡 形声。从水，喿（zào）声。喿，会意。金文从三口，从木，指群鸟在树上鸣叫。引申为嘈杂。

邊/边 会意兼形声。从辶，臱（biān）声。臱，会意。从自，从旁，金文像鼻的两翼。自，象形。像鼻形，本义为鼻子后引申为自己。简体字边用力替代臱，属符号替代字。元明时已有边字。

發/发 形声。从弓，从癶（bō 两只脚相并），从殳（投掷），本义为射箭。简体字发是繁体字發的草书楷化字。

腦/脑 象形。左为肉月旁，右部像囟门与头发。简体字脑的右边简化，但保留了繁体字腦的轮廓。旧时已有此字。

餐 形声。从食，奴声，意为吞咽、吃饭。

廳/厅 会意兼形声。从广（yǎn 敞屋，）聽声。聽，会意。甲骨文从耳，从口，指用耳听别人说话。后加悳(dé)。悳，从直，从心，表示心地正直，引申为真诚、认真。聽字表明人在听时要用心用耳，全神贯注。简体字厅将广改为厂，聽改为丁，因聽丁声音近似。古时已有此字。

報/报 会意。金文中像一只手从后按住一个像带手铐跪着的人，表示行将处决犯人。报的本义是判决犯人。因这类事情要通报，引申为报告。简体字报是繁体字报的草书楷化字，左边以扌替换幸字。

宿 会意。甲骨文从宀，从人，从丙 (tiàn 席)，像人在屋里的席子上休息。

舍 象形。舍字上部亼像房顶，中间是支撑房屋的柱子，下面的口代表墙。

甲  金 正 篆 正

正 会意。从一，从止（足）。甲骨文、金文中像人足抵达一城邑，与"征"本为同一字。引申为端正、正面、正义等。

篆 前

前 会意。金文从止（足），从舟，表示人乘船而行。

甲 告 金 告 篆 告

告 会意。甲骨文从口，从牛。本义为牛叫，引申为上报、告诉、布告等。

篆 訴

訴/诉 形声。从言，斥声，告诉、控诉之意。斥，斤字加一点，意为指责、责备。简体字诉的部首简化。

甲 己 金 己 篆 己

己 象形。甲骨文、金文、篆文均像头朝下要出生的胎儿形，引申为已经。

金 巠 篆 巠 草 经

經/经 会意兼形声。从糸，从巠（像绷在织布机上的三根经线；一说像水流与地面）；巠也兼表声。经的本意是织物的纵线，引申为经过、经历。简体字经是繁体字經的草书楷化字。

甲 封 金 封 篆 封

封 会意。甲骨文、金文中像用手在土地上植树，用种树木来划定疆界。引申为封闭，书信的量词等。

金 信 篆 信

信 会意。从人，从言，本义指人要言而有信，引申为书信。

最 会意。篆文从冃 （帽子、头盔），从取（以手割下战俘耳朵为立军功的证据）。本义指以士兵 歼敌的数目来判断谁立下头等战功，引申为总计、极度等。

近 形声。从辶，斤声。斤，象形。甲骨文中上像斧头，下像斧柄。

除 会意兼形声。篆文从阜（土山），从余；余亦声。本义为阶梯，引申为除去等。余，形声。甲 骨文、金文上像屋顶，下像支撑的木头。本义为茅屋，引申为剩下、多出来等。

專/专 形声。从寸，叀声，甲骨文像用一手转动纺锤形。本义为纺锤，后为专一，专心等。简体 字专是繁体字專的草书楷化字。

業/业 象形。金文中像悬挂钟鼓乐器带齿的木架，引申为事业、家业、学业等。简体字业仅取繁 体字業的上半部。

慣/惯 从忄，贯声，意为习惯。贯，会意兼形声。从毌（贯穿），从贝，表示把钱币穿成一串。 简体字惯中的贝简化。

清 形声。篆文从水，青声，本义指水清澈透明。

楚 形声。从林，疋(shū)声。甲骨文、金文从足，从林。本义为灌木，也叫荆，引申为杖刑、整 齐等。

甲　金　篆

步 会意。古文皆从二止，像一前一后的向前迈步行走的两只脚。

篆

希 会意。篆文从爻（篱笆交织状），从巾，指织得像篱笆一样稀疏的布或网，是"稀"的本字，引申为企求、希望。

金　篆

望 会意。金文像人睁大眼睛望月状。后加王字以表声。

甲　篆

能 象形。甲骨文像有头、背、尾、掌的熊形。本义为熊，因熊凶猛力大，后被借为能字。

甲　金　篆

用 象形。甲骨文、金文均像木桶形状。因古人日常生活中常使用木桶，引申为使用。

篆　夭　甲　金　篆

笑 会意。从竹，从夭（弯曲）。李阳冰勘定《说文》中解释说"竹得风，其体夭曲，如人之笑。"夭，像人两手摇摆起舞状。有娇媚、艳丽、茂盛、夭折等意。

甲　金　篆

祝 会意。从示/礻（用石块搭起的祭台），从人，从口。甲骨文中像人跪在祭台边向神灵或祖先祈祷。

篆

累 会意兼形声。篆文从糸，畾声，有缠绕、捆绑、牵连、拖累、劳累等意。正体字上为田，下为糸(束丝)，可想为男耕女织都是使人劳累之事.

網/网 象形。甲骨文、金文、篆文皆像一张网形。楷书加糸 字旁表意,加亡字表声。简体字网恢复了古体字的本来形状。

LESSON 9

買/买 会意。甲骨文、金文从网,从贝,像用网捞贝。古时以贝壳做为货币换取物品,意为购买。简体字买是繁体字買的草书楷化字。

東/东 会意。从木,从日,以示太阳刚从东方升起,以此来表示东边。简体字东是繁体字東的草书楷化字。

西 会意。甲骨文、金文像鸟巢形,篆字则进一步在鸟巢上添一只鸟。鸟类多半在日落时回巢,而日在西边落下,故引申为西。造字方法与东相同。

售 会意。从口,佳声,指像鸟鸣一样的叫卖声。

貨/货 会意兼形声。从化(变化),从贝(古时钱币);化亦声。指用钱购买货物。 化,会意。甲骨文中像一正立人形,一倒立人形,意为变化。简体字货中的贝是繁体字貝的草书楷化字。

員/员 指事。甲骨文、金文中贝像鼎形,口是鼎口。本义指圆形,引申为人的数额以及从事某种职业的人。简体字员中的贝字简化。

衣 象形。像衣领、衣袖、衣襟形。

服 会意。甲骨文从凡（盘），从跪人，从手，表示人跪着端盘服侍。衣服为其引申义。

件 会意。篆文从人，从牛，指人把牛分解成部分。本义为分解、分割，引申为量词。牛，象形。像带角的牛头正面。

襯/衬 形声。从衤，親声。意指内衣、衬里。親，形声。从見，亲声。本义为常见，引申为亲近。简体字衬右边以寸代替親，因寸与衬声音相近。

衫 形声。篆文从衣，三声，意为单衣。

顏/颜 形声。篆文从页，彦声。意指额头、面容、色彩等。页像人头形。彦，会意兼形声。金文从文，从弓，指文武双全、德才兼备的人。简体字颜中的页字简化。

色 会意。篆文上是站立之人，下为下跪之人，前者训斥后者。本义为怒色，引申为颜色、姿色、脸色、景色等。

黄/黄 甲骨文、金文像佩璜形。上为系带，中为佩璜，下为垂穗，本义为佩玉。因这种佩玉多为黄色，引申为黄颜色。黄是黄的异体字，后也用为黄的简体字。

紅/红 形声。从糸，工声。本义为粉红色的丝绸，后泛指红色。颜色常用丝帛表示，故从糸 。简体字红的偏旁纟 是由繁体糸 简化而来。

穿 会意。从穴，从牙，表示用牙咬穿或掘洞。本义为穿透，引申为穿戴。

條/条 形声。从木，攸(yōu)声。本义为小树枝，引申为量词。简体字条仅采用繁体字條的右边。元明已有此字。

褲/裤 形声。从衣，库声。库，会意。从车，从广。广指大棚，本义指放兵车的大棚，引申为仓库。简体字库下部的车是繁体字車的草书楷化字。

宜 会意。从宀，从且（祖宗的牌位）。把祖宗的牌位放在室内，本义为祭祀，引申为合适、应当。

付 会意。篆文从寸（手），从人，意指用手把物交与他人。

錢/钱 形声。从金，戋声。戋，会意。从二戈，本义为残杀，是残的古字。简体字钱左边部首由金 简化为钅， 右边戋简化为戋。

共 会意。金文像用双手捧一块碧玉形。本义为供奉，共给，引申义有拱手、环绕、合计、共同等。

少 象形。少是由小字分化而来，古时小、少常通用。小在甲骨文、金文中为三点，像是细小的沙粒。少为四点。

塊/块 形声。从土，鬼声。本义为土块，引申为量词。鬼，象形。在甲骨文、金文中均像大头鬼。简体字块用夬 (guài, archery) 替代鬼，因夬与块声音相似。

毛 象形。金文像皮上丛生的毛。

分 会意。上从八，下从刀，指用刀将一物体切为两半。八的本义是分，后加刀以强化此意。

百 会意。一说甲骨文字形上像一把尺子，下像白米粒，表示摆下一尺长的米粒，引申为一百。白，象形。像一粒白米。

雙/双 会意。从又（右手），从双隹（短尾鸟），表示一只手抓两只鸟。简体字双把繁体字雙该为两个又字，意为双手，属会意词。宋元时期已见双字。

鞋 从革，从双土。革，本义为剥去动物的皮毛，引申为皮革。

換/换 形声。从手，奐声，意为对换、变换等。奐，会意。篆文下有双手，上有人站在高大的洞穴之上，本义指用手建造高大洞穴以为居所，引申为盛大。简体字换是繁体字换的草书楷化字，字右部稍有改动。

黑 会意。金文字形像被烟熏火烤，大汗淋漓、满面污垢的人。

雖/虽 形声。从虫，唯声。本义指一种似蜥蜴的爬虫，今用作连词，表示转折。唯，甲骨文从口，从隹（短尾鸟），意指恭敬的应答。简体字虽仅取繁体字雖的右部，旧时已有此字。

然 会意兼形声。金文从火，从肰（狗肉）；肰亦声。意指用火烤狗肉。犬，象形。甲骨文中像一条大狗形，本义为大狗。

合 会意。下像盒子，上像盒盖，合在一起表示合拢。

適/适 形声。从辶，商声。本义指前往、来到，引申为舒适、适合、适宜等。商，甲骨文、金文、篆文中从口，从帝，意为高声。简体字适以舌代替商，因舌与適声音相似，属同音替代字。

![商]

商 象形。甲骨文、金文像古代盛酒的容器。酒器有量度，故引申为估量、商量。做生意重在双方商议，因此又引申为经商、做买卖。

![店]

店 形声。篆文从土，占声。本义为置放物品的土台子。后改土字旁为广（敞屋），有商店、旅店等意。店字展示了由在土台上售货到在大房内售货的演变过程。

如 会意。从女，从口。按照传统的价值观念，女人应该柔顺，听从男人的话。《仪礼 丧服 子夏传》道"未嫁从父，既嫁从夫，夫死从子"。如本义为顺从、遵照。引申为如同、例如、假如等。

甲　金　篆

果 象形。像树上结出的果实。甲骨文树上有三个果子，金文变成一个大果子。在楷书中方形化则变成了田字。

甲　金　篆　草

長/长 象形。古字像一长发挂杖之老人。本义为发长，引申义有长度、长久、长处、擅长等。

篆

短 形声。从矢，豆声。意为不长。矢即是箭，古人可用矢量长度，故短从矢部。豆，象形。像一种古代食器。豆本义为食器，后借用为豆类植物。

篆

種/种 形声。从禾，重声。本义指种植，引申为种子、种族、种类等。重，象形。像人身负重物。简体字种把种字的声旁重用中替代。

篆

挺 形声。从扌，廷声。本义为拔出，引申为挺立、挺拔、笔挺、突出、相当等。
廷，象形。金文像一人立于宫廷台阶前，本义为朝廷。

甲　金　篆

它 象形。古字像一头部突出、身体弯曲的蛇形。本义为蛇，后借为别的、另外等意。近代用它来指代事物、动物。而蛇的意思则由它字左边加部首虫来表示。

篆

刷 形声。左半边为声，右从刂。本义为用刀刮，引申为用刷子清洗，梳理、涂抹、划过、刷子等。

卡 会意。无古字。由上下二字合并而成，意指不上不下，卡在中间。也用作关卡，卡子等。因声音近似，还用来音译一些英文词汇，如卡片(card)，卡路里(calorie)，卡通 (cartoon) 等。

收 形声。篆文从攴(pō 手持杖击打)，丩声。本义为逮捕，收监，引申为收容、收集、收到、收复、收获等。部首攵与攴意思相同。

LESSON 10

比 会意。古文的比字像一前一后靠在一起的两个人。本义为并列，引申为靠近、亲近、比较等。

雨 象形。像天上落下的雨滴。

更 会意兼形声。甲骨文从攴（手持铲）从丙（饼铛），意指持铲翻饼。引申为更改、更加等。

而 象形。甲骨文像下巴上几缕下垂的胡须，本义为胡须。

且 象形。甲骨文、金文均像用来祭祀祖先的牌位。

暖 形声。篆文从火，爰声，本义为暖和。爰，会意。甲骨文上方像一只手持物，让下方的另一只手（又）抓住，本义为援助。

約/约 形声。从糸，勺声。本义为捆缚，引申为约束、预先约定等。勺，象形，像勺瓢形。简体字约的部首简化。

園/园 形声。从囗，袁声。袁，会意。篆文上像系带，中为玉佩，下乃衣服，意指胸前挂玉。本义为环玉，引申为环绕、长袍等。简体字园囗中以元代替袁，属同音替代字。元明已有此字。

葉/叶 象形。甲骨文中像长着三片树叶的树枝。楷书加草字头。叶字本读作 xié，是协的异体字，现用来作为葉的简体字，属近音替代。

像 形声。从人，象声，意指肖像、相像、好像等。象，象形。甲骨文简要勾画出大象的轮廓。

海 形声。金文从水，每声。每，会意。甲骨文、金文均像妇女头戴装饰物，表示女子之美，后借用为每天的每。

糟 形声。从米，曹声，意为酒渣、酒糟。米，象形。像散落的米粒。曹，会意。甲骨文从两个东，从曰，像门口挂着两个灯笼。本义为双、偶。

糕 形声。从食，羔声，意指糕饼。羔，甲骨文、金文上从羊，下从火，表示烤小羊。本义为小羊羔。

又 象形。甲骨文像右手形。

剛/刚 会意兼形声。甲骨文以刀断网来表示物体坚硬，冈也兼表声。冈，形声兼会意。篆文从山从网，指山梁如网状，意为山脊、山岭、山坡等。繁体字冈的简体字为冈。简体字刚字左边的冈简化，右边不变。

出 会意。甲骨文中本字上部从止，下部像洞穴，表示人从穴居走出。

熱/热 形声。从火，埶声。埶，会意。甲骨文中像一人手持树苗栽种状，本义为种植。简体字热是繁体字热的草书楷化字，左上方以才代替。

舒 会意兼形声。从舍，从予；予亦声。舍和予都有给与、放开之意，故舒本义为伸展，缓解。舍，象形。像房舍形，引申为施与，放弃等。予，像以手把物推给他人。

夏 象形。金文中像人形，有头（页）、身、手、足，像个四肢发达、高大强壮的人。一说像夏天天热，人的手足都露在外面。

涼/凉 形声。从水，京声。京，象形。甲骨文、金文字形像在高丘上建造的宫殿，引申为京城。凉过去为涼的俗写字，现用作涼的简体字。冫的意思是冰，例如用在冰、冷等字中。

春 会意兼形声。甲骨文从日，从艹，从屯（tún 植物发芽）；屯亦声。春字是春天阳光普照，草木萌发，生机勃勃的写照。

冬 会意。上部为古文终字，下部两点水代表冰，意指冬天是年终天寒结冰的日子。

冷 从冫，令声。令，甲骨文上像屋顶，下像一跪坐人形，指人于室内发号施令。

閲/闷 会意兼形声。从心，从門（表示关闭），意指人关在屋内，心中憋闷。門也兼表声。简体字闷的部首简化。

次 象形。从二，从欠（张口打呵欠），像人连连打呵欠状。引申为前后顺序以及动作的次数。

秋 会意。从禾，从火。秋天谷物成熟颜色变深，高粱变红，故加义符火。禾，象形。甲骨文中像禾苗形。

臺/台 会意。篆字整体像是高台：上部像高台上的建筑，中间是高字的省略，下部为至（到达），意指人可到高台上眺望四方。早在金元时期台已在作为臺字的简化字而使用。

北 会意。甲骨文中像二人背对背站着，本义为违背，引申为脊背。后来加肉月旁作"背"，表示脊背之义，而"北"则借用为方位名词。

灣/湾 会意兼形声。从水，从彎（弯曲）；彎亦声。意为水流弯曲之处、港湾、海湾等。彎，形声。从弓，䜌声。本义为拉开弓，引申为弯曲。简体字湾是繁体字灣的草书楷化字。

篆 郵

郵/邮 会意。从阝（阝 指邑，即居住区域），从垂（义为边陲）。邮本义指古代供信差食宿的驿站。引申义为邮递、邮差等。

金 城　篆 城

城 形声。从土，成声。本义指城墙。古代城市皆有墙，因而引申为城市。成，形声。从戊（古代一种斧型兵器），丁声，本义为休兵言和结盟，引申成功，完成、成为、成全、成就等。

甲 市　金 市　篆 市

市 会意兼形声。甲骨文从之（去，前往），从冂（jiǒng，划出的集市范围），之亦表声。本义指集市，市场。因有城即有市场，引申为城市。

古 特　篆 特

特 形声。从牛，寺声。本义指公牛。因牛角突出醒目，引申为独特、特别、特点、特色等。

LESSON 11

金 寒　篆 寒

寒 会意。金文、篆文中像人躲在屋内草中取暖，下面两横代表冰，表示屋内极为寒冷。

叚 金 叚　篆 叚

假 形声。从人，叚声，意为假期。叚，会意。金文左边是山崖，右边是两只手，意指用双手攀崖。叚本义为凭借、借助。

篆 飛

飛/飞 象形。篆文中上像鸟头，下像鸟身与展开的双翅，意为飞翔。简体字飞仅沿用了繁体字飛的一部分，但仍像一只飞鸟的轮廓。

機/机 形声。从木，幾声，指机器、机会、重要事务等。简体字机的右部以几替代繁体的幾，属同音替代。

票 会意。篆文中下部从火，上部意指升高，本义指火焰腾起。

場/场 形声。从土，易声。古代祭神用的平地，引申为场地、处所等。易，会意。从日，从勿（像阳光穿过云层射出状），意指日出。简体字场是由繁体字場的草书楷化而来。

汽 会意兼形声。从水，从气；气亦声。意为水蒸气、气体。气，象形。甲骨文像云气升腾浮动状。

車/车 象形。篆文像简化了的车形，只有车架、一个轮子与轴。简体字车是繁体字車的草书楷化字。

或 会意。甲骨文从戈，从口（口像城的围墙），表示以武器（戈）保卫城池。金文、篆文下部加一横以示国土疆界。本义为邦国，假借义为或者。

者 会意。甲骨文中上像架起的木架与水蒸汽，下从火。本义为烧、煮，后常用在形容词、动词后以表示某类人或事物。

地 形声。从土，也声。本义指土地，引申为地区、领域等。

鐵/铁 形声。从金，**戜**（zhì）声，意为铁制的用具。简体字铁左边部首简化，右边以失（shī）代替戜（zhì），属近音替代。元明时已见简化了的铁字。

走 会意。金文上像人摆动双臂，下从止（脚），表示人用脚快步前行。

站 形声。从立，占声。立，会意。甲骨文、金文从大（正面人形），从一(指地面)，表示人站在地上。占，会意。上从卜（龟甲烧裂后之兆纹），下从口，意指观察兆纹解说凶吉。

綠/绿 形声。从糸，录声，本义为绿色。绿是綠的异体字，部首糸 简化为纟 后变为简体字。

线/线 形声。从糸，泉声。泉，象形。甲骨文像水从泉眼流出。綫是线的异体字。简体字线是将繁体字綫左边的部首糸 简化为纟，右边戋简化为戈。参见 L.9 钱(錢)字的简化法。

藍/蓝 形声。从艹，监声。本义指蓼蓝，叶子可用来提炼蓝色染料。监，象形。甲骨文、金文中本字像人睁大眼用水盆照自己的容颜。简体字蓝是繁体字蓝的草书楷化字，将臣简化为两竖。

麻 会意。篆文从广（敞屋），从林（pài 治麻），表示人在屋下劈麻晾麻。麻是大麻、亚麻、黄麻等植物的统称。

煩/烦 会意。从頁（人头），从火，表示脑袋发热，烦躁不安。简体字烦右边的页由繁体字頁简化而来。

篆

租 形声，从禾，且(jū)声。田赋、出租、租用之意。

甲 　 金

送 会意。从辶，从关。"送"字在甲骨文、金文中左像船形，右像双手持篙，本意指以船运送。

甲 　 金 　 篆 　 草

過/过 形声。从辶，呙声。呙，形声。从口，从冎（残缺）；冎亦声。呙本义指歪嘴。简体字过用寸代替呙，是由繁体字過的草书楷化而来。

篆

讓/让 形声。从言，襄声，本义为责备。襄，从衣，其中两口表示哭声，意指办完丧事脱去丧服去耕地。襄本义为解衣耕地，借用为升高、辅助等。简体字让用上代替襄，属于近音替代字。

甲 　 金 　 篆

花 形声。从艹，化声。化，会意。甲骨文像两人一正一倒形，意指变化。

甲 　 金 　 篆

每 会意。甲骨文、金文像妇女头上戴有装饰物。本义表示女子之美，后借用为每天的每。

甲 　 金 　 篆

速 形声。从辶，束声，本义指迅速。束，会意。金文从口从木，像袋子的两端被捆扎起来。本义为束缚。

金 　 篆

路 形声。从足，从各（到来），各亦声。意指道路。

篆　　草

紧/緊 会意。上部左为竖着的眼睛，右是手，下部从丝（省为纟），本义指眼睛盯着，用手将丝弦调紧。　简体字紧是繁体字緊的草书楷化字。如同本课的蓝字，将臣简化为两竖。

甲　　　　金　　　　篆

自 象形。甲骨文像鼻形。本义为鼻子，后引申为自己，而鼻子则写作"鼻"。

甲　　　　金　　　　篆

己 象形。古文字中像人腹形，用作人称代词、自己、本身等。注意己（jǐ）和已（yǐ）的区别。(已　yǐ　象形。甲骨文、金文、篆文中本字像头朝下的胎儿，引申为已经)。

甲　　　　金　　　　篆

新 会意兼形声。从木，从斤(斧)，辛声。本义为用斧头砍柴，是薪的本字，后用作新旧的新。辛，象形。甲骨文中像凿子一类的刑具，用来在犯人脸上刺字。

CHARACTER INDEX

(by Lesson)

KEY	
*	**Bound Form** (a character that is "bound together" with another character—it appears in combination with another character, not by itself)
MW	**Measure Word**
P	**Particle**
QP	**Question Particle**

Radicals		
人（亻）	rén	man; person; humankind
刀（刂）	dāo	knife
力	lì	physical strength; power
又	yòu	right hand; again
口	kǒu	mouth
囗	wéi	enclose
土	tǔ	earth; soil
夕	xī	sunset; evening
大	dà	big; great
女	nǚ	female; woman
子	zǐ	son; child
寸	cùn	inch
小	xiǎo	little; small
工	gōng	tool; work; labor
幺	yāo	tiny; the youngest
弓	gōng	bow
心（忄）	xīn	heart
戈	gē	dagger-ax
手（扌）	shǒu	hand
日	rì	sun
月	yuè	moon; month
木	mù	tree; wood
水（氵）	shuǐ	water
火（灬）	huǒ	fire
田	tián	(a surname); farmland; field
目	mù	eye
示（礻）	shì	show

糸/纟	mì	silk
耳	ěr	ear
衣（衤）	yī	clothing
言/讠	yán	speak; speech
貝/贝	bèi	cowry shell
走	zǒu	walk
足	zú	foot
金	jīn	(a surname); gold; metal
門/门	mén	door; gate
隹	zhuī	short-tailed bird
雨	yǔ	rain
食	shí	eat
馬/马	mǎ	horse

Numerals		
一	yī	one
二	èr	two
三	sān	three
四	sì	four
五	wǔ	five
六	liù	six
七	qī	seven
八	bā	eight
九	jiǔ	nine
十	shí	ten

Lesson 1		
先	xiān	first; before; earlier

生	shēng	be born; grow		這/这	zhè/zhèi	this
你	nǐ	you		爸	bà	dad
好	hǎo/hào	good; fine; OK; like; be fond of		媽/妈	mā	mom
				個/个	gè	MW
小	xiǎo	little; small		男	nán	male
姐	jiě	elder sister		孩	hái	child
王	wáng	king; (a surname)		子	zǐ	son
李	lǐ	plum; (a surname)		誰/谁	shéi	who
請/请	qǐng	please; invite		他	tā	he
問/问	wèn	ask		弟	dì	younger brother
您	nín	polite form of "you"		女	nǚ	female; woman
貴/贵	guì	honorable; expensive		妹	mèi	younger sister
姓	xìng	surname		她	tā	she
我	wǒ	I; me		兒/儿	ér	son; child
呢	ne	QP		有	yǒu	have; there are
叫	jiào	call; shout		沒/没	méi	not have
甚/什	shén	*what		高	gāo	tall; high
麼/么	me	*QP		家	jiā	family; home
名	míng	name		幾/几	jǐ	how many; a few
字	zì	character		哥	gē	elder brother
朋	péng	friend		兩/两	liǎng	two; a couple of
友	yǒu	friend		和	hé	and; harmonious; *warm
是	shì	be		做	zuò	do
老	lǎo	old		英/英	yīng	flower; hero
師/师	shī	teacher		文	wén	script; language
嗎/吗	ma	interrogative auxiliary		律	lǜ	law; rule
不	bù	not; no		都	dōu	all; both
學/学	xué	study		醫/医	yī	doctor; cure; medicine;
也	yě	also; too		愛/爱	ài	love; be fond of
中	zhōng	center; middle				
國/国	guó	country; nation		**Lesson 3**		
人	rén	man; person; humankind				
美	měi	beautiful		月	yuè	moon; month
京	jīng	capital		號/号	hào	number
紐/纽	niǔ	knob; button		星	xīng	star
				期	qī	period of time
Lesson 2				天	tiān	sky; heaven; day
				日	rì	day
那	nà/nèi	that		今	jīn	today; now
張/张	zhāng	open; MW; (a surname)		年	nián	year
照	zhào	shine		多	duō	many
片	piàn	slice; piece; *film; slice		大	dà	big; great
的	de	P		歲/岁	suì	age; year

吃	chī	eat		看	kàn	see
晚	wǎn	evening; late		電/电	diàn	electricity
飯/饭	fàn	meal; food		視/视	shì	view
怎	zěn	*how		唱	chàng	sing
樣/样	yàng	shape; kind		歌	gē	song
太	tài	too; extremely		跳	tiào	jump
了	le	particle for the completion of an action		舞	wǔ	dance; wave
謝/谢	xiè	thank		聽/听	tīng	listen
喜	xǐ	*like; happy		音	yīn	sound; music
歡/欢	huān	joyful		樂/乐	yuè	music
還/还	hái	still; yet		對/对	duì	correct; toward
還/还	huán	return		時/时	shí	time
				候	hòu	wait; time
可	kě	but; may; permit		書/书	shū	book; write
們/们	men	*(plural suffix)		影	yǐng	shadow
點/点	diǎn	dot; o'clock		常	cháng	often
鐘/钟	zhōng	clock		去	qù	leave; go
半	bàn	half		外	wài	outside
上	shàng	above; top		客	kè	guest
見/见	jiàn	see		昨	zuó	yesterday
再	zài	again		所	suǒ	*so; place
白	bái	white		以	yǐ	with
現/现	xiàn	now; present		久	jiǔ	long time
在	zài	at; in; on		錯/错	cuò	wrong; error
刻	kè	quarter hour; carve		想	xiǎng	think
明	míng	bright		覺/觉	jiào/jué	sleep; feel; reckon
忙	máng	busy		得	dé/de	obtain; get; P
很	hěn	very		意	yì	meaning
事	shì	affair; matter		思	sī	think
為/为	wèi/wéi	for		只	zhǐ	only
因	yīn	because		睡	shuì	sleep
同	tóng	same		算	suàn	calculate; figure
認/认	rèn	recognize		找	zhǎo	look for; seek
識/识	shí	recognize		別/别	bié	other
菜	cài	vegetable; dish; food				
				Lesson 5		
Lesson 4						
				呀	ya	(exclamation)
週/周	zhōu	week		進/进	jìn	enter
末	mò	end		快	kuài	fast; quick
打	dǎ	hit; strike		來/来	lái	come
球	qiú	ball		介	jiè	between
				紹/绍	shào	carry on

下	xià	below; under
興/兴	xìng	mood; interest
漂	piào	*pretty
亮	liàng	bright
坐	zuò	sit
哪	nǎ/něi	which
工	gōng	tool; work; labor
作	zuò	work; do
校	xiào	school
喝	hē	drink
茶	chá	tea
咖	kā	*coffee
啡	fēi	*coffee
啤	pí	*beer
酒	jiǔ	wine
吧	ba	question indicator; onomatopoeic
要	yào	want
杯	bēi	cup; glass
起	qǐ	rise
給/给	gěi	give
水	shuǐ	water
玩	wán	play; visit
圖/图	tú	drawing
館/馆	guǎn	accommodations
瓶	píng	bottle
聊	liáo	chat
才	cái	just; not until; only
回	huí	return

Lesson 6

話/话	huà	speech
喂	wèi	hello; hey
就	jiù	just
位	wèi	polite MW for a person
午	wǔ	noon
間/间	jiān	between; MW for rooms
題/题	tí	topic; question
開/开	kāi	open
會/会	huì	meet
節/节	jié	MW for classes
課/课	kè	class; lesson

級/级	jí	grade; level
考	kǎo	test
試/试	shì	try
後/后	hòu	after; behind
空	kòng	free time
方	fāng	square; side
便	biàn	convenient
到	dào	go to; arrive
辦/办	bàn	manage
公	gōng	public
室	shì	room
行	xíng	all right; okay
等	děng	wait
氣/气	qì	air
幫/帮	bāng	help
練/练	liàn	drill
習/习	xí	practice
說/说	shuō	speak
啊	a	P
但	dàn	but
知	zhī	know
道	dào	road; way
準/准	zhǔn	standard; criterion; allow; accurate
備/备	bèi	prepare
面	miàn	face

Lesson 7

跟	gēn	with; and; follow
助	zhù	assist
復/复	fù	duplicate
寫/写	xiě	write
慢	màn	slow
教/教	jiāo	teach
筆/笔	bǐ	pen
難/难	nán	difficult; hard
裏/裡/里	lǐ	inside
第	dì	(ordinal prefix)
預/预	yù	prepare
語/语	yǔ	language
法	fǎ	method; way
容	róng	hold; contain; allow

易	yì	easy		最	zuì	most
懂/懂	dǒng	understand		近	jìn	near
詞/词	cí	word		除	chú	except
漢/汉	hàn	Chinese		專/专	zhuān	special
平	píng	level; even		業/业	yè	occupation
早	zǎo	early		慣/惯	guàn	be used to
夜	yè	night		清	qīng	clear; clean
功	gōng	skill		楚	chǔ	clear; neat
眞/真	zhēn	true; real		步	bù	step
始	shǐ	begin		希	xī	hope
唸/念	niàn	read		望	wàng	look into the distance; hope; wish
錄/录	lù	record		能	néng	be able
帥/帅	shuài	handsome; smart		用	yòng	use
枝	zhī	twig; branch; MW for long, thin objects		笑	xiào	laugh
紙/纸	zhǐ	paper		祝	zhù	wish
酷	kù	cruel; extremely		累	lèi	tired; fatigued
				網/网	wǎng	net

Lesson 8		
篇	piān	MW for articles
記/记	jì	record
牀/床	chuáng	bed
洗	xǐ	wash
澡	zǎo	bath
邊/边	biān	side
教/教	jiào	teaching
發(发)	fā	emit; issue
新	xīn	new
腦/脑	nǎo	brain
餐	cān	meal
廳/厅	tīng	hall
報/报	bào	newspaper
宿	sù	stay
舍	shè	house
正	zhèng	just; straight
前	qián	front; before
告	gào	tell; inform
訴/诉	sù	tell; relate
已	yǐ	already
經/经	jīng	pass through
封	fēng	MW for letters
信	xìn	letter

Lesson 9		
買/买	mǎi	buy
東/东	dōng	east
西	xī	west
售	shòu	sell
貨/货	huò	merchandise
員/员	yuán	personnel
衣	yī	clothing
服	fú	clothing
件	jiàn	MW for items
襯/衬	chèn	lining
衫	shān	shirt
顏/颜	yán	face; countenance
色	sè	color
黃/黄	huáng	yellow
紅/红	hóng	red
穿	chuān	wear
條/条	tiáo	MW for long objects
褲/裤	kù	pants
宜	yí	suitable
付	fù	pay
錢/钱	qián	money
共	gòng	altogether

少	shǎo	few; little
塊/块	kuài	piece; dollar
毛	máo	hair; dime
分	fēn	penny; minute
百	bǎi	hundred
雙/双	shuāng	pair
鞋	xié	shoes
換/换	huàn	change
黑	hēi	black
雖/虽	suī	though; while
然	rán	like that; so
合	hé	suit; agree
適/适	shì	suit; fit
商	shāng	commerce; business
店	diàn	shop; store
如	rú	as; if
果	guǒ	fruit; result
長/长	cháng	long
短	duǎn	short; brief
種/种	zhǒng/zhòng	species; kind; sort; grow; plant
挺	tǐng	erect; straighten up; very; rather
它	tā	it
刷	shuā	scrub; brush; swipe
卡	qiǎ/kǎ	wedge; get stuck; be jammed; card
收	shōu	receive; accept

Lesson 10

比	bǐ	compare
雨	yǔ	rain
更	gèng	even more
而	ér	and; in addition
且	qiě	for the time being
暖	nuǎn	warm
約/约	yuē	make an appointment
園/园	yuán	garden
葉/叶	yè	leaf
像	xiàng	image
海	hǎi	sea
糟	zāo	messy

糕	gāo	cake
又	yòu	right hand; again
剛/刚	gāng	just now
出	chū	go out
熱/热	rè	hot
舒	shū	stretch
夏	xià	summer
涼/凉	liáng	cool
春	chūn	spring
冬	dōng	winter
冷	lěng	cold
悶/闷	mēn	stuffy
次	cì	MW for occurrence
秋	qiū	autumn; fall
臺/台	tái	platform
北	běi	north
灣/湾	wān	strait; bay
郵/邮	yóu	post; mail; postal
城	chéng	wall; city wall; city
市	shì	market; city
特	tè	special; unusual

Lesson 11

寒	hán	cold
假	jià	vacation
飛/飞	fēi	fly
機/机	jī	machine
票	piào	ticket
場/场	chǎng	field
汽	qì	steam
車/车	chē	car
或	huò	or
者	zhě	auxiliary used to indicate a class of persons or things
地	dì	earth
鐵/铁	tiě	iron
走	zǒu	walk
站	zhàn	stand; station
綠/绿	lǜ	green
線/线	xiàn	line
藍/蓝	lán	blue
麻	má	hemp; numb

煩/烦	fán	bother
租	zū	rent
送	sòng	deliver
過/过	guò	pass
讓/让	ràng	let
花	huā	spend; flower
每	měi	every
速	sù	speed
路	lù	road; way
緊/紧	jǐn	tight
自	zì	self
己	jǐ	oneself

CHARACTER INDEX

(by Pinyin)

KEY		
*	**Bound Form** (a character that is "bound together" with another character—it appears in combination with another character, not by itself)	
MW	**Measure Word**	
P	**Particle**	
QP	**Question Particle**	

A			
啊	a	P	137
愛/爱	ài	love; be fond of	61
B			
八	bā	eight	24
爸	bà	dad	48
吧	ba	question indicator; onomatopoeic	115
白	bái	white	78
百	bǎi	hundred	190
半	bàn	half	76
辦/半	bàn	manage	132
幫/帮	bāng	help	135
報/报	bào	newspaper	162
杯	bēi	cup; glass	116
北	běi	north	214
貝/贝	bèi	cowry shell	16
備/备	bèi	prepare	140
筆/笔	bǐ	pen	144
比	bǐ	compare	201
邊/边	biān	side	159
便	biàn	convenient	131
別/别	bié	other	103
不	bù	not; no	40
步	bù	step	171
C			

才	cái	just; not until; only	121
菜	cài	vegetable; dish; food	84
餐	cān	meal	161
茶	chá	tea	113
常	cháng	often	94
長/长	cháng	long	196
場/场	chǎng	field	221
唱	chàng	sing	88
車/车	chē	car	222
襯/衬	chèn	lining	181
城	chéng	wall; city wall; city	216
吃	chī	eat	68
出	chū	go out	208
除	chú	except	168
楚	chǔ	clear; neat	171
穿	chuān	wear	184
牀/床	chuáng	bed	158
春	chūn	spring	211
詞/词	cí	word	149
次	cì	MW for occurrence	213
寸	cùn	inch	6
錯/错	cuò	wrong; error	98
D			
打	dǎ	hit; strike	86
大	dà	big; great	5, 67
但	dàn	but	138

刀 (刂)	dāo	knife	1
到	dào	go to; arrive	132
道	dào	road; way	139
得	dé	obtain; get	100
的	de	P	47
得	děi	must; have to	100
等	děng	wait	134
弟	dì	younger brother	52
第	dì	(ordinal prefix)	145
地	dì	earth	224
點/点	diǎn	dot; o'clock	75
電/电	diàn	electricity	87
店	diàn	shop; store	195
東/东	dōng	east	177
冬	dōng	winter	211
懂	dǒng	understand	148
都	dōu	all; both	60
短	duǎn	short; brief	197
對/对	duì	correct; toward	92
多	duō	many	67

	E		
兒/儿	ér	son; child	54
而	ér	and; in addition	202
耳	ěr	ear	15
二	èr	two	21

	F		
發/发	fā	emit; issue	160
法	fǎ	method; way	147
煩/烦	fán	bother	228
飯/饭	fàn	meal; food	69
方	fāng	square; side	131
啡	fēi	*coffee	114
飛/飞	fēi	fly	220
分	fēn	penny; minute	189
封	fēng	MW for letters	166
服	fú	clothing	180
復/复	fù	duplicate	142
付	fù	pay	186

	G		
剛/刚	gāng	just now	208
高	gāo	tall; high	55
糕	gāo	cake	207
告	gào	tell; inform	164
戈	gē	dagger-ax	9
哥	gē	elder brother	57
歌	gē	song	89
個/个	gè	MW	49
給/给	gěi	give	117
跟	gēn	with; and; follow	141
更	gèng	even more	202
弓	gōng	bow	8
工	gōng	tool; work; labor	7, 111
公	gōng	public	133
功	gōng	skill	151
共	gòng	altogether	187
館/馆	guǎn	accommodation	119
慣/惯	guàn	be used to	170
貴/贵	guì	honorable; expensive	32
國/国	guó	country; nation	42
果	guǒ	fruit; result	196
過/过	guò	pass	229

	H		
孩	hái	child	50
還/还	hái	still; yet	73
海	hǎi	sea	206
寒	hán	cold	219
漢/汉	hàn	Chinese	149
行	háng	firm	134
好	hǎo	good; fine; OK	28
好	hào	like; be fond of	28
號/号	hào	number	63
喝	hē	drink	112
和	hé	and; harmonious	58
合	hé	suit; agree	193
黑	hēi	black	192
很	hěn	very	81

紅/红	hóng	red	184
候	hòu	wait; time	93
後/后	hòu	after; behind	130
花	huā	spend; flower	230
話/话	huà	speech	123
歡/欢	huān	joyful	73
還/还	huán	return	73
換/换	huàn	change	191
黃/黄	huáng	yellow	183
回	huí	return	121
會/会	huì	meet	127
火(灬)	huǒ	fire	12
貨/货	huò	merchandise	179
或	huò	or	223
和	huo	*warm	58

		J	
機/机	jī	machine	220
級/级	jí	grade; level	128
幾/几	jǐ	how many; a few	56
己	jǐ	oneself	233
記/记	jì	record	157
家	jiā	family; home	56
假	jià	vacation	219
間/间	jiān	between; MW for rooms	125
見/见	jiàn	see	77
件	jiàn	MW for items	181
教/教	jiāo	teach	143
覺/觉	jiào	sleep	99
教/教	jiào	education	143
節/节	jié	MW (for classes)	127
姐	jiě	elder sister	29
介	jiè	between	107
金	jīn	(a surname); gold; metal	18
今	jīn	today; now	66
緊/紧	jǐn	tight	232
進/进	jìn	enter	105
近/近	jìn	near	168
京	jīng	capital	43

經/经	jīng	pass through	166
九	jiǔ	nine	24
久	jiǔ	long time	98
酒	jiǔ	wine	115
就	jiù	just	124
覺/觉	jué	feel; reckon	99

		K	
咖	kā	*coffee	113
開/开	kāi	open	126
看	kàn	see; look	87
考	kǎo	test	129
可	kě	but; may; permit	74
刻	kè	quarter hour; carve	79
客	kè	guest	96
課/课	kè	class; lesson	128
空	kòng	free time	130
口	kǒu	mouth	3
酷	kù	cruel; extremely	155
褲/裤	kù	pants	185
快	kuài	fast; quick	106
塊/块	kuài	piece; dollar	188

		L	
來/来	lái	come	106
藍/蓝	lán	blue	227
老	lǎo	old	38
了	le	particle for the completion of an action	71
樂/乐	lè	happy	91
累	lèi	tired; fatigued	175
冷	lěng	cold	212
李	lǐ	plum; (a surname)	30
裏/裡/里	lǐ	inside	145
力	lì	physical strength; power	2
練/练	liàn	practice; drill	136
涼/凉	liáng	cool	210
兩/两	liǎng	two; a couple	57

亮/亮	liàng	bright	109
聊	liáo	chat	120
六	liù	six	23
錄/录	lù	record	153
路	lù	road; way	232
律	lǜ	law; rule	60
綠/绿	lǜ	green	226
		M	
媽/妈	mā	mom	48
麻	má	hemp; numb	227
馬/马	mǎ	horse	20
嗎/吗	ma	interrogative auxiliary	39
買/买	mǎi	buy	177
慢	màn	slow	143
忙	máng	busy	80
毛	máo	hair; dime	189
麼/么	me	*QP	35
沒/没	méi	not have	55
美	měi	beautiful	43
每	měi	every	231
妹	mèi	younger sister	53
悶/闷	mēn	stuffy	212
門/门	mén	door; gate	18
們/们	men	*(plural suffix)	74
糸	mì	silk	14
面	miàn	face	140
名	míng	name	36
明	míng	bright	80
末	mò	end	85
木	mù	tree; wood	11
目	mù	eye	13
		N	
哪	nǎ/něi	which	110
那	nà/nèi	that	45
男	nán	male	49
難/难	nán	difficult; hard	144
腦/脑	nǎo	brain	160
呢	ne	QP	34

能	néng	be able	173
你	nǐ	you	28
年	nián	year	66
唸/念	niàn	read	153
您	nín	polite form of "you"	32
紐/纽	niǔ	knob; button	44
暖	nuǎn	warm	203
女	nǚ	female; woman	5, 52
		P	
朋	péng	friend	37
啤	pí	*beer	114
篇	piān	MW for articles	157
便	pián	*inexpensive	131
片	piàn	slice; piece; *film	46
漂	piào	*pretty	109
票	piào	ticket	221
瓶	píng	bottle	120
平	píng	level; even	150
		Q	
七	qī	seven	23
期	qī	period of time	64
起	qǐ	rise	117
氣/气	qì	air	135
汽	qì	steam	222
卡	qiǎ/kǎ	wedge; get stuck; be jammed; card	199
前	qián	front; before	164
錢/钱	qián	money	187
且	qiě	for the time being	203
清	qīng	clear; clean	170
請/请	qǐng	please; invite	31
秋	qiū	autumn; fall	213
球	qiú	ball	86
去	qù	leave; go	95
		R	
然	rán	like that; so	193

讓/让	ràng	let; allow	230	帥/帅	shuài	handsome	154
熱/热	rè	hot	209	雙/双	shuāng	pair	190
人（亻）	rén	man; person; humankind	1, 42	水（氵）	shuǐ	water	12, 118
認/认	rèn	recognize	83	睡	shuì	sleep	102
日	rì	sun; day	10, 65	說/说	shuō	speak	137
容	róng	hold; contain; allow	147	思	sī	think	101
如	rú	as; if	195	四	sì	four	22
				送	sòng	deliver	229
		S		宿	sù	stay	162
				訴/诉	sù	tell; relate	165
三	sān	three	21	速/速	sù	speed	231
色	sè	color	183	算	suàn	calculate; figure	102
衫	shān	shirt	182	雖/虽	suī	though; while	192
商	shāng	commerce; business	194	歲/岁	suì	age; year	68
上	shàng	above; top	76	所	suǒ	*so; place	97
少	shǎo	few; little	188				
紹/绍	shào	carry on	107			**T**	
舍	shè	house	163				
誰/谁	shéi	who	51	他	tā	he	51
甚/什	shén	*what	35	她	tā	she	53
生	shēng	be born; grow	27	它	tā	it	198
師/师	shī	teacher	39	臺/台	tái	platform	214
食	shí	eat	20	太	tài	too; extremely	71
十	shí	ten	25	特	tè	special; unusual	217
識/识	shí	recognize	84	題/题	tí	topic; question	126
時/时	shí	time	92	天	tiān	sky; heaven; day	65
始	shǐ	begin	152	田	tián	(a surname); farmland; field	13
示（礻）	shì	show	14	條/条	tiáo	MW for long objects	185
是	shì	be	38	跳	tiào	jump	89
事	shì	affair; matter	81	鐵/铁	tiě	iron	224
視/视	shì	view	88	聽/听	tīng	listen	90
室	shì	room	133	廳/厅	tīng	hall	161
試/试	shì	try	129	挺	tǐng	erect; straighten up; very; rather	198
適/适	shì	suit; fit	194	同	tóng	same	83
市	shì	market; city	216	圖/图	tú	drawing	119
收	shōu	receive; accept	200	土	tǔ	earth; soil	4
手（扌）	shǒu	hand	10				
售	shòu	sell	178			**W**	
書/书	shū	book; write	93				
舒	shū	stretch	209	外	wài	outside	95
刷	shuā	scrub; brush; swipe	199				

灣/湾	wān	strait; bay	215
玩	wán	play; visit	118
晚	wǎn	evening; late	69
王	wáng	king; (a surname)	30
網/网	wǎng	net	175
望	wàng	look into the distance; hope; wish	172
囗	wéi	enclose	3
為/为	wèi/wéi	for	82
位	wèi	polite MW for a person	124
喂	wèi	hello; hey	123
文	wén	script; language	59
問/问	wèn	ask	31
我	wǒ	I; me	33
五	wǔ	five	22
舞	wǔ	dance; wave	90
午	wǔ	noon	125
		X	
夕	xī	sunset; evening	4
希	xī	hope	172
西	xī	west	178
習/习	xí	practice	136
喜	xǐ	like; happy	72
洗	xǐ	wash	158
下	xià	below; under	108
夏	xià	summer	210
先	xiān	first; before; earlier	27
現/现	xiàn	now; present	78
線/线	xiàn	line	226
想	xiǎng	think	99
像	xiàng	image	205
小	xiǎo	little; small	7, 29
校	xiào	school	112
笑	xiào	laugh	174
鞋	xié	shoes	191
寫/写	xiě	write	142
謝/谢	xiè	thank	72
心(忄)	xīn	heart	9
新	xīn	new	234
信	xìn	letter	167

星	xīng	star	64
行	xíng	all right; okay	134
姓	xìng	surname	33
興/兴	xìng	mood; interest	108
學/学	xué	study	40
		Y	
呀	ya	(exclamation)	105
言	yán	speak; speech	16
顏/颜	yán	face; countenance	182
樣/样	yàng	shape; kind	70
幺	yāo	tiny; the youngest	8
要	yào	want	116
也	yě	also	41
夜	yè	night	151
業/业	yè	occupation	169
葉/叶	yè	leaf	205
一	yī	one	21
醫/医	yī	doctor; cure; medicine	61
衣(衤)	yī	clothing	15, 180
宜	yí	suitable	186
以	yǐ	with	97
已	yǐ	already	165
意	yì	meaning	100
易	yì	easy	148
因	yīn	because	82
音	yīn	sound; music	91
英	yīng	flower; hero	59
影	yǐng	shadow	94
用	yòng	use	173
郵/邮	yóu	post; mail; postal	215
友	yǒu	friend	37
有	yǒu	have; there are	54
又	yòu	right hand; again	2, 207
語/语	yǔ	language	146
雨	yǔ	rain	19, 201
預/预	yù	prepare	146
員/员	yuán	personnel	179
園/园	yuán	garden	204
約/约	yuē	make an appointment	204
月	yuè	moon; month	11, 63

樂/乐	yuè	music	91

		Z		

再	zài	again	77
在	zài	at; in; on	79
糟	zāo	messy	206
早	zǎo	early	150
澡	zǎo	bath	159
怎	zěn	*how	70
站	zhàn	stand; station	225
張/张	zhāng	open; MW; (a surname)	45
找	zhǎo	look for; seek	103
照	zhào	shine	46
者	zhě	auxiliary used to indicate a class of persons or things	223
這/这	zhè/zhèi	this	47
眞/真	zhēn	true; real	152
正	zhèng	just; straight	163
知	zhī	know	138
枝	zhī	twig; branch; MW for long, thin objects	154

只	zhǐ	only	101
紙/纸	zhǐ	paper	155
中	zhōng	center; middle	41
鐘/钟	zhōng	clock	75
種/种	zhǒng/zhòng	species; kind; sort; grow; plant	197
週/周	zhōu	week	85
助	zhù	assist	141
祝	zhù	wish	174
專/专	zhuān	special	169
隹	zhuī	short-tailed bird	19
準/准	zhǔn	standard; criterion; allow; accurate	139
子	zǐ	son	6, 50
字	zì	character	36
自	zì	self	233
走	zǒu	walk	17, 225
租	zū	rent	228
足	zú	foot	17
最	zuì	most	167
昨	zuó	yesterday	96
做	zuò	do	58
坐	zuò	sit	110
作	zuò	work; do	111

TRADITIONAL CHARACTER INDEX

(by Stroke Count)

```
KEY
*          Bound Form (a character that is "bound
           together" with another character—it appears in
           combination with another character, not by itself)
MW         Measure Word
P          Particle
QP         Question Particle
```

1			
一	yī	one	21
2			
八	bā	eight	24
刀（刂）	dāo	knife	1
二	èr	two	21
九	jiǔ	nine	24
了	le	particle for the completion of an action	71
力	lì	physical strength; power	2
七	qī	seven	23
人（亻）	rén	man; person; humankind	1, 42
十	shí	ten	25
又	yòu	right hand; again	2, 207
3			
才	cái	just; not until; only	121
寸	cùn	inch	6
大	dà	big; great	5, 67
工	gōng	tool; work; labor	7, 111
弓	gōng	bow	8
己	jǐ	oneself	233
久	jiǔ	long time	98

口	kǒu	mouth	3
女	nǚ	female; woman	5, 52
三	sān	three	21
上	shàng	above; top	76
土	tǔ	earth; soil	4
囗	wéi	enclose	3
夕	xī	sunset; evening	4
下	xià	below; under	108
小	xiǎo	little; small	7, 29
幺	yāo	tiny; the youngest	8
也	yě	also	41
已	yǐ	already	165
子	zǐ	son	6, 50
4			
比	bǐ	compare	201
不	bù	not; no	40
方	fāng	square; side	131
分	fēn	penny; minute	189
戈	gē	dagger-ax	9
公	gōng	public	133
火（灬）	huǒ	fire	12
介	jiè	between	107
今	jīn	today; now	66
六	liù	six	23
毛	máo	hair; dime	189
木	mù	tree; wood	11
片	piàn	slice; piece; *film	46

日	rì	sun; day	10, 65
少	shǎo	few; little	188
甚/什	shén	*what	35
手（扌）	shǒu	hand	10
水（氵）	shuǐ	water	12, 118
太	tài	too; extremely	71
天	tiān	sky; heaven; day	65
王	wáng	(a surname); king	30
文	wén	script; language	59
五	wǔ	five	22
午	wǔ	noon	125
心（忄）	xīn	heart	9
以	yǐ	with	97
友	yǒu	friend	37
月	yuè	moon; month	11, 63
中	zhōng	center; middle	41
5			
白	bái	white	78
半	bàn	half	76
北	běi	north	214
出	chū	go out	208
打	dǎ	hit; strike	86
冬	dōng	winter	211
付	fù	pay	186
功	gōng	skill	151
叫	jiào	call; shout	34
可	kě	but; may; permit	74
末	mò	end	85
目	mù	eye	13
平	píng	level; even	150
卡	qiǎ/kǎ	wedge; get stuck; be jammed; card	199
且	qiě	for the time being	203
去	qù	leave; go	95
生	shēng	be born; grow	27
示（礻）	shì	show	14
市	shì	market; city	216
四	sì	four	22
他	tā	he	51
它	tā	it	198

臺/台	tái	platform	214
田	tián	(a surname); farmland; field	13
外	wài	outside	95
用	yòng	use	173
正	zhèng	just; straight	163
只	zhǐ	only	101
6			
百	bǎi	hundred	190
吃	chī	eat	68
次	cì	MW for occurrence	213
地	dì/de	earth	224
多	duō	many	67
而	ér	and; in addition	202
耳	ěr	ear	15
共	gòng	altogether	187
行	háng	firm	134
好	hǎo	good; fine; OK	28
好	hào	like; be fond of	28
合	hé	suit; agree	193
回	huí	return	121
件	jiàn	MW for items	181
考	kǎo	test	129
老	lǎo	old	38
忙	máng	busy	80
糸	mì	silk	14
名	míng	name	36
年	nián	year	66
如	rú	as; if	195
色	sè	color	183
收	shōu	receive; accept	200
她	tā	she	53
同	tóng	same	83
西	xī	west	178
先	xiān	first; before; earlier	27
行	xíng	all right; okay	134
衣（衤）	yī	clothing	15, 180
因	yīn	because	82
有	yǒu	have; there are	54
再	zài	again	77

在	zài	at; in; on	79
早	zǎo	early	150
字	zì	character	36
自	zì	self	233
7			
吧	ba	question indicator; onomatopoeic	115
貝/贝	bèi	cowry shell	16
別/别	bié	other	103
步	bù	step	171
車/车	chē	car	222
牀/床	chuáng	bed	158
但	dàn	but	138
弟	dì	younger brother	52
告	gào	tell; inform	164
更	gèng	even more	202
見/见	jiàn	see	77
近	jìn	near	168
快	kuài	fast; quick	106
冷	lěng	cold	212
李	lǐ	plum; (a surname);	30
沒/没	méi	not have	55
每	měi	every	231
那	nà/nèi	that	45
男	nán	male	49
你	nǐ	you	28
汽	qì	steam	222
位	wèi	polite MW for a person	124
我	wǒ	I; me	33
希	xī	hope	172
呀	ya	(exclamation)	105
言	yán	speak; speech	16
找	zhǎo	look for; seek	103
助	zhù	assist	141
走	zǒu	walk	17, 225
足	zú	foot	17
坐	zuò	sit	110
作	zuò	work; do	111
8			

爸	bà	dad	48
杯	bēi	cup; glass	116
長/长	cháng	long	196
到	dào	go to; arrive	132
的	de	P	47
店	diàn	shop; store	195
東/东	dōng	east	177
兒/儿	ér	son; child	54
法	fǎ	method; way	147
服	fú	clothing	180
果	guǒ	fruit; result	196
和	hé/huo	and; harmonious; *warm	58
花	huā	spend	230
或	huò	or	223
姐	jiě	elder sister	29
金	jīn	(a surname); gold; metal	18
京	jīng	capital	43
咖	kā	*coffee	113
刻	kè	quarter hour; carve	79
空	kòng	free time	130
來/来	lái	come	106
兩/两	liǎng	two; a couple	57
妹	mèi	younger sister	53
門/门	mén	door; gate	18
明	míng	bright	80
呢	ne	QP	34
朋	péng	friend	37
衫	shān	shirt	182
舍	shè	house	163
始	shǐ	begin	152
事	shì	affair; matter	81
刷	shuā	scrub; brush; swipe	199
所	suǒ	*so; place	97
玩	wán	play; visit	118
姓	xìng	surname	33
夜	yè	night	151
宜	yí	suitable	186
易	yì	easy	148
雨	yǔ	rain	19, 201
者	zhě	auxiliary used to	223

			indicate a class of persons or things	
知	zhī	know	138
枝	zhī	twig; branch; MW for long, thin objects	154
隹	zhuī	short-tailed bird	19
	9		
便	biàn	convenient	131
城	chéng	wall; city wall; city	216
穿	chuān	wear	180
春	chūn	spring	211
飛/飞	fēi	fly	220
封	fēng	MW for letters	166
孩	hái	child	50
很	hěn	very	81
紅/红	hóng	red	184
後/后	hòu	after; behind	130
看	kàn	see; look	87
客	kè	guest	96
亮/亮	liàng	bright	109
律	lǜ	law; rule	60
美	měi	beautiful	43
面	miàn	face	140
便	pián	*inexpensive	131
前	qián	front; before	164
秋	qiū	autumn; fall	213
食	shí	eat	20
是	shì	be	38
室	shì	room	133
帥/帅	shuài	handsome	154
思	sī	think	101
挺	tǐng	erect; straighten up; very; rather	198
為/为	wèi/wéi	for	82
洗	xǐ	wash	158
信	xìn	letter	167
星	xīng	star	64
要	yào	want	116
音	yīn	sound; music	91
英	yīng	flower; hero	59

約/约	yuē	make an appointment	204
怎	zěn	*how	70
祝	zhù	wish	174
昨	zuó	yesterday	96
	10		
茶	chá	tea	113
除	chú	except	168
剛/刚	gāng	just now	208
高	gāo	tall; high	55
哥	gē	elder brother	57
個/个	gè	MW	49
海	hǎi	sea	206
候	hòu	wait; time	93
級/级	jí	grade; level	128
記/记	jì	record	157
家	jiā	family; home	56
酒	jiǔ	wine	115
馬/马	mǎ	horse	20
們/们	men	*(plural suffix)	74
哪	nǎ/něi	which	110
能	néng	be able	173
紐/纽	niǔ	knob; button	44
瓶	píng	bottle	120
起	qǐ	rise	117
氣/气	qì	air	135
容	róng	hold; contain; allow	147
師/师	shī	teacher	39
時/时	shí	time	92
書/书	shū	book; write	93
送	sòng	deliver	229
特	tè	special; unusual	217
夏	xià	summer	210
校	xiào	school	112
笑	xiào	laugh	174
郵/邮	yóu	post; mail; postal	215
員/员	yuán	personnel	179
站	zhàn	stand; station	225
真/真	zhēn	true; real	152
紙/纸	zhǐ	paper	155
租	zū	rent	228

11					**12**			
啊	a	P	137		報/报	bào	newspaper	162
菜	cài	vegetable; dish; food	84		備/备	bèi	prepare	140
常	cháng	often	94		筆/笔	bǐ	pen	144
唱	chàng	sing	88		場/场	chǎng	field	221
得	dé	obtain; get	100		詞/词	cí	word	149
得	de	P	100		等	děng	wait	134
得	děi	must; have to	100		短	duǎn	short; brief	197
第	dì	(ordinal prefix)	145		發/发	fā	emit; issue	160
都	dōu	all; both	60		飯/饭	fàn	meal; food	69
啡	fēi	*coffee	114		復/复	fù	duplicate	142
國/国	guó	country; nation	42		給/给	gěi	give	117
黃/黄	huáng	yellow	183		貴/贵	guì	honorable; expensive	32
貨/货	huò	merchandise	179		寒	hán	cold	219
假	jià	vacation	219		喝	hē	drink	112
教/教	jiāo	teach	143		黑	hēi	black	192
涼/凉	liáng	cool	210		換/换	huàn	change	191
聊	liáo	chat	120		幾/几	jǐ	how many; a few	56
麻	má	hemp; numb	227		間/间	jiān	between; MW for rooms	125
唸/念	niàn	read	153		進/进	jìn	enter	105
您	nín	polite form of "you"	32		就	jiù	just	124
啤	pí	*beer	114		開/开	kāi	open	126
票	piào	ticket	221		累	lèi	tired; fatigued	175
清	qīng	clear; clean	170		裡/裏/里	lǐ	inside	145
球	qiú	ball	86		買/买	mǎi	buy	177
紹/绍	shào	carry on	107		悶/闷	mēn	stuffy	212
視/视	shì	view	88		期	qī	period of time	64
售	shòu	sell	178		然	rán	like that; so	189
宿	sù	stay	162		商	shāng	commerce; business	194
速/速	sù	speed	231		試/试	shì	try	129
條/条	tiáo	MW for long objects	185		舒	shū	stretch	209
望	wàng	look into the distance; hope; wish	172		訴/诉	sù	tell; relate	165
問/问	wèn	ask	31		晚	wǎn	evening; late	69
習/习	xí	practice	136		喂	wèi	hello; hey	123
現/现	xiàn	now; present	78		喜	xǐ	like; happy	72
張/张	zhāng	open; MW; (a surname)	45		葉/叶	yè	leaf	205
這/这	zhè/zhèi	this	47		園/园	yuán	garden	204
專/专	zhuān	special	169		週/周	zhōu	week	85
做	zuò	do	58		最	zuì	most	167

13

愛/爱	ài	love; be fond of	61
楚	chǔ	clear; neat	171
道	dào	road; way	139
電/电	diàn	electricity	87
煩/烦	fán	bother	228
跟	gēn	with; and; follow	141
過/过	guò	pass	229
號/号	hào	number	63
話/话	huà	speech	123
會/会	huì	meet	127
塊/块	kuài	piece; dollar	188
節/节	jié	MW for classes	127
經/经	jīng	pass through	166
裏/裡/里	lǐ	inside	145
路	lù	road; way	232
媽/妈	mā	mom	48
嗎/吗	ma	interrogative auxiliary	39
腦/脑	nǎo	brain	160
暖	nuǎn	warm	203
睡	shuì	sleep	102
歲/岁	suì	age; year	68
跳	tiào	jump	89
想	xiǎng	think	99
新	xīn	new	234
業/业	yè	occupation	169
意	yì	meaning	100
預/预	yù	prepare	146
照	zhào	shine	46
準/准	zhǔn	standard; criterion; allow; accurate	139
慢	màn	slow	143
麼/么	me	*QP	35
漂	piào	*pretty	109
認/认	rèn	recognize	83
說/说	shuō	speak	137
算	suàn	calculate; figure	102
圖/图	tú	drawing	119
舞	wǔ	dance; wave	90
像	xiàng	image	205
寫/写	xiě	write	142
網/网	wǎng	net	175
語/语	yǔ	language	146
種/种	zhǒng/zhòng	species; kind; sort; grow; plant	197

14

對/对	duì	correct; toward	92
歌	gē	song	89
慣/惯	guàn	be used to	170
漢/汉	hàn	Chinese	149
緊/紧	jǐn	tight	232
酷	kù	cruel; extremely	155
綠/绿	lǜ	green	226

15

課/课	kè	class; lesson	128
褲/裤	kù	pants	185
樂/乐	lè	happy	91
練/练	liàn	practice; drill	136
篇	piān	MW for articles	157
請/请	qǐng	please; invite	31
熱/热	rè	hot	209
誰/谁	shéi	who	51
適/适	shì	suit; fit	194
線/线	xiàn	line	226
鞋	xié	shoes	191
樣/样	yàng	shape; kind	70
影	yǐng	shadow	94
樂/乐	yuè	music	91

16

辦/办	bàn	manage	132
餐	cān	meal	161
錯/错	cuò	wrong; error	98
懂	dǒng	understand	148
糕	gāo	cake	207
館/馆	guǎn	accommodation	119
機/机	jī	machine	220
錄/录	lù	record	153

錢/钱	qián	money		187
興/兴	xìng	mood; interest		108
學/学	xué	study		40
澡	zǎo	bath		159
17				
幫/帮	bāng	help		135
點/点	diǎn	dot; o'clock		75
還/还	hái	still; yet		73
還/还	huán	return		73
謝/谢	xiè	thank		72
糟	zāo	messy		206
18				
藍/蓝	lán	blue		227
雙/双	shuāng	pair		190
題/题	tí	topic; question		126
顏/颜	yán	face; countenance		182
醫/医	yī	doctor; cure; medicine		61
19				
邊/边	biān	side		159
難/难	nán	difficult; hard		144
識/识	shí	recognize		84
20				
覺/觉	jiào	sleep		99
覺/觉	jué	feel; reckon		99
鐘/钟	zhōng	clock		75
21				
襯/衬	chèn	lining		181
鐵/铁	tiě	iron		224
22				
歡/欢	huān	joyful		73

聽/听	tīng	listen	90
24			
讓/让	ràng	let	230
廳/厅	tīng	hall	161
灣/湾	wān	strait; bay	215

Traditional Character Stroke Index

SIMPLIFIED CHARACTER INDEX

(by Stroke Count)

KEY	
*	**Bound Form** (a character that is "bound together" with another character—it appears in combination with another character, not by itself)
MW	**Measure Word**
P	**Particle**
QP	**Question Particle**

		1		
一	yī	one		21

		2		
八	bā	eight		24
刀（刂）	dāo	knife		1
儿/兒	ér	son; child		54
二	èr	two		21
几/幾	jǐ	how many; a few		56
九	jiǔ	nine		24
了	le	particle for the completion of an action		71
力	lì	physical strength; power		2
七	qī	seven		23
人（亻）	rén	man; person; humankind		1, 42
十	shí	ten		25
又	yòu	right hand; again		2, 207

		3		
才	cái	just; not until; only		121
寸	cùn	inch		6
大	dà	big; great		5, 67
飞/飛	fēi	fly		220
个/個	gè	MW		49
工	gōng	craft; work		7, 111
弓	gōng	bow		8

己	jǐ	oneself		233
久	jiǔ	long time		98
口	kǒu	mouth		3
马/馬	mǎ	horse		20
么/麽	me	*QP		35
门/門	mén	door; gate		18
女	nǚ	female; woman		5, 52
三	sān	three		21
上	shàng	above; top		76
土	tǔ	earth; soil		4
囗	wéi	enclose		3
夕	xī	sunset; evening		4
习/習	xí	practice		136
下	xià	below; under		108
小	xiǎo	little; small		7, 29
幺	yāo	tiny; the youngest		8
也	yě	also		41
已	yǐ	already		165
子	zǐ	son		6, 50

		4		
办/辦	bàn	manage		132
贝/貝	bèi	cowry shell		16
比	bǐ	compare		201
不	bù	not; no		40
长/長	cháng	long		196
车/車	chē	car		222
方	fāng	square; side		131

分	fēn	penny; minute	189	
戈	gē	dagger-ax	9	
公	gōng	public	133	
火(灬)	huǒ	fire	12	
见/見	jiàn	see	77	
介	jiè	between	107	
今	jīn	today; now	66	
开/開	kāi	open	126	
六	liù	six	23	
毛	máo	hair; dime	189	
木	mù	tree; wood	11	
片	piàn	slice; piece; *film	46	
气/氣	qì	air	135	
认/認	rèn	recognize	83	
日	rì	sun; day	10, 65	
少	shǎo	few; little	188	
什/甚	shén	*what	35	
手	shǒu	hand	10	
书/書	shū	book; write	93	
双/雙	shuāng	pair	190	
水(氵)	shuǐ	water	12, 118	
太	tài	too; extremely	71	
天	tiān	sky; heaven; day	65	
厅/廳	tīng	hall	161	
王	wáng	king; (a surname)	30	
为/為	wèi/wéi	for	82	
文	wén	script; language	59	
五	wǔ	five	22	
午	wǔ	noon	125	
心(忄)	xīn	heart	9	
以	yǐ	with	97	
友	yǒu	friend	37	
月	yuè	moon; month	11, 63	
中	zhōng	center; middle	41	
专/專	zhuān	special	169	

		5		

白	bái	white	78	
半	bàn	half	76	
北	běi	north	214	
边/邊	biān	side	159	

出	chū	go out	208
打	dǎ	hit; strike	86
电/電	diàn	electricity	87
东/東	dōng	east	177
冬	dōng	winter	211
对/對	duì	correct; toward	92
发/發	fā	emit; issue	160
付	fù	pay	186
功	gōng	skill	151
汉/漢	hàn	Chinese	149
号/號	hào	number	63
记/記	jì	record	157
叫	jiào	call; shout	34
节/節	jié	MW for classes	127
可	kě	but; may; permit	74
乐/樂	lè	happy	91
们/們	men	*(plural suffix)	74
末	mò	end	85
目	mù	eye	13
平	píng	level; even	150
卡	qiǎ/kǎ	wedge; get stuck; be jammed; card	199
且	qiě	for the time being	197
去	qù	leave; go	95
让/讓	ràng	let	230
帅	shuài	handsome	154
生	shēng	be born; grow	27
示(礻)	shì	show	14
市	shì	market; city	216
四	sì	four	22
他	tā	he	51
它	tā	it	198
台/臺	tái	platform	214
田	tián	(a surname); farmland; field	13
外	wài	outside	95
写/寫	xiě	write	142
业/業	yè	occupation	169
叶/葉	yè	leaf	205
用	yòng	use	173
正	zhèng	just; straight	163
只	zhǐ	only	101

		6	
百	bǎi	hundred	190
场/場	chǎng	field	221
吃	chī	eat	68
次	cì	MW for occurrence	213
地	dì	earth	224
多	duō	many	67
而	ér	and; in addition	202
耳	ěr	ear	15
刚/剛	gāng	just now	208
共	gòng	altogether	187
过/過	guò	pass	229
行	háng	firm	134
好	hǎo	good; fine; OK	28
好	hào	like; be fond of	28
合	hé	suit; agree	193
红/紅	hóng	red	184
后/後	hòu	after; behind	130
欢/歡	huān	joyful	73
回	huí	return	121
会/會	huì	meet	127
机/機	jī	machine	220
级/級	jí	grade; level	128
件	jiàn	MW for items	181
考	kǎo	test	129
老	lǎo	old	38
妈/媽	mā	mom	48
吗/嗎	ma	interrogative auxiliary	39
买/買	mǎi	buy	177
忙	máng	busy	80
系(纟)	mì	silk	14
名	míng	name	36
那	nà/nèi	that	45
年	nián	year	66
如	rú	as; if	195
色	sè	color	183
师/師	shī	teacher	39
收	shōu	receive; accept	200
岁/歲	suì	age; year	68
她	tā	she	53

同	tóng	same	83
网/網	wǎng	net	175
问/問	wèn	ask	31
西	xī	west	178
先	xiān	first; before; earlier	27
行	xíng	all right; okay	134
兴/興	xìng	mood; interest	108
衣(衤)	yī	clothing	15, 180
因	yīn	because	82
有	yǒu	have; there are	54
约/約	yuē	make an appointment	198
再	zài	again	77
在	zài	at; in; on	79
早	zǎo	early	150
字	zì	character	36
自	zì	self	233
		7	
吧	ba	question indicator; onomatopoeic	115
报/報	bào	newspaper	162
别/別	bié	other	103
步	bù	step	171
床/牀	chuáng	bed	158
词/詞	cí	word	149
但	dàn	but	138
弟	dì	younger brother	52
饭/飯	fàn	meal; food	69
告	gào	tell; inform	164
更	gèng	even more	202
还/還	hái	still; yet	73
还/還	huán	return	73
花	huā	spend; flower	230
间/間	jiān	between; MW for rooms	125
进/進	jìn	enter	105
快	kuài	fast; quick	106
块/塊	kuài	piece; dollar	188
来/來	lái	come	106
冷	lěng	cold	212
李	lǐ	plum; (a surname)	30
里/裡/裏	lǐ	inside	145

两/兩	liǎng	two; a couple	57	
没/沒	méi	not have	55	
每	měi	every	231	
闷/悶	mēn	stuffy	212	
男	nán	male	49	
你	nǐ	you	28	
纽/紐	niǔ	knob; button	44	
汽	qì	steam	222	
识/識	shí	recognize	84	
时/時	shí	time	92	
诉/訴	sù	tell; relate	165	
条/條	tiáo	MW for long objects	185	
听/聽	tīng	listen	90	
位	wèi	polite MW for a person	124	
我	wǒ	I; me	33	
希	xī	hope	172	
呀	ya	(exclamation)	105	
言(讠)	yán	speak; speech	16	
医/醫	yī	doctor; cure; medicine	61	
邮/郵	yóu	post; mail; postal	215	
员/員	yuán	personnel	177	
园/園	yuán	garden	198	
张/張	zhāng	MW; (a surname)	45	
找	zhǎo	look for; seek	103	
这/這	zhè/zhèi	this	47	
纸/紙	zhǐ	paper	155	
助	zhù	assist	141	
走	zǒu	walk	17, 225	
足	zú	foot	17	
坐	zuò	sit	110	
作	zuò	work; do	111	
		8		
爸	bà	dad	48	
杯	bēi	cup; glass	116	
备/備	bèi	prepare	140	
衬/襯	chèn	lining	181	
到	dào	go to; arrive	132	
的	de	P	47	
店	diàn	shop; store	195	
法	fǎ	method; way	147	

服	fú	clothing	180	
国/國	guó	country; nation	42	
果	guǒ	fruit; result	196	
和	hé/huo	and; harmonious; *warm	58	
话/話	huà	speech	123	
货/貨	huò	merchandise	179	
或	huò	or	223	
姐	jiě	elder sister	29	
金(钅)	jīn	(a surname); gold; metal	18	
京	jīng	capital	43	
经/經	jīng	pass through	166	
咖	kā	*coffee	113	
刻	kè	quarter hour; carve	79	
空	kòng	free time	130	
练/練	liàn	practice; drill	136	
录/錄	lù	record	153	
妹	mèi	younger sister	53	
明	míng	bright	80	
呢	ne	QP	34	
念/唸	niàn	read	153	
朋	péng	friend	37	
绍/紹	shào	carry on	107	
衫	shān	shirt	182	
舍	shè	house	163	
始	shǐ	begin	152	
事	shì	affair; matter	81	
视/視	shì	view	88	
试/試	shì	try	129	
刷	shuā	scrub; brush; swipe	199	
所	suǒ	*so; place	97	
图/圖	tú	drawing	119	
玩	wán	play; visit	118	
现/現	xiàn	now; present	78	
线/線	xiàn	line	226	
姓	xìng	surname	33	
学/學	xué	study	40	
夜	yè	night	151	
宜	yí	suitable	186	
易	yì	easy	148	
英	yīng	flower; hero	59	
雨	yǔ	rain	19, 201	

者	zhě	auxiliary used to indicate a class of persons or things	223
知	zhī	know	138
枝	zhī	twig; branch; MW for long, thin objects	154
周/週	zhōu	week	85
隹	zhuī	short-tailed bird	19
9			
帮/幫	bāng	help	135
便	biàn	convenient	131
茶	chá	tea	113
城	chéng	wall; city wall; city	216
除	chú	except	168
穿	chuān	wear	184
春	chūn	spring	211
点/點	diǎn	dot; o'clock	75
封	fēng	MW for letters	166
复/復	fù	duplicate	142
给/給	gěi	give	117
贵/貴	guì	honorable; expensive	32
孩	hái	child	50
很	hěn	very	81
觉/覺	jiào	sleep	99
觉/覺	jué	feel; reckon	99
看	kàn	see; look	87
客	kè	guest	96
亮/亮	liàng	bright	109
律	lǜ	law; rule	60
美	měi	beautiful	43
面	miàn	face	140
哪	nǎ/něi	which	110
便	pián	*inexpensive	131
前	qián	front; before	164
秋	qiū	autumn; fall	213
食（饣）	shí	eat	20
是	shì	be	38
室	shì	room	133
适/適	shì	suit; fit	194
说/說	shuō	speak	137

思	sī	think	101
送	sòng	deliver	229
虽/雖	suī	though; while	192
挺	tǐng	erect; straighten up; very; rather	198
洗	xǐ	wash	158
信	xìn	letter	167
星	xīng	star	64
要	yào	want	116
音	yīn	sound; music	91
语/語	yǔ	language	146
怎	zěn	*how	70
钟/鐘	zhōng	clock	75
种/種	zhǒng/zhòng	species; kind; sort; grow; plant	197
祝	zhù	wish	174
昨	zuó	yesterday	96
10			
啊	a	P	137
爱/愛	ài	love; be fond of	61
笔/筆	bǐ	pen	144
都	dōu	all; both	60
烦/煩	fán	bother	228
高	gāo	tall; high	55
哥	gē	elder brother	57
海	hǎi	sea	206
候	hòu	wait; time	93
换/換	huàn	change	191
家	jiā	family; home	56
紧/緊	jǐn	tight	232
酒	jiǔ	wine	115
课/課	kè	class; lesson	128
凉/涼	liáng	cool	210
难/難	nán	difficult; hard	144
脑/腦	nǎo	brain	160
能	néng	be able	173
瓶	píng	bottle	120
起	qǐ	rise	117
钱/錢	qián	money	187
请/請	qǐng	please; invite	31

热/熱	rè	hot	209	
容	róng	hold; contain; allow	147	
谁/誰	shéi	who	51	
速/速	sù	speed	231	
特	tè	special; unusual	217	
铁/鐵	tiě	iron	224	
夏	xià	summer	210	
校	xiào	school	112	
笑	xiào	laugh	174	
样/樣	yàng	shape; kind	70	
预/預	yù	prepare	146	
站	zhàn	stand; station	225	
真/眞	zhēn	true; real	152	
准/準	zhǔn	standard; criterion; allow; accurate	139	
租	zū	rent	228	

11				
菜	cài	vegetable; dish; food	84	
常	cháng	often	94	
唱	chàng	sing	88	
得	dé	obtain; get	100	
得	de	P	100	
得	děi	must; have to	100	
第	dì	(ordinal prefix)	145	
啡	fēi	*coffee	114	
馆/館	guǎn	accommodation	119	
惯/慣	guàn	be used to	170	
黄/黃	huáng	yellow	183	
假	jià	vacation	219	
教/教	jiāo	teach	143	
累	lèi	tired; fatigued	175	
聊	liáo	chat	120	
绿/綠	lù	green	226	
麻	má	hemp; numb	227	
您	nín	polite form of "you"	32	
啤	pí	*beer	114	
票	piào	ticket	221	
清	qīng	clear; clean	170	
球	qiú	ball	86	
商	shāng	commerce; business	194	

售	shòu	sell	178	
宿	sù	stay	162	
望	wàng	Look into the distance; hope; wish	172	
做	zuò	do	58	

12				
道	dào	road; way	139	
等	děng	wait	134	
短	duǎn	short; brief	197	
寒	hán	cold	219	
喝	hē	drink	112	
黑	hēi	black	192	
裤/褲	kù	pants	185	
期	qī	period of time	64	
然	rán	like that; so	193	
舒	shū	stretch	209	
湾/灣	wān	strait; bay	215	
晚	wǎn	evening; late	69	
喂	wèi	hello; hey	123	
喜	xǐ	like; happy	72	
谢/謝	xiè	thank	72	
最	zuì	most	167	

13				
楚	chǔ	clear; neat	171	
错/錯	cuò	wrong; error	98	
跟	gēn	with; and; follow	141	
蓝/藍	lán	blue	227	
路	lù	road; way	232	
暖	nuǎn	warm	203	
睡	shuì	sleep	102	
跳	tiào	jump	89	
想	xiǎng	think	99	
新	xīn	new	234	
意	yì	meaning	100	
照	zhào	shine	46	

14				

歌	gē	song		89
酷	kù	cruel; extremely		155
慢	màn	slow		143
漂	piào	*pretty		109
算	suàn	calculate; figure		102
舞	wǔ	dance; wave		90
像	xiàng	image		205
15				
懂	dǒng	understand		148
篇	piān	MW for articles		157
题/題	tí	topic; question		126
鞋	xié	shoes		191
颜/顏	yán	face; countenance		182
影	yǐng	shadow		94
16				
餐	cān	meal		161
糕	gāo	cake		207
澡	zǎo	bath		159
17				
糟	zāo	messy		206